TRADITION AND EXPERIMENT
IN ENGLISH POETRY

TRADITION AND EXPERIMENT IN ENGLISH POETRY

Philip Hobsbaum

First published 1979 by
THE MACMILLAN PRESS LTD
London and Basingstoke
Associated companies in Delhi
Dublin Hong Kong Johannesburg Lagos
Melbourne New York Singapore Tokyo

Printed in Great Britain by
LOWE AND BRYDONE PRINTERS LTD
Thetford, Norfolk

British Library Cataloguing in Publication Data

Hobsbaum, Philip
    Tradition and experiment in English poetry
    1. English poetry—History and criticism
    I. Title
    821'.009   PR502
    ISBN 0–333–14611–5

For my dear wife, Rosemary

anima candida

CONTENTS

'A tradition is the body of texts and interpretations current among a group of writers at a given time and place'—J. V. Cunningham.

'In dealing with individual poets the critic, whether explicitly or not, is dealing with tradition, for they live in it. And it is in them that tradition lives'—F. R. Leavis.

PREFACE

Tradition and Experiment was conceived as an attempt to write an informal history of poetry in English. Existing accounts leave room for a work which is neither bedevilled with names of scant literary significance nor selective to the point where it ceases to be history at all. The present survey begins with *Piers Plowman* in the fourteenth century and comes up to the present with a final chapter on those poets whom the author believes to be the major figures of the mid-twentieth century.

Necessarily, this involves some foreshortening. Of the twelve chapters, four deal with individual poets—Langland, Chaucer, Shakespeare, Wordsworth. A further chapter, centring on Ben Jonson, compares the work of this poet with that of his successors in the seventeenth century—in lyric poetry, in descriptive verse, in satire, in comedy of manners. The book is arranged in roughly chronological order, but a chapter on the rise of the dramatic monologue covers almost the entire historical range in demonstrating how this highly distinctive form grew out of the decadence of English drama. And a chapter on American verse seeks to demonstrate that America has developed a literary tradition of its own, involving Eliot, Pound, Stevens and Lowell as much as Whitman, who in many ways must be regarded as its founder.

The concept of tradition in this book is the key theme that links its several chapters together. The basic form in English is that of *Piers Plowman*: narrative verse in a highly alliterative idiom; and it is surprising how constant this métier has been.

Whole alien tracts of subject-matter—Homer's *Odyssey*, Ariosto's *Orlando Furioso*—have been assimilated into the characteristically English verse of poets such as Chapman and Harington. The mistake, as I see it, has been to imitate from time to time the style, as well as the subject-matter, of foreign modes; and this is what, in the book, is termed 'experiment'. Thus Chaucer, for all his command of native idiom, introduced a large number of novel verse forms into English and so left the door open for the Italianising tendencies of Spenser and the Elizabethan sonneteers generally. And they, in their turn, begin a by-line in English verse that includes Milton, Tennyson, Housman and the wave of Imagism that is upon us today. In much the same way, some damage was done to English verse by too close an imitation in the 1930s of the American idiom as evidenced in such poets as Eliot and Pound. The claim put forward is that the central line of English poetry—the tradition, so to speak—is earthy, alliterative, colloquial, with a strong regard for structure and the claims of plot. It is no accident that these are the characteristics of the central figures of this book.

Ancillary to this is the question of the way in which these great poets have been presented to the public. The chapters concerning *Piers Plowman*, Wordsworth and Whitman raise issues of scholarship, particularly in the matter of selecting and editing the relevant texts. Inferior texts and uncertainty of selection have considerably muffled the impact made by these poets upon their audience, and the comparison and analysis which brings out the inferiority of alternative readings and editions is an attempt to demonstrate the excellence of their work at its best.

Needless to say, no work on English poetry can be simply that, and so the counter-influence of other forms of literature must be acknowledged, indeed often analysed. Thus, Restoration comedy is a presence in the Jonson chapter; the medieval sermon takes its rightful place in the chapter on Langland; George Eliot, Hardy and Lawrence make their appearance in the Wordsworth chapter; and the chapter on the dramatic monologue takes into its purview the decline of tragedy from the Jacobeans to the Romantics.

I hope that *Tradition and Experiment* will prove of service to the university student in providing guidelines through what must often seem to be the bewildering proliferation of poetry in English. I also hope that it will assist the general reader by indicating that the development of our literature has been very much the product of a creative tension between the native idiom and the imitation of European forms.

Acknowledgments are due to the *British Journal of Aesthetics*, the *British Journal of American Studies*, the *Hudson Review*, *The Listener*, the *Michigan Quarterly Review*, the *Poetry Review* and *Wisconsin Studies in Contemporary Literature*, in which earlier versions of several chapters appeared.

As I said in *A Theory of Communication*, sister-book to the present enterprise, my debts are few but crucial. To my Head of Department, Peter Butter, who obtained for me a sabbatical year without which I would still be writing this work. To the British Library, Scottish National Library and Glasgow University Library, together with their devoted staffs. To the secretaries who, over the years, typed and retyped successive drafts of various chapters, especially Valerie Eden and Ingrid Swanson; and to Janice Bell, who undertook the typing of the final draft. And my greatest debt of all, to my dear wife Rosemary, dedicatee of this book: *anima qualem neque candidiorem terra tulit, neque cui me sit devinctior alter.*

Glasgow, 1968–77

1 *Piers Plowman* through Modern Eyes

Every great literature has some work, early in its history, which crystallises the tradition and defines its possibilities. Such a work is *Piers Plowman*. It would be difficult to exaggerate the centrality of this poem. Behind it stands the entire corpus of medieval preaching. Before it stretches English. There are very few major works in our language not influenced by *Piers Plowman*, directly or indirectly. And the language itself diminishes in efficacy as it draws farther away from its central masterpiece.

Yet which of us has read it? Is it not true of *Piers Plowman*, as of most medieval poems outside Chaucer, that its interest remains primarily for scholars? But, if this is so, these same scholars have done a very poor job. For it is the task of the editor to make his text available—not to a few select colleagues, who are in any case presumably engaged upon their own furrows, but to the literate public.

Ultimately this means that a great poem of the past must be available to poets. Only in this way can a tradition be renewed. Readers of modern poetry must be aware that the other great alliterative poem of the Middle Ages, *Sir Gawain and the Green Knight,* may be seen as an influence in the work of such writers as Ted Hughes and Peter Redgrove. How many of them realise that this is largely due to the effort of another modern poet, Francis Berry? He edited *Sir Gawain,* removed the more ludicrous manuscript spellings, and in short brought the poem into the twentieth century—where it belongs. For a great poem transcends its own time: that is what makes it a great poem. If *Piers Plowman* belongs anywhere, it is with us, in our community. And in these decadent times we more than ever have need of it. It is, in any case, useless to surmise how the early readers saw the poem. We cannot remove from our minds all memory of the Wars of the Roses, the Armada, the Civil War and the Industrial Revolution. Nor should we try: upheavals of this nature can only enhance the quality of a great poem. If the author predicts disaster, then our history does much to prove him right.

In any case, *Piers Plowman* was, in its time, a popular poem—popular in every sense of the word. To imagine it passed from hand to hand round an in-circle of scholiasts is absurd. Rather we should hear it as a clarion call from a secular platform, a lay sermon told through examples—and some of those examples define not only what our literature has done but what it can do.

But the difficulties of making *Piers Plowman* available even to an educated reader are immense—far more so than those which beset the editors of *Sir Gawain and the Green Knight*. For one thing we shall have to persuade the scholars that more than a century of reading has been wrong. When we speak so glibly of *Piers Plowman*, we are in fact referring not to one poem but to two.

It is no news that the poem can be readily bisected. We are accustomed to divide *Liber de Petro Plowman* into two parts; the *Visio Willelmi de Petro le Plowman*, and *Vita de Dowel, Dobet et Dobest*. For brevity we shall follow custom in calling them, respectively, the *Visio*, and the *Vita*.

The *Visio* is an account of a dream—the whole world milling about on a plain, misled by false priests, judged by a king who himself is misled by his councillors. One root cause of this error is my Lady Meed, a personification of bribery or reward. A whole drama is based upon the question of her marriage. The knight Conscience refuses to have anything to do with her. And Reason, an august figure based upon Brinton, Bishop of Rochester, preaches such a sermon that the Seven Deadly Sins themselves come forward to make their confession to another personified figure, Repentance. But the people still milling about on the plain—a recurrent image—cry out to know the path to truth. Kings, priests, palmers from the Holy Land—all have failed to show them the way. And, at this point, the ploughman appears: this is Piers, who is a loyal follower of Truth. He describes the way, and it is a very hard one. The people ask him to guide them, but he will not do so until he has finished his work in the world. So the different people in the crowd help him, each in their own fashion, and those who will not work are punished by Hunger. But before the pilgrims depart upon their journey, Truth sends what purports to be a pardon but what is in fact part of the Creed, in effect calling off the whole venture. The Dreamer wakes up to the sound of Piers arguing about this with a priest. The conclusion drawn is that the good life is worth all the pardons and indulgences in the world.

I have gone into this detail because it is the *Visio* with which we shall be chiefly concerned. The *Vita*, though much longer, is more easily described. It consists of a series of dialogues between the Dreamer and various allegorical figures—Thought, Wit, Study, Clergy, Scripture, etc. At first the Dreamer is seeking the Good Life (Dowel), which is a life of action. Later he seeks Dobet, which is the life of contemplation. But these can both be extended to an ideal, Dobest, which is the life of Christ. Piers the ploughman is identified with all three of these: as the Good Layman; as the Priest and, by extension, Peter; finally, with Christ.

Thus it can be seen that the poem to some extent rounds upon itself. Having in the *Visio* identified the Good Life with that of the active workman, the poem—if we accept it as a whole—proceeds to deny this in favour of a hierarchy of ascending orders which would eventually take us out of the world altogether. It would seem, then, that in the *Visio* the immediate hope in this world is in our all putting our hands to the plough, or its equivalent; while in the *Vita* there is no hope in this world at all save preparation for the next.

So, philosophically speaking, we are in the presence not of one poem but of two. The poem appears to split crucially after Piers receives his pardon and the Dreamer wakes up. But I should prefer to say that, at this point, a new poem begins. Certainly the Dreamer falls asleep all over again, and the verse resumes again on lines similar to those of the original prologue:

> Thus yrobed in russet I romed aboute
> Al a somer season for to seke dowel . . . .
>
> (B-text, VIII 1–2)

The effect is not that of a continuation so much as a parallel, though the verse is noticeably more subdued and, throughout the *Vita*, more abstract.

And this brings me to another point: the question of mode. Whereas the *Visio* is a secular sermon, packed with example always vivid and sometimes scarifying, the *Vita* is a series of theological dialogues, scant of illustration, and—most damning of all—losing little by being recast in English prose, or even that of Latin: indeed, the latter would seem to be their true medium:

> Austyn þe olde hereof made bokes,
> And hymself ordeyned to sadde vs in bileve.
> Who was his Auctour? alle þe foure Evaungelistes.
> And Crist cleped hymself so, þe [scripture] bereth
>   witnesse:
> [*Ego in patre et pater in me est, et qui videt me
>   videt et patrem meum*]
> Alle þe clerkes vnder crist ne koude þis assoille
> But þus it bilongeþ to bileve to lewed at willen dowel.
> For hadde nevere freke fyn wit þe feith to dispute,
> Ne man hadde no merite myȝte it be ypreved:
> *Fides non habet meritum ubi humana racio prebet
>   experimentum* . . . .
>
> (B, x 249–57)

If we are to argue that the *Visio* and the *Vita* are one poem, we have to explain (1) the change of moral direction from this world to the next: (2) the sharp break in continuity of argument; (3) the sudden alteration of tone, from a sermon by example to one by precept; and, perhaps most important of all, (4) the great decline in the quality of the poetry.

There are four reasons, then, for regarding this apparently divided poem as not one work but two. Certainly not one of them can be put forward as being in any way an advantage. And the last seems to me crucial if we are thinking, as we should be, in affective terms. For there can be no doubt that, whatever the formal dimensions of a poem, it ceases to communicate when it ceases to function aesthetically. Thus, for example, *Paradise Lost* cannot be very well sustained as an entity beyond the fourth book. We know that, formally speaking, there are four books of tedious exhortation and recapitulation to follow this; but, since the poem does not get going again until the great temptation scene in Book IX, it is hard to feel that these books matter very much; any more than the History of Mankind which concludes the poem. Aesthetically speaking, Books V, VI, VII, VIII, X, XI, and most of XII do not exist.

That would be my case against regarding *Paradise Lost* as a whole. The case against the *Visio* and the *Vita* as a unity is even stronger. For it is always possible to argue against an affective criterion: no critic, it may be felt, is entitled to attribute more than a limited validity to his personal response. But when one considers that, in effect, the *Vita* discounts all that the *Visio* puts forward, and does so using a totally different technique of presentation—then, indeed, we have some backing for what at first may seem a rather startling assertion: that the scholars have taken for one poem what can now be seen to be two; one of them, I might add, manifestly inferior.

To extend my Milton analogy: it is rather as though, deceived by the similarity of title, the scholars had rammed *Paradise Lost* and *Paradise Regained* together and treated them as one; using, moreover, startling ingenuity of argument to show (a) that there was, against all appearance, a cohesion of argument and style between the parts, and (b) that the disunity everywhere apparent was in some way an advantage. But the analogy, absurd though it is, is not sufficiently extreme to characterise the situation as it applies to *Piers Plowman*. The *Vita* is, indeed, another *Paradise Regained*, but a much longer and duller one. So the enforced juxtaposition of *Visio* and *Vita* is even more incongruous than that of Milton's poems would be.

I think all this would convince the poets, the literary critics, the educated readers—those, in fact, who I am seeking to convince. But what of the scholars: those whose job it is to keep this great poem before the public and who have, instead, made it into a specialist enclave? The scholars cannot be appealed to on grounds such as aesthetics or commonsense. For them we must have sterner arguments.

It is a fact that, of seventeen manuscripts surviving of the first draft, four contain merely the *Visio*—presented as though that work were a complete poem. Of the others, all but one treat the *Vita* as though it were another work entirely. Most have written on them some such legend as this: *Explicit hic visio willelmi de petro plowman Et hic incipit dowel dobet and dobest secundum wit & resoun*. But, whatever the exact form of the legend, the inference is clear: when the fifteenth-century reader came to the end of the 'Vision concerning Piers Plowman', he started a new poem called the Life of Dowel, Dobet, and Dobest'.

The scholars have little to be proud of, in having lumped together two poems of widely differing merits and in attempting to pass them on as a single entity. Every first-year honours student will remember the experience of reading with increasing interest the first few passus of the *Visio*; with mounting excitement as the language became more familiar; turning the pages after the dispute between Piers and the Priest—for, after all, we were told the poem did go on—only to find himself struggling with dismal theological abstractions and even more dismal Church Latin. Indeed, how many graduates can honestly maintain that they ploughed through—no pun intended—to the bitter end? And—another triumph for the scholars—who do they suppose, apart from honours students studying for an examination, has ever read the poem?

When one considers that the *Visio* was one of the great popular manifestos of its time and has come down to us in three main drafts on an aggregate of fifty-one manuscripts (*Sir Gawain and the Green Knight* occurs only on one), this situation seems preposterous. There seems no reason why the *Visio* should not be read at least as widely as *Pilgrim's Progress* and the *Communist Manifesto*—with both of which it has more than a little in common. What, other than the unfortunate pairing of the *Visio* with the *Vita* to form a mythical *Piers Plowman*, has prevented such a currency?

I am afraid that, once more, the answer lies in the lap of the scholars. Granted that we study the *Visio* apart from the *Vita*, what of the difficulties attendant upon the language? The most hardened layman may recoil a little when faced with this:

> In a somer seson whan softe was þe sonne
> I shoop me into [a] shrou[d] as I a sheep weere;

In habite as an heremite, vnholy of werkes,
Wente wide in þis world wondres to here.
Ac on a May morwenynge on Maluerne hilles
Me bifel a ferly, of fairy me þoʒte.
I was wery forwandred and wente me to reste
Vnder a brood bank by a bourn[e] syde,
And as I lay and lenede and loked on þe watres
I slombred into a slepyng, it sweyed so murye. . . .

(B, Prol. 1–10)

Now, to the medievalist, this presents no problem at all; which is why, perhaps, medievalists perpetuate obsolete spellings and forms of words. But if we are going to have people outside Departments of English Language reading this poem—for pleasure, mind—we are going to have to do something about the way in which we put it before the public. Personally I transliterate 'u' for 'v' and *vice versa* more or less automatically, now: I had trouble copying out this passage from the edition of Kane and Donaldson (Athlone Press, 1960–   ) without modernising the whole lot as I went along. Such are the benefits a training in English can give you. But what of a modern poet who may have been trained, like Peter Redgrove, as a scientist? Or what if, like Peter Porter and countless others, he has been denied the privilege of a university education? Would not the adherence to archaic usage cause more trouble than it was worth?

And are these usages so much worth preserving after all? Is there any particular cachet in retaining the 'ʒ' when all it can mean is a 'gh' or 'y', according to context? Do we really have to write 'somer' when we know the poet means 'summer'; or 'bourn[e] syde' when it is obvious that the modern form is 'burn-side'? Depend upon it, the medieval readers of *Piers Plowman* did not have to scratch their heads over that poem's antiquated spellings, losing the urgency and thrill of the verse in so doing. Nor were medieval scribes over-sedulous about retaining consistency of spelling. Spelling was arbitrary in those days: indeed, was barely stabilised by the time Johnson compiled his dictionary four centuries later. If we are not to bury the *Visio* beneath a mass of pedantry, or preserve it merely for pedagogues, we shall have to supply, whenever we can do so, modern forms of spelling for the arbitrary and archaic versions used by the fourteenth- or fifteenth-century copyist.

This does not mean that we should translate the *Visio*. One might just as well seek to translate Chaucer, or Shakespeare, or the Authorised Version of the Bible. Where *Piers Plowman* is, there is English: one cannot translate one stage of the language into another. Not that, once made available to the reader, the *Visio*'s English is very far removed from our own. That English is superior in concreteness, in drama, in weight, pithiness, example: a statement in the *Visio* has all the force of a metaphor in modern English—so much has the language thinned out. But the qualification to all this is that the poem must be made available: it must be seen in order to be read.

Here we are talking not of translation but of transliteration. This last is a purely visual matter, and so cannot affect the poetry. In preparing my quotations I have sought to avoid any alteration that would strike the ear: for, after all, a poem, to be effective, must be spoken. But how we are to speak it when we are puzzling over idiosyncratic spellings and obsolete forms of words—that is more than I can tell. Let us then modernise, as Francis Berry did *Sir Gawain*, but modernise, as he did, with discretion: not bringing the poem up to date as much as recognising it for what it is: a great work of art that has survived endless upheavals and which, divested of the irrelevant growths of centuries, stands clear as when it was first written. An analogy might be the cleaning of a Titian.

At first sight this analogy seems rather startling. Those violent colours, that far from tasteful sharpness of definition—is that really how the picture looks? Yes, and the mysterious darkness that obfuscates our Rembrandts, that, too, is the irrelevant overlay of time—as irrelevant as the scholarly apparatus, the faithful reproduction of minutiae, the attempt to bottle in a far-off century the contemporaneity of the *Visio*, the tedious truth to the letter that has long shaded the exuberant scenes of England's greatest allegory.

If we repeat the beginning of the poem, but in slightly rationalised spelling, it will be seen that this is no museum piece or even survival from the past but a living voice speaking to us as contemporaries. We shall now be better able to appreciate the quiet authority of one of the most enchanting openings in English poetry.

In a summer season   when soft was the sun,
I shoop me into a shroud   as I a sheep were;
In habit as an hermit   unholy of works,
Went wide in this world   wonders to hear.
Ac on a May morning   on Malvern hills
Me befell a ferly,   of fairy methought.
I was weary forwandered   and went me to rest
Under a broad bank   by a burn-side,
And as I lay and leaned   and looked on the waters
I slumbered into a sleeping   it swayed so merry.
Then 'gan I meten   a marvellous sweven,
That I was in a wilderness,   wist I never where.
Ac as I beheld into the east   an high to the sun,
I saw a tower on a toft   trierly made,
A deep dale beneath,   a dungeon therein
With deep ditches and dark   and dreadful of sight.
A fair field full of folk   found I there between
Of all manner of men,   the mean and the rich,
Working and wandering   as the world asketh.
Some putten hem to plough,   playden full seld,
In setting and sowing   swonken full hard;
Wonnen that these wasters   with gluttony destroyeth.
And some putten hem to pride,   apparelled hem thereafter
In countenance of clothing   comen disguised. . . .

                              (B, Prol. 1–24)

In little, here we have the main themes of the *Visio*. We are
never allowed to forget that this is a dream: the drowsy yet
hypnotic opening lines put us into a state receptive enough to
hear the amazing truths the Dreamer has to tell us. The image
which occurs throughout the poem, the 'fair field of folk', is
placed before us here for the first time. And we are not allowed
to forget that this 'fair field'—our world—is held in suspension,
as it were, between a 'tower on a toft' (heaven) and 'a deep
dale beneath' (hell). So, without any strain in the verse, the allegory
is suggested through the recounting of particular, observed details.
Indeed—and this is a lesson which runs throughout English literature—if it were not real, how could it be an allegory?

The picture is one of a world sadly at odds with itself: the

people 'working and wandering' in search of some solace which
their present state cannot afford them. They are battened upon
by 'bidders and beggars', by 'pilgrims and palmers', by friars—'all
the four orders' and by that most sinister of medieval figures,
the pardoner preaching 'as he a priest were'. The people kneel
to kiss his bulls and to press gifts upon him—'thus ye given
your gold gluttons to help' (B, Prol. 76). And nobody interferes:
the parish priest is in league with the pardoner, and the bishop,
wrongly it seems, trusts to the priest to protect his flock. Indeed,
this bishop is represented as an absentee landlord, living it up
in London around the king's court. And the king himself is
represented as, in the sharpest sense of the word, misguided.
How, after all, can the people safeguard themselves against tyranny? The problem is demonstrated in the form of a parable.
Suddenly the field is flooded with rats:

> With that ran there a rout   of ratons at once
> And small mice mid hem;   more than a thousand
> Comen to a council   for the common profit.
> For a cat of a court   came when him liked
> And overleap hem lightly   and laught hem at will
> And played with hem perilously   and possed about.
> 'For doubt of diverse deeds   we dare not well look,
> And if we grouch of his gamen   he wol grieven us all,
> Cratchen us or clawen us,   and in his clutches hold
> That us lotheth the life   ere he let us pass.
> Might we with any wit   his will withstand
> We might be lords aloft   and liven at our ease.'
> A raton of renown   most renable of tongue
> Said for a sovereign   salve to hem all:
> 'I have ye-seyen segges,' quod he,   'in the City of London
> Bearen bighes full bright   abouten hire necks,
> And some collars of crafty work   uncoupled they wenden
> Both in warren and in waste   where hem lief liketh;
> And otherwhile they aren elsewhere,   as I hear tell.
> Were there a bell on hire bighe   by Jesu, as me thinketh,
> Men might witten where they went   and hire way roam.
> And right so,' quod that raton,   'reason me showeth
> To buy a bell of brass   or of bright silver
> And knitten it on a collar   for our common profit
> And hangen it upon the cat's halse   then hear we mowen

Where he ride or rest   or roameth to play;
And if him list for to laik   then look we mowen
And 'pearen in his presence   there while him play liketh,
And if him wratheth beware   and his way shony.'
All the rout of ratons   to this reason assented.
Ac though the bell was y-brought   and on the bighe
   hanged
Then ne was raton in the rout   for all the realm of
   France
That durst have bounden the bell   about the cat's neck.
Ne hangen it about his halse   all England to win;
Ac helden hem unhardy   and hir council feeble
And leten hire labour lost   and all hire long study. . . .
(B, Prol. 146–81)

This direct and concise narrative shows the *Visio*'s mastery of
plot. So clear-cut a tale saves hundreds of lines of commentary.
Indeed, the king's powers must be curbed, but how are the
commons to do it? In our days of ruthlessly presidential government, this problem from the age of Edward III must seem
peculiarly pressing. Who can bell the cat? I need hardly stress
the point that the sharpness of the allegory would have been
much muted if we adhered to the manuscript spellings and forms
of words. Consider the words of the oldest rat, for example:

'I have yseyen segges', quod he, 'in þe Cite of Londoun
Bere beiȝes ful briȝte abouten hire nekkes,
And somme colers of crafty werk; vncoupled þei wen[d]en
Boþe in wareyne and in waast where hem [leue] like[þ] . . . .

This puts a pressing parable back into the dusty past, and gives
us a 'period' flavour wholly at variance with the claim of the
poem upon our attention. So I hope it will be taken as an
axiom that we edit the *Visio* for readers to experience now.

Even so, we have not cleared our way into the poem. Earlier
medievalists held that there were two main drafts of *Piers Plowman*;
the Victorian editor W. W. Skeat insisted that there were three,
and modern scholarship has upheld his opinion. Any one of
these drafts must necessarily be compiled from a multiplicity
of manuscripts, and it has proved immensely difficult to determine
a hierarchy among them. It can be seen that the modern editor
of *Piers Plowman* has his problems.

They are, first of all, problems of presentation. Skeat put all three drafts forward simultaneously. Those who, like myself, were brought up on his old Clarendon edition will testify to the eye-rending experience of turning over the page and landing oneself on the wrong text, wrong passus or both. The poem disports itself over the double page in all three of its guises simultaneously: text A holding the fort above on both sides, text B guarding the lower part of the left-hand page, text C equally zealous upon the right. A more unsatisfactory way of reading a great poem cannot well be imagined.

Modern editors have not emulated these demands upon the reader's patience. The Athlone Press edition of *Piers Plowman* prefers to bring out each main text in an individual volume, and at the time of writing two of these, the A-text and B-text, have appeared. This is much less of a strain on the reader's eyes, but it does bring forward an important aesthetic problem. Which of the three major drafts should we study?

The A-text is the briefest and most rough in technique. Much is left out in this earliest draft that one would far rather have in. For example, the fable of the rats which we have just looked at is omitted altogether. Much, also, that is baldly stated in text A is given a greater resonance and play elsewhere. So, except for purposes of comparison, the A-text cannot be recommended for those who want a definitive version of the *Visio*. The description of Meed, the lady of reward and/or bribery, is only half as long in A as in B: a brief statement of her presence is all we are given, with a most perfunctory reference to what she wears. But, as a hundred sermons tell us, clothing was of the first importance, as a guide to a person's social status and character. Moreover, much of the drama of Lady Meed turns upon her availability, her beauty, and, above all, what is to be done with her. Therefore it is essential that she be felt as a living presence in the poem. This condition is, I think, upheld in the B-text:

> I looked on my left half   as the lady me taught
> And was 'ware of a woman   wonderly y-clothed,
> Purfled with pelour,   the purest on earth,
> Y-crowned in a crown,   the King hath none better.
> Fetisly her fingers   were fretted with gold wire
> And thereon rich rubies   as red as any glede

> And diamonds of dearest price   and double-manner
>   sapphires
> Orientals and ewages   envenoms to destroy.
> Her robe was full rich   of red scarlet ingrained,
> With ribbons of red gold   and of rich stones.
> Her array me ravished;   such richesse saw I never.
> I had wonder what she was   and whose wife she were. . . .
>   (B, II 7–18)

What of the C-text? As a student I used to frequent this, mainly because there was more of it—one had more detail for one's money. Certainly there is a great weight of autobiographical matter, especially in the later passus, that texts A and B rather tend to spare us. But such matter is only important if we are interested in Langland rather than in *Piers Plowman*. And, as I hope to show later, the identity and personality of this author is of less moment than that of any other major poet. The *Visio*, far more than 'Lycidas', is 'a poem nearly anonymous'.

The copious details of the C-text do not clarify the plot-line; they obfuscate it. Time and time again poetry is lost in favour of factual statement. Keeping to the personification of Meed for the moment, we find her rich dress a little impoverished in the presentation which the C-text chooses to afford us:

> Fetisly her fingers   were fretted with gold wire
> And thereon rich rubies   as red as any glede
>   (B, II 11–12)

becomes, in the C-text,

> On all her five fingers   richly y-ringed,
> And thereon red rubies   and other rich stones.
>   (C, III 12–13)

The simile is dropped in favour of a vague amplification, and the dazzling 'fretted with gold wire' is thinned out to the bald statement of fact, 'richly ringed'.

A kindred lessening of pressure from B-text to C can be found in the description of Meed's costume. B-text has

> Her robe was full rich   of red scarlet ingrained,

With ribbons of red gold   and of rich stones

(B, II 15–16)

while all C can give us is

Her robe was richer   than I rede couthe,
For to tell of her attire   no time have I now.

(C, III 14–15)

No, indeed: text C dates from the 1390s, by which time the author's powers were manifestly failing. It was all he could do to revise and enlarge the whole effort before he died. But, earlier on, the author had the time, and could 'rede': the B-text comes from 1377, or thereabout, when the author was in the full vigour and prime of his life. Not that it matters: from internal evidence alone—the evidence of the poetry—it is the B-text we must read if we would read the *Visio* and not, on the one hand, a rough preliminary draft, or, on the other, a laboured rewriting which habitually replaces poetry with diffuse explanation.

For, time and time again, the C-text adds circumstance that nobody could possibly want. For example, the ninety-two lines of hectoring about 'Meed' which are added to the third passus of text B hammer home what is already unmistakable:

Thus is mede and mercede   as two manner relations,
Rect and indirect   running both
On a sad and a siker   semblable to himself—
As adjective and substantive   unity asken,
Accordance in kind   in case and in number,
And either is other's help   of them cometh retribution,
That is the gift that God giveth   to all leal living,
Grace of good end   and great joy after;
*Retribuere dignare, domine deus, omnibus nobis, et
cetera.* . . .

(C, IV 335–42)

One salient example, one dramatic circumstance, is worth a hundred lines of such abstract statement—that is what the *Visio*'s B-text can tell us. And it is one of the half-dozen supreme masterpieces in English.

Yet we cannot regard it, as we might a Romantic poem, in terms of personal achievement. What we can envy in the Middle Ages is their extraordinary community of radical vision. This had little or nothing to do with the Establishment: Church and Court were as corrupt as ever they were, and, like all civilisations, Western Europe was a more or less stable tyranny. But the outcry against both ecclesiastical and secular abuse was astonishingly directed and focused. Langland's was not an individual voice. Nor, though the people took up his cry to an amazing extent, was he simply *vox populi*. Behind him are centuries of denunciation: the poor priests criticising on the one hand the absentee bishops, on the other the parasitical itinerants who preyed upon the people.

Keeping with Lady Meed for a moment, we should be very rash to identify Langland with some early form of socialism. He has great doubts as to the extent to which the Church should involve itself directly in secular matters, and yet he is not against the Church. If he shows a link-up between Meed and the bishops, the cry is for reform, not abolition. In the words of Conscience,

'. . . She is assoiled as soon   as herself liketh.
She may nigh as much do   in a month one
As your secret seal   in six score days.
She is privy with the Pope,   provisors it knoweth:
Sir Simony and herself   sealeth the bulls.
She blesseth these bishops   if they be lewd;
Provenders parsons   and priests she maintaineth
To hold lemans and lotebies   all hire life-days . . . .'

(B, III 144–51)

Behind all this is the kind of radical conscience which, as a former student of mine, Mr Gerard Doherty, has pointed out to me, characterises the voice of William of Ockham (*fl.* 1321). This Franciscan, vowed to poverty, was deeply concerned about the ceaseless interference of the Church with the Court and *vice versa*. For example, he bitterly opposed the right of the Pope to have any say in the election of the German Emperor. For him, such trafficking in politics demeaned the Papacy and was, in any case, at the other extreme of conduct from that demanded by his Franciscan vows, themselves revealed by the life of Christ. The only expropriation the Pope is entitled to make is that which is necessary in order to support his divine work upon earth. Those familiar with Langland will recognise a kindred stand in Ockham. It leads on to the ferocious complaints of John Ball and Jack Upland, to anonymous satires such as the *Ploughman's Tale* and the *Satire on the Consistory Courts*, and to such uprisings as the Peasants' Revolt. Yet we should beware of attributing to these phenomena either the vision of an individual prophet or the viewpoint of a socialist. For Langland and Ockham are part of a movement directed against a malaise general in Europe: the secularisation of the Church, the wanton interference of the State in divine matters; indeed, the two problems are one and the same. G. R. Owst's great book on medieval preaching (1933) gives us countless examples of denunciations on this theme. Bishop Fitzralph, the fourteenth-century Archbishop of Armagh, attacked the very prelates of whom he was one as fornicators, gluttons, plunderers, thieves and robbers. And an anonymous vernacular preacher deputising for the bishop before whom he was preaching took the opportunity to lash out at abuse in high places:

Wold God that ther longed not so meche riches as ther dose to that office [the Pope]; but that itt were pore as Crist left it with Petur! And than ther wold no man make no debate ne striff ther fore. And than shuld all othur clerkes lese meche of here covetize, and eve hem to prechynge and to teche the pepull goddes lawe aftur tho gospell; and than shuld muche flaterynge in sermons be lefte . . . .

Where do these ideas come from? What is the emotional pressure that drives theologians and popular preachers alike, crystallising most memorably in the *Visio* itself? To the left of Ockham stand Marsilius of Padua and John of Jandun, who proclaimed the sovereignty of the people as the source of all political power. And to his right stand St Bernard's *De Consideratione ad Eugenium Papam* and perhaps the *De Monarchia* of Dante. And, if it is true to say that Ockham provided us with the most persuasive formulation of medieval radical conscience, it is equally true that the verse of Langland kindled it into a consuming fire.

For, when we look at Meed's relationship with the Court in the *Visio*, it is clear that no ranks and no orders are to be spared. To prevent her disastrous marriage to False she is brought before the king; but there are intermediaries:

> Gently with joy   the justices some
> Busked hem to the bower   there the bird dwelleth,
> Comforted her kindly   by Clergy's leave,
> And saiden 'mourn not, Meed,   ne make thou no sorwe,
> For we will wisse the king   and thy way shape
> To be wedded at thy will   and where thee lief liketh
> For all Conscience's cast   and craft, as I trow.'
> Mildly Meed then   mercied hem all
> Of hire great goodness   and gave hem each one
> Coupes of clean gold   and cups of silver,
> Rings with rubies   and richesses many,
> The least man of her meinie   a mouton of gold.
> Then laught they leave,   these lords, at Meed.
>   (B, III 13–25)

Bribery, or reward—this is it that troubles the Conscience of the king. He denounces Meed as a bawd and corrupter of popes, kings, wives, and holy Church itself. So, though the King would marry Meed to Conscience—or, to break the allegory, would try to inculcate a system of just reward—it appears to be impossible: the whole idea of material gain is itself corrupting. The only chance, says Conscience, is to take merely that reward which enables one to continue one's work in the world:

> '. . . That labourers and low folk   taken of hire maistres
> It is no manner Meed   but a measurable hire.
> In merchandise is no Meed,   I may it well avow:
> It is a permutation apertly   a pennyworth for another. . . .'
>   (B, III 255–8)

So we are back with the concept of Piers the ploughman: the honest labourer who asks only just recognition for his daily work. It is doubtful whether this figure could have gained such popularity so quickly if he were the personal idea of one man. Over and over again we find the medieval preachers insisting on the sanctity of labour. 'To labourers it falleth to travail bodelich and with their sore swete geten out of the earth bodelich lifelode for hem and other partes'; and, as Professor Owst points out, we may discern in that vast storehouse of sermon-lore, John Bromyard's *Summa Predicantium* (c.1390), the lineaments of Piers as the pawn among the world's chessmen. He, it is, who 'moves only one square at a time . . . who in this world seeks the maintenance of life alone'. It is in Piers, rather than in the various orders of the Church, that Ockham's ideal of poverty and devotion is to be found. And before this is put down to a characteristically ecclesiastical regard for the status quo—flatter the poor lest they overcome us—we should remember that we find this concept in the vernacular preachers, the lay clerks like Langland himself, and in such radicals as Ockham, who was expelled from the Church for what the Establishment felt were his heresies. Moreover, the labourer is the only figure not denounced as a class: king, bishop, knight, all feel the weight of the preacher's tongue. The humble pawn alone is spared.

This, then, is the 'positive' of *Piers Plowman*: grand, simple, clear-cut. When the official leaders of the people fail, the man of the people himself must lead the way. Where is truth?

> 'Peter!' quod a ploughman   and put forth his head:
> 'I know Him as kindly   as a clerk doth his books.
> Conscience and Kindwit   kenned me to His place,
> And did me sure Him sithe   to serve Him for ever,
> Both sow and set   the while I swink might.
> I have been His follower   all this forty winter,
> Both y-sowen His seed   and 'sued His beasts,
> Within and withouten   waited His profit.
> I dyked and I dolve,   I do that He hoteth.
> Some time I sow   and some time I thresh,
> In tailors' craft and tinkers' craft   what Truth can devise,
> I weave and I wind   and do what Truth hoteth. . . .'
>
> (B, V 537–48)

And of Truth himself Piers says,

> '. . . He withhold none hewe his hire   that he ne hath
>   it at even.
> He is as low as a lamb   and lovely of speech.
> And if ye wilneth wit   where that Wye dwelleth
> I wol wisse yow well   right to His place.'
>
> (B, V 552–5)

Simple, direct, but with a strong grip on circumstance: the
literal narrative and the divine allegory are one. For Piers refuses
to guide the people until he has completed his work in the
world:

> '. . . I have a half-acre to erie   by the highway;
> Had I eried this half-acre   and sown it after
> I would wend with yow   and the way teach.'
>
> (B, vi 4–6)

This is a stand against the life merely contemplative. The way
of truth lies close to our hand: in doing the job well. We
may remember that Jesus was a carpenter and made his friends
among fishermen. No wonder that the ploughman stood in popular
mythology as a figure against all the power of the church and
the glitter of the court. Here, in the poem, we find him putting
the people to work—even the women:

> 'Some shall sew the sack   for shedding of the wheat;
> And ye lovely ladies   with your long fingers,
> That ye have silk and sendel   to sew, when time is,
> Chasubles for chaplains   churches to honour.
> Wives and widows   wool and flax spinneth;
> Maketh cloth, I counsel yow,   and kenneth so your
>   daughters.
> The needy and the naked   nimmeth heed how they lieth;
> Casteth hem clothes for cold   for so wol Truth. . . .'
>
> (B, vi 9–16)

The tone is urgent—that of a war leader in a time of crisis.
Even the knight offers to cast in his services on the plough.
But Piers tells him that he will be more use in other labours—pro-
tecting the people from robbers, keeping the land free from
vermin, both human and animal. From being a scene of aimless
milling around, the plain is transformed to one of frenzied activity:

> Now is Perkin and his pilgrims   to the plough faren.
> To erie this half-acre   holpen him many;
> Dykers and delvers   digged up the balks . . . .
>
> (B, vi 105–7)

But, of course, in any community there are the shiftless and
the idle. They are dealt with by the author in terms sternly
ironical:

> Then sitten some   and sungen atten ale
> And holpen ere his half-acre   with 'how trolly lolly'.
>
> (B, VI 115–16)

Not only drunkards, either, but also other malingerers:

> Tho were faitours afeared   and feigned hem blind;
> Some laid hir leg a-leary   as such lorels kenneth
> And made hir moan to Piers   how they might not work:
> 'We have no limbs to labour with;   Lord, y-graced be
>   ye. . . .'
>
> (B, VI 121–4)

And, as ever, one of the wasters is particularised as an individual,
without, however, losing his allegorical significance:

> 'I was not wont to work,' quod Waster,   'now wol I
>   not begin!'
> And leet light of the law   and less of the Knight
> And set Piers at a pease   and his plough both,
> And menaced him and his men   if they met eftsoon.
>
> (B, VI 167–70)

But Piers has a simple credo: if you don't work, you don't
eat. So he sets another allegorical figure, Hunger, to beat Waster
and his parasitic friend, a Breton immigrant:

> Hunger in haste thoo   hent Waster by the maw
> And wrung him so by the womb   that all watered his
>   eyen.
> He buffeted the Bretoner   about the cheeks
> That he looked like a lantern   all his life after.
> He beat hem so both   he burst near hire maws.
> Ne had Piers with a pease-loaf   prayed Hunger him bileve
> They had been dead and dolven,   ne deem thou noon
>   other.
>
> (B, VI 174–80)

The view of life, then, is communal, shared by preachers, theologians, satirists, and, so far as we can make out, by the bulk of the people themselves. The achievement of the *Visio* is not so much in creation as in re-creation. What is best of the tradition is selected and sifted here. Where the sermons treat the community *en masse*, the *Visio* is aware of it as a collection of separate entities. Consider the flurry that the incursion of hunger causes among the wasters:

> Faitours for fear   flowen into barns
> And flapten on with flails   fro morwe til even
> That Hunger was not hardy   on hem for to look.
> For a potful of peas   that Piers had y-maked
> An heap of hermits   henten hem spades
> And cutten hir copes   and courtepies made,
> And went as workmen   to weeding and mowing
> And dolven drit and dung   to dit out hunger....
>
> (B, VI 183-90)

This is graphic ('flapten on with flails') and particular ('a potful of peas'). The distinction between this and the sermons is in the quality of reference. The *Visio* talks about an external, tangible world all right, but it also selects the most salient particulars and puts them forward with unequalled force.

This is seen clearly even when the poem is at its most traditional. M. W. Bloomfield wrote a study of the Seven Deadly Sins (1952) showing that their origin was composite. The Gnostics derived from such sources as the Egyptian 'Book of the Dead' and the Apocryphal 'Life of Joseph the Carpenter' the concept of a soul journey. Origen in his *Contra Celsum* (*ante* 254, VI 22) described the soul leaving this world by a series of steps, each guarded by a demon. The process was one in which the fleshly lusts of earthly being were progressively sloughed off before the spirit met its God. This linked up with various references in the Bible to sins (2 Timothy 3:2; Matthew 15:19; Acts 15:20); to demons (Acts 15:29; 1 Peter 5:8; Philippians 3:2); and, once more, to the mystic number seven (Proverbs 26:25; Luke, 8:2, 11:26, 17:4). Such concepts became a convenient way of defining the evil that the Fathers of the Church saw in the world. The

Seven Deadly Sins were codified by John Cassian (*De Institutis Coenobiorum*, c. 420) and given final authority by Pope Gregory, whose *Moralia* (*ante* 604) discussed them in an exegesis of Job 39. From this stemmed such widespread rehandling as that of the *Cursor Mundi* (early 14th century) and of the *Summa de Viciis* (*ante* 1261) of Gulielmus Peraldus, which so greatly influenced Chaucer. But the Sins had already become, by the new millennium, a stamping-ground for monkish homilies, vernacular sermons and innumerable tracts and treatises. Thus, the greatest literary treatment of the theme, that of Langland, was based upon an intensely felt and genuinely popular tradition. There is, nevertheless, something eerie in the ability of the Deadly Sins to survive all kinds of experiments in our literature. We may attribute some of their persistence to the ready assimilation of heathen superstitions into the Christian belief that the fallen angels were transmogrified into the hobgoblins and trolls of the earth. From Babylon through Grosseteste's *Chasteau d'Amour* (c. 1230) to Bunyan, Mansoul was felt to be God's peculiar castle, and it seems to have been felt that this was constantly under threat, as though the Devil had to have his fortress, too. In fact, one sermon is based upon the Castle of Sin and Misery, whose proprietor had the sinister name of Oldcastle. But, we remember, it was an Oldcastle who was the historical prototype of Falstaff; in his turn, perhaps the greatest Vice of our literature. It is in matters such as these that the individual genius is reinforced: often the tradition appears to be doing most of the work. What are we to make of the preachers' denunciations of gluttony?

> Glotenie maketh a man or a woman nat onliche blynd bodiliche but also gostliche. Vor it bryngeth him, as we se wel, anon rith in to drunkunhode, and thanne i sei he is blynd. Thow a now se thre candeles, ye, thre mones ther a nother man seth but on, yit i seye he is blynd. . . . I pray the, is nat this a grete blendnes, thynkis te, whan a man hath sete ate nale hows or ate taverne alday,—ye, nat onliche alday, but also meche of the nith therto,—and ate laste cumth hom as drunke as a dosel, and chit his wyf, reprevith his children, bet his meyne, ye, unnethe a kan go to bedde but as a his browth therto with his servauntes hondis! . . .

Or again:

God biddeth hym aryse erliche out of his bed and goo to chirche to the servise of God. The wombe seith 'Nay: that may not be doo! ffor I am so foul of mete, and drinke undefied that I mote abide til I have swet and bettir slept; ffor the chirche wole abide in to that I come.' And whan suche oon . . . gynneth to ryse of his bed, he bygynneth not to seie his matynes or other prayers. But anone he asketh what he schal ete and what he schal drynke, and whether eny such mete may be founde, or drinke. . . .

Or yet again:

glotons sittynge in the taverne, puttynge hire mouthes into the bolle, til thei ben drunke. Thenne thei crien with grete voice, boostynge, swerynge, lyynge and slaunderynge, and al hire evele dedes which thei have doun of many yeres afore freschli rehercynge and reiosynge. . . .

I could double or quadruple the number of quotations quite easily. Gluttony, or, to be specific, drunkenness, was evidently regarded as a curse of the age. But it was left to Langland to select the minute particulars which make up a portrait of Gluttony. Whereas the sermons denounce 'gluttony', 'gluttons' or, as a generic type, 'a glutton', Langland, without forgetting the general, implies this in a particular presentation: one Glutton who, setting out, as in our second quotation, to go to church, unfortunately stumbles across a tavern on the way:

Now beginneth Glutton   for to go to shrift
And caryeth him to kirkward   his *culpa* to show
Ac Betton the brewster   bade him good morwe
And heo asked him with that   whitherward he would.
'To holy church', quod he,   'for to hear mass,
And sithen I wole be shriven   and sin namoore.'
'I have good ale, gossip,' quod she,   'Glutton, woltou
    assay?'
'Hastou', quod he,   'any hot spices?'
'I have pepper and peony   and a pound of garlic,
A farthingworth of fennel-seed   for fasting days.'
Then goeth Glutton in   and great oaths after.

Cis the Sowester   sat on the bench,
Wat the Warner   and his wife both,
Tim the Tinker   and twain of his knaves,
Hick the Hackneyman   and Hugh the Needler,
Clarice of Cock's Lane   and the Clerk of the church,
Sir Piers of Pridie   and Peronelle of Flanders,
Daw the Dyker   and a dozen other,
A ribibour, a ratoner,   a raker of Cheap,
A roper, a redingking   and Rose the Disher,
Godfrey of Garlic-hithe   and Griffin the Welsh,
Of upholders a heap,   early by the morwe,
Give Glutton with glad cheer   good ale to hansel. . . .
(B, v 296–318)

This is one of the great comic portraits in literature; none the less comic for having as its basis an undercurrent of moral indignation. Glutton is all the more a person for being defined by his bad companions. Each of their names has a meaning. Take Clarice of Cock's Lane, for example: quite apart from the obvious pun, Cock's Lane was where women of ill repute were led after they had been placed in the pillory. Or, for another instance, Sir Piers of Pridie—Sir Piers was a usual name for a monk, and Pridie, according to Skeat (1886 edition), is a sort of pun on prie-dieu or praying stool. And, 'by a severe stroke of satire', this ecclesiastic is found on a tavern-bench next to Peronelle of Flanders: Peronelle (or purnel) being a cant-name for any bold-faced woman, and Flemish women being especially notorious as street-walkers. One could go on, but it is fairly clear from all this that Glutton has found himself in congenial company.

The whole passage, though, is subtler than even this would suggest. For we are never allowed to forget that Glutton should be in church. There is what appears to be a senseless game of barter whereby the difference of value between two articles of clothing is estimated by the friends of the barterers, the difference to be taken out in ale:

Hick the Hostler   then had the cloak
In covenant that Clement   should the cup fill,
And have Hick's hood, the hostler, and holden him
    y-served,
And whoso repenteth rathest   should arise after

And greeten Sir Glutton   with a gallon ale.

(B, v 331–5)

Senseless game, indeed; but does not this irresistibly call to mind the soldiers dicing for Christ's clothes after the Crucifixion? And just as telling, there are intimations of time passing—of time, indeed, running out; and all these are done in terms of the church from which Glutton has absented himself:

There was laughing and louring   and 'let go the cup!'
Bargains and beverages   began to arise,
And sitten so till evensong   and sungen umwhile
Till Glutton had y-glubbed   a gallon and a gill.
His guts began to gothlen   as two greedy sows;
He pissed a pottle   in a paternoster-while,
And blew his round rewet   at the rug-bone's end
That all who heard that horn   held hir nose after
And wished it had been waxed   with a wisp of furzes.

(B, v 336–44)

Evensong, the paternoster, even the last trump most dangerously parodied in Glutton's final fart: all inform us, though not Glutton, that the Day of Judgment is at hand. Yet the author never loses hold of the comic aspect of things: this is a character presented with a Jonsonian or Shakespearean comic gusto. Glutton staggers, spews, collapses, is got home to bed; then the cycle starts all over again:

With all the woe of the world   his wife and his wench
Bearen him to his bed   and brought him therein,
And after all this excess   he had an accidie
That he sleep Saturday and Sunday   till sun yede to rest.
Then waked he of his winking   and wiped his eyen;
The first word that he spake was   'where is the bowl?'

(B, v 357–62)

The lad of the old castle, indeed, and with no ambiguity at all looking forward through two centuries of Vices to *Henry IV. 1* and *2*. We remember the words of the Justice, a personification of justice itself, to the reprobate Falstaff: 'Your means are very slender, and your waste is great. . . . You follow the young prince up and down, like his ill angel.'

Equally traditional, and equally forward-looking, is the portrait of Covetous. In the sermons, he usually appears as a merchant dealing in short measure:

> I muste nedys weyin falsly chese and wolle, spyserye and othere thinges, and selle be false mesurys as othere don; ellys schulde I loose ther-on. . . .

Or again:

> as when a marchant can sotelliche adresse his ware to make hit seme better than it is, and scheweth it in derke place, to hyde the defaute therof, or to make seme the better, as doth drapers, mercers, and many other suche. . . .

But it was left to Langland to clothe these traditional elements— 'false othys and auncerys' in a lousy hat and a torn tabard, to give them a meagre allowance of flesh and set them to walk through the world.

> Then came Covetise   I can him not describe,
> So hungrily and holwe   Sir Harvey him looked.
> He was beetle-browed and baber-lipped   with two bleared
>   eyen
> And like a leathern purse   lolled his cheeks
> Well sidder than his chin;   they chivelled for eld;
> And as a bondman's bacon   his beard was y-shave.
> With a hood on his head,   a hat above,
> In a torn tabard   of twelve winter age;
> But if a louse could leap,   I 'lieve and I trow,
> She should not wander on that welsh,   so was it threadbare.
>   (B, v 188–97)

In the case of Glutton, Langland provided a milieu and a situation set in the present. For Covetous he provides a singularly convincing biography:

> 'I have been covetous,' quod this caitiff,   'I beknow it
>   here.
> For some time I served   Sim atten Oak

And was his prentice y-plight   his profit to look.
First I learned to lie   a leaf other twain;
Wickedly to weigh   was my first lesson.
To Wye and to Winchester   I went to the Fair
With many manner merchandise   as my master me hight.
Ne had the grace of guile   y-go amongst my ware
It had been unsold this seven year   so me God help.
Then drew me among drapers   my donat to learn,
To draw the list along,   the longer it seemed;
Among the rich rays   I rendered a lesson;
Proached hem with a pack-needle   and plait hem together
Put hem in a presser   and pinned hem therein,
Till ten yards or twelve   told out thirteen. . . .'

(B, v 198–212)

In Langland's hands, then, the Deadly Sins are anything but two-dimensional. They have a vividness of appearance, a depth of characterisation and a wealth of antecedent that puts them among the great characters of literature. Behind them, as with all of Langland, is the corpus of medieval preaching. And, as I said earlier, before them lies English. The outbreak of Pardoner plays and morality plays with personified vices owes far more in mode and subject matter to Langland than to Chaucer. Even the miracle plays proper, which owe most directly to the sermons and to the Scriptures behind them, show the influence of our central allegory; not just in simple-minded processions of the Deadly Sins as in the Coventry Doomsday Play—'on Covetyse was all thy thought'—but also in far more sophisticated productions. The character of Mac, for example, in the Towneley Second Shepherd's Play (c.1420) has progressed far from the medieval sermon, but not from Langland's scheming shyster:

Now were time for a man that lacks what he would
To stalk privily then unto a fold,
And nimbly to work then, and be not too bold,
For he might aby the bargain, if it were told
At the ending.
Now were time for to rail
But he needs good council
That fain would fare well
And has but little spending . . . .

Notice the rather off-beat rhythms, the general air of elusiveness. This looks forward to the conjuror figure—he puts a spell on the sleeping shepherds—of the starving and still vicious Subtle in *The Alchemist* (1610):

> at Pie-Corner
> Taking your meal of steam in, from cooks' stalls,
> Where, like the father of hunger, you did walk
> Piteously costive, with your pinched-horn-nose,
> And your complexion of the Roman wash,
> Stuck full of black and melancholic worms,
> Like powder corns shot at the artillery yard. . . .
> When you went pinned up in the several rags
> You had raked and picked from dunghills, before
>   day;
> Your feet in mouldy slippers for your kibes;
> A felt of rug, and a thin threaden cloak,
> That scarce would cover your no buttocks . . . .

Visually this relates to the *Visio*. More important, it demonstrates how Langland was part of the central tradition of English and to what extent he helped to shape it. A figure common to *Piers Plowman*, the *Second Shepherd's Play* and *The Alchemist* is something more than a static representation of sin or vice. And, indeed, Covetous has other guises: as Barabas in the *Jew of Malta* counting his treasure, or Volpone, in Jonson's play of that name (1605), even more blasphemously worshipping it:

> Good morrow to the day; and next, my gold!—
> Open the shrine that I may see my saint.
> Hail the world's soul, and mine!

Kindred figures are Meercraft in *The Devil is an Ass* by the same author, or Luke Frugal in Massinger's *City Madam*; also his threatening figure of Overreach in *A New Way to Pay Old Debts* followed by the ever-hungry Greedy. And the tradition goes on, through channels so apparently diverse as the courtly Restoration comedy and the homely John Bunyan. This is the stuff not just of English drama but the English language itself; and if we find the allegory receding a little in the eighteenth century, so that the particular details of Pope's Cotta or Fielding's

Parson Trulliber remain unbacked by representative significance, this is only to suggest that already Romanticism was coming and the great weight of tradition and sense of community was being gradually replaced by the artist's lonely voice. Fagin, Scrooge and Boffin are all in their different ways embodiments of Covetous, but the allegory is subsumed in the realism. Yet even as far as the late nineteenth century the force of the *Visio* can be felt. Through interludes and miracle plays, through Shakespeare and Jonson, through Restoration comedy into Fielding on the one hand and Bunyan on the other, the moralised figure capers and grimaces: we think of the myriads of fluttering and buzzing creatures that in *Our Mutual Friend* are attracted to the dunghills of the Golden Dustman.

This is what I meant when, at the beginning of this chapter, I insisted that the *Visio* crystallises and defines the possibilities of English literary tradition. And why we should be indignant at the way in which our greatest non-dramatic poem outside Chaucer has been treated by its scholars. For *Piers Plowman* is the triumph, not of one particular man, but of a community, past and present; though sifted, it is true, through an extraordinary sensibility. Wherever we go in our language we come up against figures deriving at one, two or three removes from *Piers Plowman*. And English poetry itself is at its best when, like Langland, it is pithy, proverbial, local, alliterative. Therefore it is true to say that he who does not know Langland does not know English.

2 Chaucer: Experimentalist Extraordinary

The history of English poetry is, for the most part, an attestation of unoriginality. Poet has learned from previous poet and, all too often, takes over as characteristics his master's mannerisms. But there is an exception to this, and he occurs early in our literature. Chaucer, as W. W. Skeat said many years ago, was our first great English metrist. He employed for the first time in English the ottava rima of the Monk's Tale; the rhyme royal of *Troilus and Criseyde*; the terza rima of 'A Complaint to his Lady'; the roundel of the birds' song at the end of *The Parlement of Foules*; and the heroic couplet, which is the standard metre of *The Canterbury Tales*.

This points to a study of literature taking place well away from home. Alone among English poets, Chaucer's antecedents are predominantly Continental. The other great medieval poets, Langland and the author of *Sir Gawain and the Green Knight*, are his contemporaries, not his predecessors. He knew no Anglo-Saxon. Apart from a few lyrics, there was nothing in the vernacular from which he could learn.

We can tell very clearly what Chaucer thought of English poetry before his time. It consisted largely of verse romances. They make painful reading now, and we have no reason to suppose they would be much more attractive to a cultivated sensibility of the fourteenth century. They halt, they limp, they thrust forward stock phrases in a painful effort to achieve a rhyme. They are repetitive, objurgatory, conventional in all the

least appropriate ways. A modern author might try to write
an essay on the topic, privative though it would be, but there
are other ways of voicing an adverse criticism. The way Chaucer
took involved yet another form which he was the first to use
in English: the verse parody. 'Sir Thopas' is the item he put
forward in his pilgrim persona as his own contribution to *The
Canterbury Tales*. And there is hardly a phrase in it that is
not a caricature of some pre-existing phrase out of stock. Consider
the stylised beginning:

> Listeth, lordes, in good entent,
> And I wol telle verrayment
>   Of mirthe and of solas;
> Al of a knight was fair and gent
> In bataille and in tourneyment,
>   His name was sire Thopas.

This clearly derives from the beginning of *St Alexius* (early
14th century):

> Lesteneth alle, and herkeneth me,
> Yonge and olde, bonde & fre,
>   And ich you telle sone,
> How a yong man, gent and fre
> By-gan this worldis wele to fle
>   Y-born he was in Rome.

But the beginning of 'Sir Thopas' could as well derive from
Guy of Warwick (early 14th century), or any of a dozen such
stock romances. The same is true of Chaucer's stylised description
of his hero with his yellow beard hanging down to his girdle.
One finds this in 'Libeaus Desconus', but there are figures like
it in 'The Seven Sages of Rome' or 'Launfal'. The rejection
of all such nonsense is couched as parody rather than analysis,
but that does not make the adverse judgement any the less
firm. If Chaucer was to learn his craft, it would have to be
from craftsmen.

Of all texts, the one most useful to him seems to have been
La Roman de la Rose. This began as an allegory by Guillaume
de Lorris (c. 1225) and was completed as a satire by Jean de
Meun (c. 1275). The dependence of Chaucer upon this work

is no less astonishing than his independence. The point can be made, once more, through Chaucer's criticism; taking the shape this time, not of parody, but of translation.

The English version of the poem, *The Romaunt of the Rose*, survives in three fragments, the first of which is certainly by Chaucer (c. 1360s). It represents an apprenticeship which was to serve him through his working career. Yet, even while studying de Lorris, Chaucer brought to bear a focus not to be found in the high idealism of the French poet. The portrait of Elde, for instance, is distanced in the *Roman*:

> Ce ne fust mie grant morie
> S'ele morist, ne granz pechiez,
> Car toz ses cors estoit sechiez
> De vieillece e aneientiz. . . .

Chaucer's personification of age is more physically graphic:

> Y-wis, great qualm ne were it non,
> Ne sinne, although her lyf were gon.
> Al woxen was her body unwelde,
> And drie and dwined al for elde. . . .

'Unwelde', 'drie', 'dwined' seem more actual than their French equivalents. Partly this is a matter of alliteration, partly homeliness of speech.

In Chaucer's earliest 'original' poem, *The Book of the Duchess* (c. 1369), the first few lines, describing a state of sleeplessness, are imitated from Jean Froissart, who has

> Je sui de moi en grant merveille
> Comment je vifs quant tant je veille
> Et on ne point veillant. . . .
>
>   (*Paradys d'Amour*, c. 1360s)

Chaucer, in contrast, aims for the tone of the speaking voice:

> I have gret wonder, be this light,
> How that I live, for day ne night
> I may nat slepe wel nigh noght . . . .

'Be this light', 'day ne night', 'wel nigh noght'—these are Chaucer's additions. In altering the French, he is promulgating English. One can see how his asseverations are adapted from vernacular romance, but they could not have lived outside the French subject matter. The freedom and ease is, in any case, a technical triumph. According to Joseph Mersand (*Chaucer's Romance Vocabulary*, 1937), Chaucer introduced into the language over a thousand words of Romance origin. No doubt a good many of these were current in France and even in England, but Chaucer used them in his own way. There seems no reason to disagree with the verdict of John Skelton: 'oure englisshe rude so fresshely hath set out'. The new words were not eccentric. They included such items as 'dotard', 'laxatif', 'envoluped' and 'riotoures', which are familiar to readers of Chaucer as climactic to the poems in which they appear. Because they have lasted in the language, they appear to be 'modern' as well. Notes are sounded which are often not heard again in English poetry until many centuries later.

Here, for example, we have a tone of voice normally associated with the great satirists of the Augustan age:

> A thousand times have I herd men telle
> That ther is joy in hevene and peyne in helle,
> And I acorde wel that it is so;
> But, natheles, yet wot I wel also
> That ther nis noon dwelling in this contree,
> That eyther hath in hevene or helle y-be,
> Ne may of hit noon other weyes witen,
> But as he hath herd seyd, or founde it writen . . . .

One can see why Chaucer was so much admired by Dryden. This is from the Prologue to *The Legend of Good Women*. In text F (c. 1385), which is the earlier of the two versions, it is one of the greatest poems Chaucer wrote. Its felicity of style can be localised in the cadence that puts a case at leisure before going on to show what other possibilities there are. There is a sense of epigram which, unlike the constricting Augustan antithesis, liberates the explicit statement into wider areas of meaning. 'Bernard the monk ne saw not all, pardee!'—one has the sense of the author looking all round a question. Further, the style is inseparable from a sense of personality. There is the note of experience here, certainly, but it is never overweening:

> And as for me, though that I konne but lite,
> On bokes for to rede I me delite . . . .

This tone, at once expository and self-deprecating, disperses itself through dozens of masks and semblances. Here, in *The Parlement of Foules* (c. 1380), we find the wisdom of the achieved poet:

> The lyf so short, the craft so long to lerne,
> Th'assay so hard, so sharp the conqueringe,
> The dredful joye, alwey that slit so yerne:
> Al this mene I by Love . . . .

But such wisdom co-exists with a modesty at once impish and deliberated:

> For al be that I knowe nat Love in dede,
> Ne wot how that he quiteth folk here hire,
> Yit happeth me ful ofte in bokes reede
> Of his mirakles and his crewel ire . . . .

The one tone informs and affects the other. In this way, Chaucer becomes a character in his own poetry. The narrative mode of *Troilus and Criseyde* (1380–85) is, like that of *The Parlement of Foules*, biased personally. But the bias makes for a deliberately composed personality:

> For I, that God of Loves servantz serve,
> Ne dar to Love, for myn unliklinesse . . . .

Indeed, the tone is subtly deflected into the distinct character that Chaucer built up from the conventional go-between he found in Boccaccio:

> 'Ye, Troilus, now herke,' quod Pandare;
> 'Though I be nice, it happeth often so,
> That oon that excesse doth ful yvele fare
> By good counseil kan kepe his frend therfro.
> I have myself ek seyn a blind man goo
> There as he fel that couthe loken wide;
> A fool may ek a wis-man ofte gide. . . .'

Here, again, we have indebtedness to a foreign source—*Il Filostrato*
(1336)—compounded with an ingenuity owing nothing to anyone
but the poet himself. The tone is more complex than the quotation
suggests. It is clear from the action, and the various reactions
of Pandarus, that he is anything but a fool. The very self-deprecation acts as a guarantee of intelligence. And the epigrammatic
quality which is the essence of Chaucer's style is given even
more dramatic point by the character developed into Pandarus,
a man who tends to favour wise saws and modern instances.
Even Troilus, not the most discerning of mortals, says, '"For
thi proverbes may me naught availle"'.

Pandarus, then, is a character, like his author, who tends to
talk in proverbs. There is, therefore, a continuity between Pandarus's asseverations and the narrative tone:

> '... What! many a man hath love ful deere y-bought
> Twenty winter that his lady wiste,
> That nevere yet his lady mouth he kiste. ...'

This, in fact, is Pandarus talking to Troilus, but it might as aptly
have been the narrator. In this way Chaucer conflates what
critics have often thought to be two properties of fiction in
the last century. The Trapped Spectator is the non-participant
who judges the action, influences more than he knows, and
acts as mediator between the characters and the reader. The Dramatised Consciousness is the medium through which the action
is seen. Both, in *Troilus and Criseyde*, combine in the figure
of Pandarus and his interrelationship with a sharply slanted narrative.

Chaucer found no imitator in this area until the onset of
the nineteenth-century novel. He is the first relativistic writer,
and remained unique for 400 years after his time. Nothing in
his stories is to be taken for granted. One thing is certain:
he was a deeply Christian poet. And, being so, his relativism
in narrative may be due to the fact that he feels that God
alone knows all the answers.

This recognition of Chaucer's relativistic approach to his characters should clear up a number of pseudo-problems that have
vexed students of the General Prologue to *The Canterbury Tales*
(c. 1387). The travellers who set out from Southwark at sunrise
(4.45 a.m.) on 17 April 1387—the poem is amazingly specific—are
a motley company. It is as though Chaucer had collected together

some thirty of the most remarkable characters he had encountered in a busy life and worked them into immortality. Each of these figures is at once typical and also individual—the best of his kind. One cannot imagine the modern occasion that would have brought together a company of people so fortuitously and fruitfully. The Knight says,

> '. . . This world nis but a thurghfare ful of wo,
> And we been pilgrimes, passing to and fro. . . .'

Similarly, the Parson preaches his sermon on a text from Jeremiah concerned with 'wayes' and 'pathis'. An allegorical dimension is present, intermittently, through the poem. At times it seems as though the pilgrims' destination, Canterbury itself, is a semblance of the Heavenly City. And the people journeying there, 'God's plenty' as Dryden called them, are a simulacrum of mankind.

This being so, one would hardly expect to find the pilgrims faultless. Each has his own reason for going on a pilgrimage—an act of devotion, it may be, a holiday, an escape from domesticity, a means of evading justice. Therefore Chaucer has the intriguing difficulty of rendering his characters fresh and alive without at the same time seeming to endorse their shortcomings. His answer is to take the relativism of *The Parlement of Foules*, of the Prologue to *The Legend of Good Women* and of *Troilus and Criseyde* even further; perhaps, as far as it will go. As Talbot Donaldson remarked in a perceptive essay (*PMLA*, 1954), Chaucer is very much a pilgrim on this journey, and he transforms himself into one of his own characters. The pilgrim Chaucer is naïf and bourgeois; he applauds excellence of performance and seems unconcerned as to whether what is being performed is desirable or even necessary; in brief, he is a lover of good company. In other words, the persona is a good deal less sophisticated and critical than the poet. This is plain if we go no further than the General Prologue. It is not a matter of simple reduction: the opening of the poem is as blithe as anything in English:

> Whan that Aprill with his shoures soote
> The droghte of March hath perced to the roote,
> And bathed every veine in swich licour
> Of which vertu engendred is the flour . . .

Chaucer the pilgrim invokes the spring with an innocent passion that Chaucer the poet understands. The whole passage breathes the sense of rebirth, the impregnation of March by April, the bringing forth from the barren winter the plants and portents of spring. It may well be that, behind the figure of the pilgrim, the poet himself feels a yearning inspired into creation.

As ever with Chaucer, this attitude is qualified. The pilgrim has his limitations. Some of them are endearing: his innocent acceptance of strangers, for example, and his anxiety to be excused if his report of their sayings offends any delicate ear—'My wit is short, ye may wel understonde'. This is sleight of hand, designed to suspend disbelief and to make us feel that a churl, for example, is a real churl—speaking through Chaucer, perhaps, but having his own independent existence which the narrative relays to us. The result is that all the pilgrims are seen appreciatively, but only the truly good receive an unqualified endorsement. In such a case, the poet allows the narrative to take on an authoritative resonance beyond the range of the 'short' wit which he allows his *alter ego*, the innocent pilgrim.

We hear this resonance in the characterisation of the Knight, who is seen as the finest type of secular manhood:

> A Knight ther was, and that a worthy man,
> That fro the time that he first bigan
> To riden out, he loved chivalrie,
> Trouthe and honour, fredom and curteisie. . . .

This ringing encomium is reinforced by a description of the Knight's career in terms of war: 'At mortal batailles hadde he been fiftene'. These, as J. M. Manly pointed out (*Transactions of the American Philological Association*, 1907), can be expressed in terms of three separate wars fought against, respectively, the Moors, the Saracens and the Tartars. The Knight's career, in fact, has been a sustained crusade against paganism. It is strange to find that, far-fetched as his exploits seem, they match those of an acquaintance of Chaucer, Sir Stephen le Scrope of Masham. The battles have certainly taken their toll of the Knight. He presents a faded appearance, his tunic stained from his recently discarded coat of mail. This suggests that he has lost no time in fulfilling a vow made on the last of his fifteen battles:

> For he was late y-come from his viage,
> And wente for to doon his pilgrimage.

The Parson, on the other hand, is one of the meek who shall inherit the earth. Initially he is presented in terms of his positive qualities:

> A good man was ther of religioun,
> And was a povre Persoun of a Toun,
> But riche he was of hooly thoght and werk. . . .

Chaucer at first creates him in terms of the cardinal virtues which are later to be defined in the Parson's own tale as humilitee, abstinence, charitee, pitee, fortitudo, pacience and chastity. The Parson is further defined by the faults which he avoids: chiefly, the usual curse of the fourteenth-century Church, persistent absenteeism. In this way, Chaucer succeeds in portraying a genuinely good man by invoking negative elements that occur elsewhere. It is the poet, rather than the pilgrim, who has the vigorous sense not only of virtue but of default:

> He waited after no pompe and reverence,
> Ne maked him a spiced conscience,
> But Cristes loore and his apostles twelve
> He taughte, but first he folwed it himselve.

But, for most of the General Prologue, Chaucer deals with people more or less morally culpable. In spite of this, the device of the pilgrim as narrator allows the poet to make the most of any redeeming qualities the characters possess. This is seen, for example, in the rendering of those members of the clerisy who do not quite match up to the highest Christian expectations. The first in consequence—far outranking the Parson—are the Prioress and the Monk. It is no accident that great emphasis is laid on their physical attributes as fine specimens of their respective sexes. The Prioress is evoked in terms of lyric and romance:

> Ther was also a Nonne, a Prioresse,
> That of hir smiling was ful simple and coy . . . .

That phrase, 'simple et coie', is found, as J. L. Lowes tells

us (*Anglia*, 1910), in a hundred love-songs of medieval France.
The description of the Prioress, with her 'nose tretys', her 'eyen
grey as glas' and 'her mouth ful smal' is very much that of
the Lady Idleness in *The Romaunt of the Rose*. And idleness
was one of the charges most frequently brought against the
regular clergy of Chaucer's time. The Prioress is praised for
her fair forehead, her corals and beads, her kindness to her
dogs. But nuns were not supposed to reveal their foreheads,
wear jewellery, keep pets, or, indeed, go on pilgrimages. All
this suggests that the lady's vocation would have been—had she
been better connected—to bloom in the world of court and
assembly. It is true that she has temporarily triumphed over
her nun's livery and the shady cloister where she is habitually
mewed. There was in fact a Madame Argentyne at St Leonard's,
Stratford-atte-Bowe. But, in spite of the piety of her tale, and
the admiration of the pilgrim, the Prioress remains a dubious
figure. Several interpretations can be put upon her motto 'Amor
vincit omnia'; derived, as it is, from the Eclogues of Virgil
and worked—characteristically—into a gold brooch.

The gullible pilgrim, Chaucer's *alter ego*, is equally impressed
by the Prioress's contemporary, the virile Monk. He reports
his conversation in a magnificently heard *oratio obliqua*:

> He yaf nat of that text a pulled hen,
> That seith that hunters ben nat hooly men . . . .

The text in question may be found in St Augustine and in
the *Breviarium in Psalmos*, and Rudolf Willard (*Texas Studies
in English*, 1947) has pointed out many other instances. Field
sports were held incompatible with the monastic ideal:

> But thilke text heeld he nat worth an oystre;
> And I seyde his opinion was good.

Through the acquiescence of the meek little pilgrim filters the
assertiveness of the earthy Monk:

> What sholde he studie and make himselven wood,
> Upon a book in cloistre alwey to poure,
> Or swinken with his handes, and laboure,
> As Austin bit? How shal the world be served?

The answer to this is beyond the purview of the pilgrim Chaucer, but well within that of the great Christian poet. The world will be served by the Merchant, the Man of Law, the Franklin and their kind. The Monk is, like the Prioress, a fine specimen of humanity who has found himself in the wrong job. A prototype may be William de Cloune, Abbot of Leicester, who coursed the field with John of Gaunt. And he has been defended by Fr Paul Beichner (*Speculum*, 1959) in terms which might well recommend him for the post of manager of a great estate. But this goes to show that the terms of his evocation are powerfully secular:

> And whan he rood, men mighte his bridel heere
> Ginglen in a whistlinge wind als cleere
> And eek as loude as dooth the chapel belle . . . .

The ironic contrast between secular propensity and clerical employment runs throughout. The pilgrim sees, and makes us see, the Monk's shining bald head, sweating face, gleaming eyes, oiled boots—he is oiled, it seems, all over, but in no ecclesiastical unguent:

> A fat swan loved he best of any roost,
> His palfrey was as broun as is a berie.

This admixture of appreciation from the pilgrim and criticism from the poet runs throughout the General Prologue. The distance between appreciation and criticism widens when the Prologue deals with characters in greater want of forgiveness than the Prioress and the Monk. The narrative may seem to side with a rogue or hypocrite, but the mode of representation is rich enough to imply a sterner view of human conduct. The effect is that of epigram, as though the pressure of knowledge in an exiguity of space projected the language into intense and directed specificity:

> (Friar)   He was the beste beggere in his hous
>
> (Merchant)   Ther wiste no wight that he was in dette
>
> (Sergeant of the Law)   And yet he semed bisier than he was
>
> (Franklin)   For he was Epicurus' owene sone . . . .

Each of these approbations carries a strong negative charge. For example, it is impossible for the Friar to be a good beggar. Beggars are a curse, and if he is 'good' at promulgating this particular curse, he is behaving very badly. The characters, for the most part, get progressively worse through the remainder of the General Prologue:

(Shipman)	Of nice conscience took he no keep
(Doctor)	Therefore he lovede gold in special
(Miller)	And yet he hadde a thombe of gold, pardee
(Reve)	They were adrad of him as of the deeth
(Summoner)	As hoot he was and lecherous as a sparwe
(Pardoner)	He made the person and the peple his apes.

In the General Prologue, Chaucer shows up each life's tragedy or farce in a score of witty lines. But several of the characters are given prologues of their own later on, and in this way they speak for themselves and carry their histories and obsessions further. As J. M. Manly said in *Some New Light on Chaucer* (1926), characterisation by significant speech was original to Chaucer in English literature. There are headlinks, too, where relationships and conflicts take place that create the feel of a living community. Another factor in the sense of development that runs through the poem is the relationship of each pilgrim to the tale assigned him.

This is, usually, done with astonishing adroitness; not least in the case of the Knight. Whether or not the story of Palamon and Arcite existed in Chaucer's version before *The Canterbury Tales* was conceived, it fits the personality of the Knight as to the manner born. It is adapted from Boccaccio's *Teseida* (1339–40), but Chaucer made many alterations, all of them directed to what may be termed depersonalisation. For example, he reduces the difference of character between the two knights, rivals for the hand of Emily, until the figures of Palamon and Arcite are stylised equivalents of one another. The heroine herself becomes a lovely cipher: a thing to be contested for, not a woman with a choice of her own. If character is reduced in scale, the background becomes overwhelmingly into focus and detail, so that the properties of the poem become as important as the personalities. The poem may seem to sacrifice drama to symbolism, but, given its basic philosophy, this is to its advantage. One thinks of the Temple of Mars before which Arcite prays. It is described by the much-travelled Knight in the manner of an eye-witness:

> Ther saugh I first the derke imagining
> Of Felonye, and al the compassing;
> The crueel Ire, reed as any gleede;
> The pykepurs, and eek the pale Drede;
> The smilere with the knyf under the cloke . . . .

Changes of fashion in verse or dress have not diminished the sharpness of that last image. It is even more impressive if one thinks of Boccaccio's restrained original: 'E con gli occulti ferri i Tradimenti'. The conversation among the gods, too, is given with a sense of human passion that transcends period:

> '. . . Myn is the strangling and hanging by the throte,
> The murmure and the cherles rebelling,
> The groininge, and the privee empoisoning . . . .'

Whether or not this is one of Chaucer's rare allusions to the Peasants' Revolt, the general current of argument is clear. A simple reading from adverse effect to immediate cause would suggest that the gods, if they exist, are malign. Yet Christianity teaches its followers to regard the universe as the product of a beneficent providence. The Knight's Tale does much to resolve this paradox. It suffuses the plot of the *Teseida* with the philosophy of Boethius (c. 524), which seeks to reconcile human misfortune and divine benevolence. Boethius reasons that the prime impulse from godhead passes through stage after stage of increasing imperfection until, in its immediate action upon our world, it feels like the buffeting of blind chance. The Knight's stance is that of a man able to endure misfortune in the belief that, if we knew all, we would see that every event leads back, link by link, to the stability and perfection of God. There is no help for it but to accept the role that immediate chance thrusts upon us. We cannot see any reason why Arcite should die rather than Palamon: their roles appear, as they do not in Boccaccio, interchangeable. Chaucer, however, has his own critical comment here. In translating *De Consolatione Philosophiae* (c. 1380) he puts a personal emphasis upon Boethian stoicism:

> That the world with stable feyth varieth accordable chaungynges ... al this accordaunce of thynges is bounde with love, that governeth erthe and see, and hath also comandement to the hevene.... (II, metre 8)

There is love: not the courtly or knightly variety, but a universal benevolence, cast so wide that men fail to understand it. The Boethian vocabulary tinctures the Knight's Tale: it is full of such words as 'stable', 'chaungynge', 'bounds'. Its air of abstract thought and noble resignation is unusual, even in Chaucer. One can see the effect in such passages as Theseus's great speech on Destiny:

> 'The First Moevere of the cause above,
> Whan he first made the faire cheyne of love,
> Greet was th'effect, and heigh was his entente.
> Wel wiste he why, and what thereof he mente;
> For with that faire cheyne of love he bond
> The fyr, the eyr, the water, and the lond
> In certeyn boundes, that they may nat flee....'

The key to the whole poem is in the same speech: a point made epigrammatically—

> '...Thanne is it wisdom, as it thinketh me,
> To maken vertu of necessitee...'

(cf. *Con. Phil.*, v, prose 6). Even though the death of Arcite is incomprehensible to himself, to Palamon or Emily, clearly it is intended by the First Mover and therefore must be good. In the Knight's Tale we have not only an acting out of Christian stoicism but also an explanation of how the Knight rose above the dangers that beset him in fifteen mortal battles during three Crusades. *The Canterbury Tales* start off on a lofty plane.

They are not allowed so to continue. The Host, a virile figure who has put himself in charge of proceedings, calls upon the Monk to tell the other travellers a story. This is probably because he ranks highest among the clergy present. But the Miller intervenes 'in Pilate's voice' and proposes 'a noble tale' which, even at this point, one can infer will dismember the Knight's carefully composed Boethian Christianity. When the tale comes into evidence, it proves to be at once an answer to the Knight's Tale and a parody of it. The Miller shows conclusively that there is a way of regarding human affairs quite other than the exalted path of Christian stoicism. He is of the earth, earthy, and gives Chaucer a chance to concentrate his preferred images of farm and country to an extraordinary degree of richness. No knights are in question here: the contenders for a young lady's hand are a pair of comic clerks. Their duel is a mockery: one young man is tricked into kissing the lady's bottom while the other gets a heated poker thrust up his own. The heroine herself is no walking flower, no distant vision. She is presented in terms highly physical, not to say animal: she is lissom as a weasel, she sings like a swallow, skips like a calf:

> Winsinge she was, as is a joly colt,
> Long as a mast, and upright as a bolt.

Whereas Emily was wedded to virginity, Alison has an old and jealous carpenter for a mate. Her state, in other words, is barren.

The Host, suggesting that 'some better man' should tell a tale, had called the Miller 'Robin, my leeve brother'. It is an odd fact, as Robert Pratt pointed out (*Modern Language Notes*, 1944), that a similar, though younger, Robin occurs in the Miller's Tale as the carpenter's servant. We are told in the General Prologue, 'The Millere was a stout carl for the nones'. Likewise, we are told of the carpenter's Robin that he 'was a strong carl for the nones'. There was no door, we are assured, that the Miller could not heave off its hinges, and the carpenter's knave is seen doing precisely that with the door of the clerk Nicholas. There is the further fact that the Reeve tells us he was a carpenter before the days of his stewardship. He objects strongly to the Miller's intervention as a storyteller:

> '. . . It is a sinne and eek a greet folie

To apeyren any man, or him defame . . . .'

This is before the Miller has even started his tale. It is as though
the Reeve knew that his own withers were about to be wrung.
He has been riding 'the hindmoste of our route', as far as
possible removed from the Miller, who is represented with a
set of bagpipes leading the procession out of town. Clearly,
there is a deep antipathy between the men. The richness of
the Miller's Tale, in dramatic context, stems from his recollection
of an incident of his youth when he was in the service of
that jealous carpenter who eventually became the envious Reeve.

The Reeve, in his prologue, picks up the theme of age and
barrenness. He has already been described in the General Prologue
as lean and sapless—a further contrast with the Miller—but he
now extends that description *in propria persona*:

'. . . But ik am oold, me list not pley for age;
Gras time is doon, my fodder is now forage . . . .'

The robust Miller told a robust tale, redolent of a huge delight
in all things physical. The Reeve's story is similar in plot, but
the vision is alienated. The joke figure in the Miller's Tale is
a cuckolded carpenter; and the old carpenter, in his turn, retails
a similar downfall in the household of a miller. But he sees
these events with an eye at once cynical and goatish. The Miller's
daughter, compared with Alison, is gross: 'With buttokes brode,
and brestes rounde and hye'. As in the Miller's Tale, there
are two clerks in search of female flesh; but they are much
debased. Through a crude stratagem, one of the young men
beds the daughter while the other makes do with the Miller's
wife. Chaucer furthers the debasing effect by letting the Reeve
ridicule their Northern dialect. One of them bids farewell to
the Miller's daughter in grandiose fashion:

'. . . But everemo, wher so I go or ride,
I is thyn awen clerk, swa have I seel.'

It is a parody of knighthood, more rancorous than that of the
Miller. But it serves to indicate the connection of the first three
Canterbury Tales. What we have in the stories of the Knight,
the Miller and the Reeve are three views of love: stoic, sensual

and cynical.

Similar interconnections exist among the next group of tales. It was G. L. Kittredge (*Modern Philology*, 1912) who first pointed out the community of theme between the prologue and tale of the Wife of Bath and the tales of the Clerk, Merchant and Franklin. What we have here is a dramatisation of differing views of marriage.

The Wife of Bath is a striking physical presence in the General Prologue—gat-toothed, bold-faced, broad-hipped, a hat broad as a buckler on her head, on her feet a pair of sharp spurs. This embattled appearance goes along with the statement, repeated in her own prologue, 'Housbondes at chirche dore she hadde fyve'. It is clear where Chaucer got this notion. This is Jesus speaking to the Samaritan woman; in Wycliffe's version 'Thou seidist wel, for I have not an hosebonde; for soth thou hast had fyve hosebondis' (John 4). The Wife of Bath's Prologue is, among many other things, a dramatised conflict between this and a proposition in 1 Corinthians 7: 'Forsoth if thou hast taken a wyf, thou hast not synned ... nethelees suche schulen have tribulacioun of fleisch ....'

The Wife of Bath's Prologue is one of the most startlingly original works that even Chaucer, the restless experimentalist, produced. It is the first fictional autobiography in English; it is the first and most successful attempt at a stream of consciousness; except that it transcends the form, we would say it is the first dramatic monologue. The Bible provides, as has been seen, some kind of moral antecedent; but it is very freely handled. And literary antecedents can be found, as so often in Chaucer, in *La Roman de la Rose*. But the revelations even of La Vielle are stylised compared with the rich plasticity of

> 'Experience, though noon auctoritee
> Were in this world, is right ynogh for me
> To speke of wo that is in mariage ....'

We will find no equivalent for this in *La Roman de la Rose*. The air of colloquial question and debate, the implied presence of an audience, are highly characteristic:

> '... Tell me also, to what conclusion
> Were membres maad of generacion,

> And of so parfit wys a wight y-wroght?
> Trusteth right wel, they were nat maad for noght. . . .'

Colloquial though this seems, a good deal of it derives from 'auctoritee'—of a sort. The Wife's cheerful remarks about organs of generation stem from the highly unorthodox monk Jovinian, who wrote in praise of marriage. His work survives only in the indignant comments of St Jerome's tract against him (c. 395). A clever transition (lines 162–92) from this preamble on marriage reminds us of the other pilgrims and leads us into the practical aspect of the matter; namely, the Wife's account of her first three husbands (193–450). Chaucer short-cuts very ingeniously by conflating them into one composite figure, rich and old. She harangues and frightens this figure by claiming that when he is drunk, he incessantly scolds her:

> '"Thou seist that oxen, asses, hors, and houndes,
> They been assayed at diverse stoundes . . .
> But folk of wives maken noon assay . . . ."'

This is straight Jerome, after Theophrastus, and yet it is also a brilliant application of indirect speech. The pattern 'Thou seist . . . , thou seist . . .' persists through this section, and this is how the composite voice of the old husbands is got across. But the poem is dramatic: even in this fancied exchange, the Wife dominates all with her demands for information:

> '". . . But tel me this: why hidestow, with sorwe,
> The keyes of thy cheste awey fro me?
> It is my good as wel as thyn, pardee! . . ."'

It is, in spite of its immediacy of speech, an answer only in form. The Wife's idea of defence, we see, is attack. And it is attack more lethal even than the old husband realises. For the fact is that none of the exchange took place. The Wife has invented all these scoldings herself. In order to give herself a lever, she has pretended that they were spoken by the old man:

> '. . . And al was fals, but that I took witnesse
> On Janekin . . . .'

He has been mentioned before, but it is from this point (line 383) that the poem more or less elliptically approaches the subject of Jankin, who is to be husband number five. At this stage he is a young clerk, and we may infer a continuity between him and the amorous young fellows in the Miller's Tale and the Reeve's Tale. We next see him walking the Wife and her friend in the fields. This is after a transition passage (451–502) which succinctly treats of the unfaithful fourth husband. And it is during this husband's funeral procession (596 ff.) that the Wife of Bath notices Jankin's fine pair of legs. We realise that it is no accident that her name is Alison, for a similar incident takes place in a charming lyric (Sloane 2593):

> Jankin began the offis
>   On the Yole day;
> And yit me thinketh it dos me good,
>   So merie gan he say
>   Kyrieleyson.

The solemn phrase of the Mass puns on her own name and sounds in Jankin's mouth, as John Speirs remarks (*Medieval English Poetry*, 1957) like a wooing call. But Chaucer has deepened and civilised the little goliardic carol, which may have given him the idea for the final phase of the Wife's Prologue (502–828). Jankin becomes a sharply recognisable character approached—since he is a clerk—appropriately enough through his books. The Wife takes us by degrees nearer the crucial clash with her fifth husband. Already we have heard in the General Prologue that she is partly deaf. By line 634 we begin to see why:

> '. . . By God! he smoot me ones on the list,
> For that I rente out of his book a leef . . . .'

But at this point she avoids completing the anecdote and insteads quotes Jankin quoting one of the authors from his book—Valerius Maximus on female depravity. Jankin has emerged from behind his youthful gaiety and appears now as a resolute misogynist. No doubt some of this is motivated by the disappointment of a youth of twenty in finding himself married to a woman of forty. He is better informed and therefore more formidable than

the previous husbands. The Wife once more (line 666) tries
to get down to her story:

> '... Now wol I sey yow sooth, by Seint Thomas,
> Why that I rente out of his book a leef ....'

But she gets deflected, this time into a kind of Legend of Bad
Women (as Speirs calls it, *Chaucer the Maker*, 1951) drawn from
this same book of Jankin's. It appears to be a compilation of
several works: a treatise against marriage by Walter Map; an
attack on the luxury of women by the early Christian convert,
Tertullian; the account of the 'abbess' Heloïse which is found
in *La Roman de la Rose*; the stories about lovers in Ovid's
Ars Amatoria. Most of the other references—Theofraste, Crisippus,
Trotula, Jovinian again—come from the inevitable St Jerome.
By no means are all these anti-feminist, though, of course, Jankin
uses the texts for his own purpose in much the same way
as the Wife bends 'auctoritee' to hers. This set of legends has
the further advantage of providing a window out of the main
action which gives Chaucer a chance to comment on his story
and effect an amplitude of application. But these *exempla* are
integral to the plot. Jankin quotes so many cases so extensively
and abusively that at last the story reaches the situation repeatedly
prefigured by the Wife:

> '... And whan I saugh he wolde nevere fine
> To reden on this cursed book al night,
> Al sodeynly thre leves have I plight
> Out of his book, right as he radde ....'

and he, retaliating,

> '... up stirte as dooth a wood leoun,
> And with his fest he smoot me on the heed,
> That in the floor I lay as I were deed. ...'

Alison, however, turns the blow to her advantage. Jankin, shocked
at what he has done, accords her for the future the dominant
role in the marriage, or, as the Wife graphically puts it, '"He
yaf me al the bridel in myn hond"'. And, in return, she claims
that she was as kind '"As any wyf from Denmark unto Inde"'.

So a concordat is drawn up, and, after 828 lines of impetuous monologue, the Wife now declares that she is ready to tell her tale. We may be forgiven if we feel we have already heard it. And it is a fine statement of feminine individuality in an age when a married woman was a piece of property. Nothing is more entrancing in the whole of Chaucer than the way in which these long dead figures parade and jangle through the rich medium of the Wife's inconsequential memories. Inconsequential, that is to say, so far as the Wife is concerned, but the inner pattern evidenced by the form is that of consummate art.

By comparison, the Wife of Bath's Tale is a slight affair. The knight who is compelled by a rash promise to marry a loathly lady—this figure is found, as G. H. Maynardier painstakingly chronicled (1901); in English, Irish, French and German legends. The parallel between this and the elderly Wife of Bath with her young husband is obvious. But, once the knight puts himself into the hands of his ancient bride, 'His herte bathed in a bath of blisse'. The meaning of the tale seems to be that joy in marriage is attainable if the husband submits to the rule of the wife. The next few tales carry on the debate, each in its own distinctive mode of dramatisation.

The Clerk's Tale may be taken as the Church's answer to the Wife, but it is not so simple as that. It is true that the Wife insists on the limitation of the clerisy:

> '. . . By God! if wommen hadde writen stories
> As clerkes han withinne hire oratories . . . .'

And the Host joins in the badinage, calling upon the Clerk to tell his tale as though he were a young woman devoid of experience. It is true, also, that out of context the Clerk's story of patient Griselda looks like a plot designed to show the virtues of feminine submission. Her children are taken from her and she herself is cast out by her lordly husband into her former peasant state. But the tale comes from Petrarch, a clerk very different from the ascetic St Jerome; and in what Griselda has to say there is a note of bitterness that is absent even in Petrarch: '"Love is noght oold as whan that it is newe"'.

Chaucer also adds a current of indignant commentary that

runs throughout the poem:

> He hadde assayed hire ynogh bifore,
> And foond hire evere good . . . .

This in its turn answers the old husband's complaint in the Wife's Prologue,

> '"But folk of wives maken noon assay . . . ."'

It brings the Clerk nearer than might have been expected to the Wife's point of view; certainly it is not an orthodox view of the Church. The Clerk's pity and indignation redeem from brutality the tale of a husband of mature years and high station who holds in bondage a young and inexperienced girl of low degree.

In saying this I have—not unintentionally—described the basic plot of the Merchant's Tale. It is a sign of Chaucer's range and technique that the Wife's, the Clerk's and the Merchant's tales, superficially so little alike, can be shown to be related. The end of the Clerk's Tale refers back to the Wife of Bath and anticipates the Merchant. The Clerk ironically advises 'arche-wives' on how to deal with their husbands: 'And lat him care, and wepe, and wringe, and waille!' This note is taken up in his prologue by the elderly Merchant, who, it appears, has recently been married to a wife 'the worste that may be'. He says,

> 'Weping and wailing, care and oother sorwe
> I knowe ynogh, on even and a-morwe'. . . .

We can see why he is escaping on a pilgrimage. The story he tells is one worthy of an Iago; it is the most bitter of all the tales. The tone of the prologue shows some restraint, and is carried over in the observations against marriage of Justinus, a minor character in the story: 'For, God it woot, I have wept many a teere'. But the basic narrative of the tale itself is couched in a tone of scalding sarcasm. Even out of context, it would be difficult to read the praise of marriage with which the tale begins as completely straight:

> And certeinly, as sooth as God is king,
> To tak a wyf it is a glorious thing,

> And namely whan a man is oold and hoor
> Thanne is a wyf the fruit of his tresor. . . .

And on, and on, with the same mock-innocence until the term
'wyf', often repeated, assumes jangling and rancorous connotations.
The effect is all the more discordant because this is at once
a preface to and a commentary on the tale of an old man
blatantly deceived, through his uxoriousness and jealousy, by
a lively young wife.

The balance of the poem is preserved by a remarkable technical
feat. To the Merchant as narrator the wife is no more than
a sound piece of horse-flesh. But he tells us more than he knows:
through the narrative, she seems to develop. At first, she is
a passively beautiful object brought to her bridal bed as still as
a stone. On the wedding night, however, we receive a hint
as to an inner being:

> But God woot what that May thoughte in hir herte,
> Whan she him saugh up sittinge in his sherte,
> In his night-cappe, and with his nekke lene . . . .

Gradually her thoughts begin to rise nearer the surface. She
is attracted by her husband's squire; he manages to pass her
a note, and—'Who studieth now but faire fresshe May?' Her
first words, reported in indirect speech, are addressed to this
squire who appears to be dying of love for her; she bids him
be whole. Meanwhile she finds herself more and more a prisoner.
Her husband has acted out his proprietorial attitude towards
her by enclosing her in a garden so that she is, in the words
of the Song of Solomon, 'a welle selid'. A further limitation
is that the moral blindness of January becomes physical as well.
He loses his sight and this further sharpens his jealousy. In reply
to all this, the first words of May in direct speech are an assertion
of her individuality:

> 'I have,' quod she, 'a soule for to kepe
> As wel as ye . . .'

—words which belong as much in the Wife of Bath's Prologue,
for all its differences, as in this apparently cynical Merchant's
Tale. For, behind the constricting bitterness of the Merchant,

there is the wealth of Chaucer's understanding. Both views coexist and arise out of the basic situation, 'whan tendre youthe hath wedded stouping age'. The wholesale condemnation from the Merchant is undermined by the wholesale understanding of the poet.

The climax of the tale, therefore, is at once black farce and tragi-comedy. It takes place in January's walled garden. May persuades him that she is pregnant and desires a pear. January helps her up the pear-tree and into the arms of the squire who is waiting for her on a bough. The god Pluto, whose relationship with his own spouse in its turn represents a half-life, suddenly restores January's sight. The first thing the old man sees is his wife copulating with his squire in a pear-tree. May has become active with a vengeance. She even has the impudence to tell him that this was done to make him see again! The doting January is reassured, and the tale ends with a definite hint that the encounter in the tree has left her—a condition she falsely claimed before—with child.

For the Merchant this is a crowning irony. But for the poet, behind the Merchant's rancorous utterance, it suggests that even out of the most incongruous situation can come blessing and fruition:

> Now, goode men, I pray yow to be glad.
> Thus endeth heere my tale of Januarie;
> God blesse us, and his mooder Seinte Marie!

The Franklin's Tale in some degree takes up the pattern of the previous story. The marriage of a knight and a lady is jeopardised by the advances of a squire. The tale is at one with the high astounding terms in which it is couched. A clue to the reason for this is afforded by the Franklin's Prologue. The Franklin declares himself to be 'a burel man' and disclaims the colours of rhetoric. In doing so, he manages to use in eleven lines such rhetorical figures as *diminutio, interpretatio, circumlocutio, traductio* and *adnominatio*. In the tale itself I have counted, not exhaustively, twenty-two different figures of rhetoric, most of them used two or three times over. The style acts as a refracting medium: it colours that which it transmits.

Arveragus and Dorigen cannot do enough for each other. The knight's submission to Dorigen causes her to declare, '"Sire,

I wol be youre humble trewe wyf"'. This may well remind
us of Jankin's reconciliation with the Wife of Bath at the end
of her prologue or of the bargain struck by the loathly lady
in her tale. But it also, together with the elaborate style, suggests
the Franklin's unease. Concepts such as 'treuthe', 'freedom' and
'gentillesse' glide in and out of the narrative with differing
areas of connotation. The story permits this. Dorigen has promised
the squire Aurelius that she will never love him until he has
removed the black rocks on the coast of Brittany that menace
her husband's ship. He goes to a clerk who creates the illusion
that the rocks have gone; then he claims his reward. Dorigen
takes her dilemma to her husband, who advises her to keep
to her word. This concession on the part of Arveragus is termed
by Aurelius 'gentillesse'. But Aurelius, seeing Dorigen's distress,
releases her from the obligation she feels towards him; and this
might be termed 'gentillesse' in its turn. Even here, the problem
is passed on to the clerk who caused the rocks to disappear.
He is asked 'of his gentillesse' to give Aurelius time to pay.
But the clerk wishes to be as 'gentil' as a knight, and, in
his turn, absolves the squire from his debt. The denouement
of the poem, then, turns upon successive manumissions. Arveragus
has declared 'truth' to be the highest thing that man can keep,
but what, in this shifting context, is the truth? It is significant
that the poem ends, not with a statement or judgment, but
with the Franklin's favourite 'colour', *interrogatio*:

> Lordinges, this question, thanne, wol I aske now,
> Which was the mooste fre, as thinketh yow?
> Now telleth me, er that ye ferther wende.
> I kan namoore; my tale is at an ende.

There has been a moral slide from 'truth' to 'gentillesse' to
'freedom'. It may be felt that the question has been left open
as far as the Franklin is concerned; but, once more, the poet
implies a wider reality.

In the prologue the Franklin is seen deploring the lack of
'gentillesse' in his son, at least as compared with the squire.
But just as all Alisons and all clerks (with one exemplary exception)
in Chaucer have a family resemblance, so do all squires. The
qualities that the Franklin sees in the young man may not add
up to what is required of a Christian gentleman; this may be

all the more so if we consider the refractive nature of the Franklin's medium of expression. His 'colours' betoken an unease regarding his position in society, and it links up with the ambiguity of Arveragus and Dorigen. In showing gentillesse to Aurelius, it is not Dorigen doing an injustice to her husband and is not Arveragus likewise being unjust to his reluctant wife? And, however 'gentil' we may take the squire Aurelius to be, we must not forget that the problem was brought about by his 'ungentil' advances in the first place. This links up with the Janus figure inserted in a startling *descriptio*. The god of doorways and winters has two faces looking in different directions and is associated with the general air of Santa Claus that suffuses the Franklin in the General Prologue. The Franklin is a JP, an MP and a landowner, and may have been based on John Bussy, Sheriff of Lincoln, who, with all these inducements to recognition, seems not to have been accorded his rank by his enemies and was to come to grief at the end of the reign of Richard. However this may be, it is significant that the Franklin bears a purse and a dagger in lieu of a sword. This suggest that he lacks the stamp of true knighthood: military honours. The way in which Chaucer takes leave of him is telling: 'Was nowher swich a worthy vavasour'. This rare word has the implication of wealth but also of vassalage. The Franklin harps upon 'gentillesse' because he is not a parfit knight and therefore has no way of knowing what 'gentillesse' is. It is significant that he rides with the *nouveau-riche* lawyer, of whom it is said, 'So greet a purchasour was nowher noon'. All this atmosphere of entrepreneurism, as well as the basic plot, relates the Franklin's Tale to that of the Merchant; it also, however, relates to that of the Clerk. The Franklin's nobleman is as wrong-headed as Griselda's husband, though in another direction. The refusal to take 'maistrie' in marriage can, it seems, be as much of a mistake as the assumption of total dominance. This, in its turn, is a further answer to the Wife of Bath. The Franklin's rhetoric—his Dorigen has an *exclamatio* of 101 lines—is a way of colouring this fact, but he still cannot make it palatable. We need have no doubt as to how the Gordian knot of the Franklin's problem would have been cut had he submitted it for unravelment to the Parson.

The marriage debate, then, comes to no very firm conclusion in this relativist context of *The Canterbury Tales*. What we have here are four tenable attitudes: the Archwife's, the Clerk's, the

Cynic's and that of the Epicurean; the last loose and open-ended. *The Canterbury Tales* goes on to consider marriage, like love, in a wider context; a universal context: that of the Fall of Man.

The most direct treatment of this may be found in the Prioress's Tale. This is based upon a miracle told in many extant versions, not always with the tragic ending that Chaucer decided to use. On the positive side, the poem is a hymn to chastity with the Massacre of the Innocents implied in the background. Words like 'litel', 'child' and 'innocent' are insisted upon, and give the poem its somewhat frenetic atmosphere. A little child has learned a hymn to the Virgin, 'O Alma redemptoris', and says this on his way to and from school. This enrages the Jews of the district and they, possessed of a devil, cut his throat and cast him in a cess-pit. The shock of the image enhances our realisation that nothing can sully true innocence. We are very conscious of the thrilling voice of the Prioress as she pitches the note of exaltation higher and higher:

> O martir, sowded to virginitee,
> Now maistow singen, folwinge evere in oon
> The white Lamb celestial—quod she—
> Of which the grete evaungelist, Seint John,
> In Pathmos wroot, which seith that they that goon
> Biforn this Lamb, and singe a song al newe,
> That nevere, flesshly, wommen they ne knewe.

The miracle of chastity, voiced in these romantic terms by the Prioress, triumphs over the pit. It is the Host, placed on the tongue of the child by the Virgin herself, that enables his hymn to resound—'So loude that al the place gan to ringe'.

But this lyrical story is flanked by the numerous 'tragedies' recited by the Monk. Perhaps the best of these is the story of Ugolino and his children, who are starved to death in prison:

> His yonge sone, that thre yeer was of age,
> Unto him seyde, 'Father, why do ye wepe?...'

These tragedies, in their turn, relate to the series of *exempla* on the subject of dreams which form one of the numerous windows out of the great tale of the Cock and the Fox, told by the Nun's Priest. The Monk has spoken of Croesus's dream, when he thought he sat in a tree and was tended by Gods. Chanticleer, defending the authority of dreams to his wife, recounts the same story:

> '. . . Lo Cresus, which that was of Lyde king,
> Mette he nat that he sat upon a tree,
> Which signified he sholde anhanged be? . . .'

The difference is that this is part of a dialogue between two chickens. At times we are almost allowed to forget the fact. The tones of Chanticleer resonate on his plenitude of open vowels. Therefore, when we are recalled to context, the gap between the sententious conversation and the feathered controversialists becomes a simulacrum of the contrast between the brief authority of man and the fantastic tricks he plays before high heaven. The tale as a whole is an audacious conception: nothing less than the Fall of Man seen as a gigantic comedy. Like Croesus, Chanticleer is panoplied in pride: coral comb, black bill, azure legs, golden feathers, crowned with a comb, crenellated 'as it were a castel wall'; the medieval image of Mansoul. This description, L. P. Boone tells us (*Modern Language Notes*, 1949), is that of the Golden Spangled Hamburg, but the heraldic effect of the language is to present Chanticleer in the armour of a great baron—the colours of Henry Bolingbroke—or the vestments of an exalted ecclesiastic. He is pride personified before a fall.

The cock is, indeed, formidable. Chaucer causes him to quote Cicero, Macrobius and Vincent de Beauvais, among others. And the poem departs sharply from its sources in giving Chanticleer, rather than his hen, percipience enough to take note of dreams. To this extent, he is wiser than the various figures of his *exempla*, who all succumb through ignorance. But, with all this advantage of forewarning, Chanticleer falls. An array of parallels compares this, in mock-heroic vein, with the Crucifixion; the betrayal of Roland at Roncevaux; the Fall of Troy; the Roman sack of Carthage; the burning of Rome by Nero! This shows how embattled pride is proof even against intelligence. Chanticleer is the comic archetype of martyrs, tragic heroes, and, *pace* Croesus, he is well-washed with the fox's flattery. Daun Russell says,

> '. . . My lord youre fader—God his soule blesse—

> And eek youre mooder, of hire gentillesse,
> Han in myn hous y-been to my greet ese . . . .'

It is clear enough how the elder Chanticleer and his wife contributed to the fox's ease. Russell speaks with double tongue. The debate dissolves into graphic and auditory drama when the widow who owns the cock finds her treasure is taken

> 'Out, harrow and weylaway.
> Ha, ha, the fox!' and after him they ran,
> And eek with staves many another man.
> Ran Colle oure dogge, and Talbot and Gerland,
> And Malkin, with a distaf in hir hand . . .

and the cow and the calf and the hogs—and the ducks cry and the geese fly, and the bees . . . . It is as though the whole world has engaged itself in hunting down the devil. Yet, energetically told and lively as the story is, it takes up only 252 lines out of a total of 626. The rest of the tale is given over to such matters as the *exempla* (one, a miniature Canterbury Tale), the mock-heroic citation of parallels, and the wonderfully funny conversation between the two chickens:

> '. . . For whan I se the beautee of youre face,
> Ye been so scarlet reed aboute youre yen,
> It maketh al my drede for to dien;
> For al so siker as *In principio*,
> *Mulier est hominis confusio*,—
> Madame, the sentence of this Latin is,
> "Womman is mannes joye and al his blis". . . .'

The elements of the tale join together and form the vision of a world where men and beasts pitch their opinion of themselves too high and come to grief. The story is a vast *exemplum*, in other words; but, unlike the Monk's various tales, it is told as comedy: '"But I be myrie, y-wis I wol be blamed"' explains the mysterious narrator, who, alone among the pilgrims, is given no explicit personality. No doubt this is a further irony of Chaucer, since the Nun's Priest certainly wins the prize for the best story. And so the cock gains his release to live and crow in his back garden another day.

The picture of Chanticleer standing upon his toes and stretching his neck flows on into a tale told in a different manner, but also concerned with the sin of pride and the fall of man. It is a sophisticated irony of Chaucer that this highly moral tale is put into the mouth of the least equivocally condemned of all the pilgrims: the Pardoner. Yet this pardoner is allowed to boast of his virtuosity as a preacher in terms that irresistibly recall the cock carried away by his own eloquence—

> '. . . I preche so as ye han herd bifoore,
> And telle an hundred false japes moore.
> Thanne peyne I me to strecche forth the nekke,
> And est and west upon the peple I bekke . . .'

—except that, with his usual impudence, this predatory bird compares himself with a dove. However, virtuosity without spirituality is like Chanticleer's song; resonance without consonance. That is why we can criticise the pilgrim Chaucer's encomium in the General Prologue: 'He was in chirche a noble ecclesiast'.

Nevertheless the claim for technical adroitness is buttressed by what we see of the Pardoner in action. It is difficult to separate prologue from tale. The Pardoner begins the former with an unabashed description of his methods, which show him to be nothing more than a confidence trickster. Originally a pardoner or *quaestor* was a kind of fund-raiser. His job was to travel the parishes, to inform people of good works such as the building of a hospital, and to invite contributions as a means of allowing contributors to help themselves towards a state of grace (see Kellogg and Haselmayer, *PMLA*, 1951). But, by Chaucer's time, the system had got thoroughly out of hand. To say his Pardoner is 'of Rouncivale' is to condemn him. The branch of the hospice of St Mary Roncesvalles established at Charing Cross had been closed by the Crown in 1379 with considerable attendant scandal. Yet blackguardism was often harnessed to oratory. The Pardoner's Tale proper begins with a sermon of such power (lines 463–659) that some scholars have thought it was originally intended for the Parson. Unlike the Merchant's prolation in praise of marriage, there is no irony in this impassioned attack on cupidity, drunkenness, gambling and blasphemy:

> And forther over, I wol thee telle al plat,
> That vengeance shal nat parten from his hous
> That of his othes is to outrageous.
> 'By Goddes precious herte,' and 'By his nailes,'
> And 'By the blood of Crist that is in Hayles,
> Sevene is my chaunce, and thyn is cynk and treye!...'

There is a familiarity with the habits of gamblers and also an emphasis upon the details of sin rather than the delights of virtue. But these are traits found in many medieval sermons. However, the moral indignation comes oddly from the mouth of the Pardoner, who himself appears involved with all the sins he denounces. Further: the very cohesiveness of this sermon brings out the contrast between moral and moraliser. This is not only to cast a dazzling light on the Pardoner's role as hypocrite-in-chief among the pilgrims. It is also to say that an evil instrument can serve a divine purpose.

The sermon occupies the same proportion with regard to the rest of the poem that Chanticleer's 173 lines of *exempla* do in the Nun's Priest's Tale. The effect is to thrust at us, as a montage, the main sins of which the characters are guilty. The Pardoner's series of references to biblical and historical figures overtaken by 'hasardrye' acts as a set of windows which reveal a breadth of reference beyond the scope of the grim story he finally tells us. If the Prioress's Tale gives us a glimpse of heaven, the Pardoner's Tale is a chronicle of the damned. It carries, in fable as well as sermon, a powerful moral charge. All of the Deadly Sins act themselves out in the person of the revellers in the story. The young men are significantly anonymous; their possibilities are open to all sinners. They frequent stews and taverns; they gamble and swear; they envy the prowess of death, who has slain so many people; they rush out in a rage; and in their pride they vow, '"Deeth shal be deed, if that they may him hente."' Their frenzied search for death brings the revellers up against an old man at the extremity of old age:

> '...Ne Deeth, allas, ne wol nat han my lyf.
> Thus walke I, lyk a restelees kaitif,
> And on the ground, which is my moodres gate,
> I knokke with my staf, bothe erly and late,
> And seye, "Leeve mooder, leet me in!..."'

This haunting image is the turning point of the poem. The old man seems to be an exception to the common lot of humanity. In all analogues the figure fulfils a role at once prophetic and benign. And in this case he tells the revellers where death is. They find, at the spot he indicates, a heap of gold under a tree. They arrange that two of them will guard the gold until they are able to get it safely away, while the third will go to town for provisions. The last decides to poison the wine that he brings back, so that he can claim the treasure for himself. Meanwhile the other two have formed their own plans; and here one may remark that it is not only the story that is so compulsive, but also the purged and terse manner of the telling:

> What nedeth it to sermone of it moore?
> For right as they hadde cast his deeth bifoore,
> Right so they han him slain, and that anon.
> And whan that this was doon, thus spak that oon:
> 'Now lat us sitte and drinke, and make us merie,
> And afterward we wol his body berie.'
> And with that word it happed him, par cas,
> To take the botel ther the poison was,
> And drank, and yaf his felawe drinke also,
> For which anon they storven bothe two.

We can see that Chaucer was not making a vain boast for his Pardoner's expertise: 'Wel koude he rede a lessoun or a storie'. But the thing is not done yet. Though the story is over, the Pardoner modulates through a brief reversion to the impassioned tone of his sermon into an appeal to the pilgrims for funds. The oddity is that he has in his prologue boasted of his capacity to deceive the 'lewed peple' with stories, clouts and stones. Now, in his unmatchable impudence, he leaps out of his story to offer his rubbish for sale to the pilgrims like so many hot pies—'Al newe and fressh at every miles ende'— or safety insurance:

> Looke which a seuretee it is to yow alle
> That I am in youre felaweshipe y-falle,
> That may assoille yow . . .

—a thing, by the way, that he had no power to do. He caps his general sales talk with an appeal to the Host, whom he bids kiss his relics. This is the fraud seeking to supplant the virile leader of the company. But he receives, in answer, the most devastating retort in English literature:

> '. . . I wolde I hadde thy coillons in myn hond
> In stide of relikes or of seintuarie.
> Lat kutte hem of, I wol thee helpe hem carie;
> They shul be shrined in an hogges toord.'

This scornfully exposes the Pardoner, who, despite his boasts of sexual prowess, is presented as *eunuchus ex nativitate*: 'I trowe he were a gelding or a mare'. It suggests that his testicles are no more genuine than his vernicles. This, the climax of the interreaction between characters that forms the essential framework of *The Canterbury Tales*, is not driven to a conclusion; for the poem is a human comedy. The Knight, as befits his rank, intervenes and bids them make peace: 'Anon they kiste, and riden forth hir weye'.

But this framework is subjected to an extraordinary assault towards the end. The pilgrims have just heard the tale of St Cecilia, told by the Second Nun, when a Canon and his Yeoman gallop into the poem, they and their horses exhausted and sweating. Even before the pilgrim Chaucer identifies these sinister companions, the poet hints at their trade: 'His foreheed dropped as a stillatorie'. The forthcoming nature of the Yeoman's conversation causes his master to flee away. Thereupon he launches into his tale, the first part of which is as much exposition as the Pardoner's sermon. It is a flurry of words; a riot of technical terms; and we realise that the Canon is an apostate from his order (see Marie Hamilton, *Speculum*, 1941) and that he makes an illicit living as an alchemist. The apparent disorder of the Yeoman's speech, as ever in Chaucer, conceals a deliberated art. His imagery is in marked contradistinction from that which Chaucer uses elsewhere. A world is disclosed that is coagulated, combustible, crammed with materials lacking any touch of the spirit: a world, in short, fallen into corruption. The Yeoman himself speaks in the accents of a sorcerer's apprentice:

> Ful ofte it happeth so,

The pot tobreketh, and farewel, al is go!
Thise metals been of so greet violence,
Our walles mowe nat make hem resistence . . .
And somme are scatered al the floor aboute;
Somme lepe into the roof. Withouten doute,
Though that the feend noght in oure sighte him shewe,
I trowe he with us be, that ilke shrewe.

The properties, inspired by the devil, have a life of their own. But the evil intent of the alchemists is limited by their capacity. From this welter of images, smoking and exploding, precipitates a story in which a canon defrauds a priest. His three tricks are described in the same detail as the prefatory matter of the Yeoman's discourse, but, bewilderingly enough, the Yeoman insists that this was another canon and not his late master. This is a bluff calculated by the poet to fail, for the Yeoman speaks of the Canon in exactly the same terms, whether he is the historical alchemist of the prologue or the fictional alchemist of the tale. And an urgent autobiographical force runs throughout, compounded of awe at the Canon's knowledge and annoyance at himself for being involved with him—'Of his falsnesse it dulleth me to rime', and so on, through many examples. The true reason for the Yeoman's attempt to conceal the identity of the Canon in the tale is that the tale relates their last exploit together. The cause of the impetuosity of their descent upon the Canterbury pilgrims is that they are in full flight from the consequences of their crime.

Among the extraordinary effects of *The Canterbury Tales* is the way in which the Canon is mirrored by his counterpart in the Canon's Yeoman's Tale; the way the Monk in the framework—outrider and sensualist—is mirrored by a monk in the Shipman's Tale; the way in which the Friar and the Summoner compete for attention, each producing a working model of his rival in *his* tale; and, indeed, the way in which every tale picks up verbal elements of at least some of the others, so that *The Canterbury Tales* is aesthetically, if not formally, complete.

The Parson's Tale, for example, is an integral part of the poem. It plays much the same role in the structure as, on a very reduced scale, the commentary of the knights does in Eliot's *Murder in the Cathedral*. That is to say, it provides a review of the events so far retailed, but its very decisiveness renders

it yet another of those events. The Parson calls his contribution
'a myrie tale', and so it is, if to bring good news is to make
the hearers merry. For it conflates two works, a chapter on
penitence by St Raymund of Pennaforte (*ante* 1243) and a treatise
on the Deadly Sins by Gulielmus Peraldus (*ante* 1261). The
latter is freely handled by Chaucer, presumably to bring it into
closer relation with the poem; and the Parson's Tale, though
making no claims to being poetry, is a good deal richer linguistically than its reputation would suggest. If we take only a few
of the parallels between this commentary by the Parson and
the other Canterbury Tales, the nature of the relationship should
be clear.

The text on which the Parson preaches (Jeremiah 6) refers
to 'olde pathis' and he himself goes on to speak of 'wayes
espirituals' and the enjoinment put upon men 'for to goon pera-
venture naked in pilgrimages'. But the vices of the various pilgrims
are liable to lead them only to destruction. The Parson is a
good deal more critical than the pilgrim Chaucer. In the General
Prologue we are told of the Franklin,

> It snewed in his hous of mete and drinke,
> Of alle deyntees that men koude thinke.

But in the Parson's account of the sin gluttony we find, 'Glotonie
... is expres eek agayn the comandement of God ... whan
a man get him to delicaate mete or drinke' (verses 818, 828).
'Poynaunt and sharp' is the Franklin's sauce but, the Parson
says, 'sharp and poynaunt' is the manner of contrition (130).
The mention of drink reminds us of grimmer considerations.
The Parson terms drunkenness 'the horrible sepulture of mannes
resoun' (822). We think of the reproof of the Host to the
Miller and that of the Manciple to the Cook, but most of
all the Pardoner:

> For dronkenesse is verray sepulture
> Of mannes wit and his discrecioun

—this said, of course, after he himself has drunk deeply as a
means of preparing for the very tale in which he condemns
drunkenness. The Parson is forthright; the poet Chaucer is ironic
and devious.

But there are sins worse than gluttony. The Parson himself allows it in many ways to be 'venial'. He speaks with far more force of women who do not know their place, and has a definite eye, it seems, trained on the Wife of Bath. We saw her in the General Prologue sporting red stockings and we hear about her conduct in church—wearing coverchiefs weighing ten pounds, pushing her way first to the offering. All these faults are condemned by the Parson: 'hoses in whit and reed' (425); 'outrageous array of clothing' (412, 417); 'goon to offring biforn his neighebor' (407). The Wife boasts of her old husbands that she 'chidde hem spitously'. But the Parson quotes 2 Timothy 2 on the evil of chiding (630), and, moreover, uses against the Wife a proverb that she herself put into her husbands' mouths:

A man that is in a droppinge hous in manye places, though he eschewe the droppinge in o place, it droppeth on him in another place. So fareth it by a chidinge wyf; but she chide him in o place, she wol chide him in another. (632)

However, the Parson has, unlike the 'olde housbondes', a regard for woman's individuality. One of the reasons why a man and his wife 'flesshly mowen assemble' (939) is 'to yelden everich of hem to oother the dette of hire bodies, for neither of hem hath power of his owene body' (940)—language that recalls, in some measure, the Wife's own diction. The Parson is totally against the domination of the husband over the wife that is confidently assumed by January in the Merchant's Tale—

A man may do no sinne with his wyf,
Ne hurte himselven with his owene knyf

—and answers him almost in his own words:

And for that many man weneth that he may nat sinne, for no likerousnesse that he dooth with his wyf, certes, that opinion is fals. God woot, a man may sleen himself with his owene knyf.... (859)

Pilgrim after pilgrim, tale after tale, comes under the Parson's deliberate and systematic survey. The Knight has 'a noble herte and a diligent, to attayne to heighe vertuouse thinges' (469), and this is a sign of that 'gentillesse' (464) the definition of which so puzzled the Franklin. The survey takes in the envious Reve—'Murmure eek is ofte amonges servauntz' (506); and the angry Miller—'the fervent blood of man y-quiked in his herte' (536); and their mutual quarrel—

> Pride . . . ay bloweth and encreesseth the fir by chidinge and wikked wordes; thanne stant Envye, and holdeth the hoote iren upon the herte of man with a peire of longe toonges of long rancour . . . . (554–5)

The Parson will use the Pardoner's terms in condemning gambling—'thise cursede hasardours in diverse contrees' (580); and in deploring blasphemy—'For certes, it semeth that ye thinke that the cursede Jewes ne dismembred nat ynough the preciouse persone of Crist' (591). But this does not prevent him from utterly anathematising the Pardoner and his like for being venal priests, and from once more taking over the Pardoner's own language to do so:

> thise false enchauntours or nigromanciens in bacyns ful of water, or in a bright swerd, in a cercle, or in a fyr,[1] or in a shulderboon of a sheep. I kan nat seye but that they doon cursedly and dampnably agayns Crist and al the feith of hooly chirche. (603–4)

The 'fyr' reminds us of the Canon's Yeoman's Tale, which resembles the Parson's vision of hell when 'hir sighte shal be ful of derknesse and of smoke, and . . . hir nosethirles shullen be ful of stinkinge stink' (208–9) and

> The brenninge of the fyr of this world shal God yeven in helle to hem that been dampned . . . . wel may that man that no good werk ne dooth singe thilke newe Frenshe song, 'Jay tout perdu mon temps et mon labour' (221, 248)

or, as the Yeoman put it, 'For lost is al oure labour and travaille'.

Yet all is not lost. The Parson has begun by telling the pilgrims that confession is very showing of sins to the priest. This, intentionally or unintentionally, they have done, in their prologues and headlinks as in their tales. And, after the account of the

Deadly Sins, in which they all, in one way or another, are involved, the Parson ends on a note of hope—'Crist is more strong for to unbinde than sinne is strong for to binde' (1072)—and his last paragraph is a litany of love, in which the dominant words are 'bliss' and 'joy'.

This, then, is the 'myrie tale' which subsumes the comments on all the many tales we have heard on the long journey. But, though placed last, it is not Chaucer's final word on the matter. Throughout the tales, other commentaries have super-vened: the gullible pilgrim Chaucer, the secular Host, the 'gentil' authority of the Knight, the eternal feminine of the Wife, the romantic pietism of the Prioress. No one view is the final outcome of this relativist poem. Each pilgrim says what is appropriate to him, woken into drama by the great poet's narrative skill and power of characterisation. It is the process that sensitised the prototypes of his tales, whether they are in *La Roman de la Rose* or the *Novelle* of Sercambi (c. 1374) or the *fabliaux*, legends and romances of the four languages under his hand. Whatever Chaucer touches, he does not so much adapt as utterly transform. His technique of digression, too, seems wholly original. He often holds a story back, especially if it is a familiar one, while he brings in, under one pretext or another, analogues and *exempla* designed to show that the tale in question is only one instance of the many contretemps and disasters that beset mankind. It is no wonder that this ultimate stage manager of the human comedy had neither predecessor nor successor. Gigantic as he is, he seems extraordinarily isolated in his time. It is part of another comedy, that of literary history, that the first and almost the greatest of our classics should also be by far our greatest experimental poet.

3 Elizabethan Poetry

Elizabethan poetry has remained under a cloud for generations. There can be few who have not opened their Palgrave and experienced a familiar sinking of the spirits on encountering this:

> Spring, the sweet spring, is the year's pleasant king;
> Then blows each thing, then maids dance in a ring,
> Cold doth not sting, the pretty birds do sing,
>   Cuckoo, jug-jug, pu-we, to-witta-woo!...
>   (from *Summer's Last Will and Testament*, c. 1592)

That, in little, represents the traditional view of Elizabethan poetry. It also presents us with a summary of its defects: a forced jollity, a conscientious simplesse, a conventionalised view of nature. The very imitation of the nightingale—'jug-jug'—seems to us ludicrous now. This is a sophisticated writer pretending to rustic simplicity.

One's feelings about Elizabethan sophistication are confirmed on going through the first book of Palgrave's *Golden Treasury* (1861). There is the aureate diction of 'Phoebus, arise' by William Drummond of Hawthornden (1616), and Thomas Lodge's conventionalised portrait of Rosalynde (1590) with sapphire eyes and rosebud lips. Nor will the reader be reassured by this:

Diaphenia like the daffadowndilly,
White as the sun, fair as the lily,
Heigh ho, how I do love thee!
I do love thee as my lambs
Are belovéd of their dams;
How blest were I if thou would'st prove me. . . .

(from *England's Helicon*, 1600)

This is attributed to Henry Constable, and he was the nineteenth-century's idea of an Elizabethan poet, if one can judge by his representation in anthologies of the period. The melting diction, the pretty-pretty images would appeal to a taste which regarded women as legless angels. There is an area in which Petrarch and Dante Gabriel Rossetti meet; but there is no need for us to inhabit it now.

This kind of poetry has, for the most part, been rejected by the educated reader; but with it, tacitly, has gone the entire corpus of Elizabethan verse. The usual account would term it aureate, accomplished, conventionalised, pastoral—very much in the line of

Or, che'l ciel e la terra e'l vento tace,
E le fere e gli augelli il sonno affrena,
Notte'l carro stellato in giro mena,
E nel suo letto il mar senz' onda giace;
Veggio, penso, ardo, piango; e chi mi sface,
Sempre m'è innanzi per mia dolce pena

(Petrarch, c. 1340s)

which appears in one of Drummond's sonnets as

While sleep, in triumph, closed hath all eyes,
And birds and beasts a silence sweet do keep,
And Proteus' monstrous people in the deep,
The winds and waves, hushed up, to rest entice;
I wake, muse, weep, and who my heart hath slain
See still before me to augment my pain.

(from *Poems*, 1616)

What is sweet in Petrarch becomes, in Drummond, saccharine. This form of polished elegance has never sat easily on English verse, and may be regarded as an excrescence, and not only in the sixteenth century. One sees Wyatt struggle against it, Surrey succumb to it, Sidney make it popular, and Spenser bring it to a climax in the purple passages of *The Faerie Queene*. And yet the Petrarchan convention is a by-line in Elizabethan verse. Behind the major poetry of the period is the earthy force of the great alliterative poems of the Middle Ages—*Piers Plowman* and *Sir Gawain and the Green Knight*.

This may seem a surprising point to make, in view of the usual account of medieval poetry: that it came to a halt with the Wars of the Roses and that therefore it was necessary for English poets to look abroad for their technique. There was no need for Wyatt to tether his genius to the Italianate school of Petrarch, and in fact he is at his best when he departs most sharply from his master. Few admirers of 'Whoso list to hunt' know that it is an adaptation from 'Una candida cerva sopra l'erba'; and why should they? Wyatt is at his best when he aggregates Petrarch and Alamanni to his proverbial and earthy Englishness. And this is occasionally true, also, of his much lesser contemporary Surrey—who is a poet only in his all-too-few glimpses of a personal past.

But Surrey proved to be the more popular of the two, and his lack of confidence in the native tradition affected later poets adversely. And so we find the bulk of verse in this period betraying a certain instability, between native speech and Italianate polish. That which tends towards the latter is far inferior. No doubt modern anthologists would disagree with me here: the *Oxford Book of Sixteenth Century Verse* (1932) showed remarkably little advance upon the Victorian taste of Palgrave. Like Palgrave, Sir Edmund Chambers favoured lyric at the expense of satire and translation; even though these were forms at least as central to the Elizabethan temperament. There was all the more reason, then, to welcome Edward Lucie-Smith's *Penguin Book of Elizabethan Verse* (1965), which represented Constable and Nash very sparingly, showed a totally unexpected side of Lodge, and left out Drummond of Hawthornden altogether.

Clearly Lucie-Smith was not interested in the Petrarchan line of aureate diction, any more than the quasi-Petrarchan mock-sim-plesse. What did he put in its place? Well, with all his percipience, he was to some extent under the spell of another heresy—that of the scholars, who now are almost alone in reading Elizabethan poetry. They talk about the 'plain style' and Elizabethan 'classi-cism', without in either case appearing to know what they are committing themselves to. Classicism is a word without reference to the context of English literature, and the plain style is bearable only if it is not dull. But Daniel, Drayton and Davies—poets whom Lucie-Smith seemed to admire—are frequently dull; and it was poets such as these that F. R. Leavis deprecated when, in the first chapter of *Revaluation* (1936), he spoke of 'respectable figures who ... serve at any rate to set up a critically useful background'. As against these, Leavis applauds Donne, whom we read 'as we read the living'.

Unfortunately this, and the fact that Leavis begins his book at the seventeenth rather than the sixteenth century, has been taken as a general condemnation of all that went before Donne. Students have been left with the idea that Donne set up a welcome revolution against large, heavy, critically respectable figures; who need no longer be read, because they have been superseded.

Certainly the Elizabethans had few other poets of Donne's stature—has any period?—but those they had were impressive: Shakespeare and Jonson are as much the last great poets of the sixteenth century as the initiating forces behind the seventeenth. And though Donne himself was characteristically forward-looking, and can hardly be called an Elizabethan without some qualifica-tions, his restless intellect brought to a fine focus much that was troubling other poets of this transition period.

One could make a rough division between those Elizabethans who died before the new century and those who survived it. Sidney and Spenser spent their lives mastering the Petrarchan convention; but, in comparison with these, Chapman and Greville seem grown-up, disillusioned, grave—in a good sense of the word, serious poets. It is, therefore, a pity that Leavis lumped these two together with Drayton et al. as 'critically respectable figures'; and that Lucie-Smith, in his anthology, represented them all in much the same way. The fact is that Daniel, Drayton and Davies are dull sticks that sometimes rub up against a few sparks of poetry, while Chapman and Greville, together with Marston and Raleigh, are major poets by any reckoning; and their work is neglected.

One reason for this is certainly the nineteenth-century anthol-ogists' fixation upon the sweet and conventionalised treatment of love. Another is the twentieth-century academics' respect for the dull. Chapman, Marston, Raleigh and Greville get caught in the cross-fire. And yet a third reason is the curiously British reluctance to consider any but watertight categories of literature as being acceptable.

Chapman, for example, was one of the great playwrights of his time, itself the crux of our drama, and perhaps its greatest translator. His finest poetry is found in these two connections; much of his 'original' work is digressive, rhetorical and obscure. A case for Chapman's political tragedies can hardly be made from extracts; it is rather to the translations that we must turn for an idea of his poetic texture. The *Odyssey* (1611–16) is far superior to the *Iliad* (1598–1611), which would not now attract so much attention if Keats had not praised it; but both are thoroughly English poems—far more so than *The Faerie Queene*, for instance. Translation acted upon Chapman as a discipline; and it was a discipline that he thoroughly understood. Perhaps his greatest single poem is the explanation of his methods which he prefixed to his version of the *Iliad*. Here the poetic interest comes in the numerous similes, rammed with life, which act out his meaning. This sample from it is aimed savagely at the stupid public that hankers after rubbish. The whole section, in fact, is the working out of a double pun upon the meanings of 'ass' and 'taste':

> But as an ass, that in a field of weeds
>   Affects a thistle, and falls fiercely to it;
> That pricks, and galls him; yet he feeds, and bleeds;
>   Forbears a while, and licks; but cannot woo it
> To leave the sharpness; when (to wreak his smart)
>   He beats it with his foot; then backward kicks,
> Because the thistle galled his forward part:
>   Nor leaves till all be ate, for all the pricks . . .
>   So, in this world of weeds, you worldlings taste
> Your most-loved dainties; with such war, buy peace;
>   Hunger for torments; virtue kick for vice;
> Cares, for your states, do with your states increase:
>   And though you dream you feast in Paradise,
> Yet Reason's daylight shows ye at your meat,
>   Asses at thistles, bleeding as ye eat.

This is hardly a 'respectable' attitude, nor is it 'classical'; but it is certainly very considerable poetry. The subject-matter does not seem, in the abstract, rewarding—the translation of poetry is hardly an obvious theme for poetry itself. Yet the truth is that Chapman feels the theme so powerfully that all kinds of telling metaphors rush into his mind; and there can be no doubt that, in his poetry, the life is in the metaphor. Here, for example, the ass is observed with lifelike realism: 'Affects a thistle, and falls fiercely to it'. That word 'fiercely' gives us at once the savagery of the beast and of its appetite. Without reaching out of the context, the ass nevertheless takes on a life of its own. Its agonies and temptations are felt sharply: so richly understood that it gives the poet the authority to condemn, from the inside so to speak, an ass's tastes.

This poetic realism is the chief weapon of a number of poets who can be loosely associated with Chapman: in particular Jonson and Marston. After Eliot and Leavis and, more recently, Mr Johnston's edition (1954) and Mr Trimpi's study (1962), it may be taken that a cultivated reader would regard Jonson as a great non-dramatic poet, as well as the greatest English writer of comedies. But it is still worth saying that Jonson's vein of savagery was always controlled; and that, when he, like Chapman, castigated his audience, he knew exactly what he was doing:

> Say that thou pour'st 'hem wheat,
>   And they would acorns eat:
> 'Twere simple fury still thy self to waste
>   On such as have no taste:
> To offer them a surfeit of pure bread
>   Whose appetites are dead:
>   No, give them grains their fill,
>   Husks, draff to drink and swill:
> If they love lees, and leave the lusty wine,
> Envy them not, their palate's with the swine.

This is from Jonson's 'Ode to Himself' (1629). And it proves that great learning in the Elizabethan period went along with a racy and idiomatic command of English. The alliterative clusters—'grains', 'fill', 'husks', 'draff', 'drink', 'swill'—show Jonson within hailing distance of the medieval morality. This vein is

never more manifest in Jonson than when he is reviling the
unlearned masses. And here we may remember that Jonson, like
Chapman, was an Elizabethan who lived on into another, and
less appreciative, age.

Though this didn't prevent their friend and collaborator, John
Marston, from doing the same sort of thing in his earlier years.
Marston has some claim to be the most neglected major figure
of the period, mainly because he is persistently regarded primarily
as a playwright. He was, indeed, a most original dramatist, and
Shakespeare found *The Malcontent* (c. 1600) worth study, as the
many echoes of Marston in *Hamlet* go to show. But Marston's
best poetry comes only as flashes in his tragedies, which will
never again be read as wholes. For more sustained work we
must turn to his satires.

The Scourge of Villainy (1598) has an unfortunate reputation
for being coarse and savage: Hall's satires are rated far higher.
May I say here that Marston's satires are not unworthy of comparison with those of Donne; and both these poets, racy and idiomatic,
leave Hall standing sententiously on the sidelines? Marston knows
no restraint, not even that of Chapman, and he speaks of satire
not as a task but as a joyful duty:

> Fie, Satire, fie! shall each mechanic slave,
> Each dunghill peasant, free perusal have
> Of thy well-laboured lines? Each satin suit,
> Each quaint fashion-monger, whose sole repute
> Rests in his trim gay clothes, lie slavering,
> Tainting thy lines with his lewd censuring? . . .
> Fie! wilt thou make thy wit a courtesan
> For every broken handcraft's artisan?
> Shall brainless cithern-heads, each jobbernoll,
> Pocket the very genius of thy soul?

This associates itself with John Donne's account of the broken-
down adventurer in his Satire IV (1597):

> Sleeveless his jerkin was, and it had been
> Velvet, but 'twas now, so much ground was seen,
> Become tufftaffatie . . . .

It has also something in common with the medieval Scots poet William Dunbar describing the courtiers in his 'Complaint to the King' (c. 1500), 'foul jow-jowrdane-hedit jevellis, / cowkin kenseis and culroun kevellis . . .'. One is reminded of Swift denouncing the Irish Parliament in his 'Legion Club' (1736), or Joyce Cary in *The Horse's Mouth* (1944) on the subject of the British government: 'the belly ripping abortionist, the batter-brained, cak-handed, wall-eyed welsher, the club-foot trampler, the block-eared raper that would sell its sister for a cheer . . .'. To be in the ambience of Dunbar, Swift and Cary is to be in a central tradition of satire. Marston exhibits the dual quality we saw in Jonson, and in Chapman, too: a keen knowledge of society and a violent revulsion from it—both characteristics of Elizabethan satirists at their best. Notice the detail in the passage from Marston. It is so vivid as to seem fascinated by what it denounces. The 'dunghill peasant' is attacked along with the gay suit, the courtier known only by his clothes, themselves subject to meaningless changes of fashion. And notice, too, the earthiness of the language—'cithern-heads', 'jobbernolls'. The people are reduced to caricatures by the very vehemence with which they are described.

But it would be a mistake to regard Marston as being merely negative. There is a positive force even in the ingenuity and vividness of his condemnation; and the concept of the soul, merely stated here, finds realisation in other poems. In his eighth satire, for instance, Marston represents the stupidity that he hates in people as a natural characteristic of the body. Reason, a superior being, naturally flies from so vile a tenement:

> Our adverse body, being earthly, cold,
> Heavy, dull, mortal, would not long enfold
> A stranger inmate, that was backward still
> To all his dungy, brutish, sensual will:
> Now hereupon our intellectual,
> Compact of fire all celestial,
> Invisible, immortal, and divine,
> Grew straight to scorn his landlord's muddy slime;
> And therefore now is closely slunk away
> Leaving his smoky house of mortal clay,
> Adorned with all his beauty's lineaments
> And brightest gems of shining ornaments,

His parts divine, sacred, spiritual,
Attending on him . . . .

The denunciation here is sharpened and particularised by means
of Marston's fictional invention: soul identified with reason, reason
as tenant of the dungy body. The poetry arises out of this
conflict; and it is not too far-fetched to say that Marston felt
himself an unwanted inmate of a foul society, as the 'reason'
which he describes fights against the 'adverse body' which con-
stricts it.

Easiness, directness, pithiness, then, are characteristics of the
best Elizabethan poetry; and in such a context Donne and Jonson
seem at home. This is a native English tradition; and, because
of that, it can afford to assimilate a good deal of foreign material,
as the great translations of the period show. But there is a
distinction to be made here. Sidney, Spenser, Constable and Drummond, imitating Marino, Guarini, Petrarch and the rest, sought
to Italianise their subject-matter. The great translators, on the
other hand, assimilated foreign material into their English, essentially medieval and alliterative, tradition.

The first, and nearly the best, of these translators was Wyatt.
One has only to consider his famous version of Seneca's attack
on public life, 'stet quicunque volet potens', to see how he
racks the dignified Latin into the urgency of personal statement—
'Stand whoso list upon the slipper top . . . .' (c. 1630s). And H.
A. Mason, in his excellent study of early Tudor poetry (1959),
has pointed out how the received and conventional 'ignotus
moritur sibi' is replaced with what seems to be an eye-witness
account of a hanging:

himself, alas,
Doth die unknown, dazed, with dreadful face.

There is a great distinction between this and Surrey's glacial
version of Virgil. Wyatt's major translation, however, is that
of the Penitential Psalms (c. 1630s). This has the same dramatic
felicity as the poem just quoted, even though it comes after
Alamanni and Aretino:

O Lord I dread, and that I did not dread
I me repent and evermore desire

Thee, thee to dread . . . .

This, in its obsessively involuted rhythms, looks forward to
Donne's 'Hymn to God the Father' (1623):

> When thou hast done, thou hast not done
> For I have more.

And, between these two great poems, there is a body of incomparable work, technically translation, but in fact the most inventive
writing of the period.

Some of it has proved a little too inventive for the critics.
Richard Stanyhurst's version of the *Aeneid* (1582), for example,
was treated as a joke even by so discerning a reader of Elizabethan
verse as W. A. Edwards (*Scrutiny*, 1933). I suppose one might
say that Stanyhurst's accounts of battle are inclined to melodrama—

> In person Pyrrhus with fast-wrought twi-bill in handling
> Down beats with pealing the doors, and post-metal
> heaveth . . .

—though even here there is a dramatic appropriateness in the
onomatopoeia and inversion. But Stanyhurst is probably at his
best in country scenes, such as Aeneas's first sight of the fertile
terrain of Carthage, with its 'clustrous herd-flock . . . in green
frith browsing.' Another example is the Royal Hunt in Book
IV. After contrasting the 'rustical hoblobs' with the 'Lucifer-heav-
enly-in-beauty Aeneas', Stanyhurst goes on:

> Then lo, behold ye, breaking, the goats do trip from
>   the rock-tops
> Near to the plain; the herd deer doth stray from mountain
>   unharboured,
> The chase is ensued with passage dusty bepowdered.
> But the lad Ascanius, with prancing courser high-mounted,
> Doth manage in valley, now them, now these over-ambling.
> He scorns these rascal tame games, but a sounder of hogsters
> Or the browny lion to stalk fro mountain he wisheth. . . .

The freshness and authenticity of this annoyed Stanyhurst's Dutch
editor, who apologised for his tendency to dress Trojan subjects

in an English garb. And Professor Van Der Haar (1933 edition) went on to say that Stanyhurst added over 400 words to the language. This alone would be a striking achievement; but what impresses me, however, is the great translator's pithiness and proverbial quality of speech—'a sounder of hogsters', 'seams up the bedmatch', 'stand ye to your tacklings'. For all his coinage of new words and coupling of old ones, Stanyhurst's English is, at its best, as vivid as that of Hopkins. And, like Hopkins, he demonstrates that one need not be static in order to write within a tradition.

But most readers will find the translations of Arthur Golding more easy and direct. And, indeed, Ezra Pound praised Golding sixty years ago ('Notes on Elizabethan Classicists', 1917) for his freshness and felicity, although for the greater part of its existence Golding's Ovid (1565–67) has remained inaccessible to the general reader. This freshness is perhaps best seen in his numerous rural descriptions. For example:

> country carles were gathering there these osier twigs
>   that grow
> So thick upon a shrubby stalk, and of these rushes green,
> And flags that in these moorish plots so rife of growing
>   been. . . .

There is surely no need to apologise for the English setting of these poems? Golding does not Latinise his diction into pseudo-Ovid; rather he regards it as his task to supply a local referent for Ovid's Latin. He does not translate his original so much as give him an English equivalent. Here, for example, Golding fully lives up to the Roman poet in providing us with a startling example of metamorphosis; Thracian women turned into trees:

> But everyone was stayed
> With winding root which held her down: her frisking
>   could not boot.
> And while she looked what was become of toe, of nail,
>   and foot,
> She saw her legs grow round in one, and turning into
>   wood.
> And, as her thighs with violent hand she sadly striking
>   stood,

She felt them tree; her breast was tree; her shoulders
    eke were tree,
Her arms long boughs ye might have thought, and not
    deceived be. . . .

Possibly the reader may feel that Golding is a little circumscribed,
as Chapman was in his *Iliad*, by his chosen metre and rhyme.
But this is certainly not a charge that could be brought against
John Harington, the author of several pithy epigrams, but primarily
the translator (*ante* 1591) of the sixteenth-century Italian poet
Ariosto. This, far more than Fairfax's Tasso (1600), stands in
urgent need of dissemination; for it is an English classic. Unlike
Fairfax, Harington absorbs his Italian masters and has no need
for Spenser as an intermediary:

For at the chink was plainly to be seen
    A chamber hanged with fair and rich array
    Where none might come but such as trusty been.
    The Princess here in part doth spend the day,
    And here he saw a dwarf embrace the Queen
    And strive awhile, and, after homely play,
    His skill was such that ere they went asunder
    The dwarf was got aloft, and she lay under.

This is a more urbane poetry than that of Stanyhurst and Golding;
urban, too—it serves to remind us how constant the colloquial
mode of satire was from this English version of Italian mock-heroic
to Byron:

And Julia's voice was lost, except in sighs,
    Until too late for useful conversation.
    The tears were gushing from her gentle eyes;
    I wish indeed they had not had occasion,
    But who, alas, can love and then be wise?
    Not that remorse did not oppose temptation;
    A little while she strove and much repented,
    And whispering, 'I will ne'er consent'—consented.
                 (*Don Juan*, Canto 1, 1818–20)

As with Byron, there is a kind of mocking irreverence about
Harington's work, both 'original' and 'translated'. He may begin

with a gesture in the direction of Spenser; but, whereas Fairfax would have carried it on as elaborate simile, in Harington it is included only to be debunked:

> Astolfo, whilom King of Lombardy
>   To whom his elder brother left his reign,
>   Was in his youth so fresh and fair to see
> As few to such perfection could attain.
> Apelles' match or Zeuxis' he might be,
> That such a shape could paint without much pain.
> Great was his grace, and all the world so deemed it,
> But yet himself of all men most esteemed it.

This mocking quality carries on, too, into Harington's epigrams (*ante* 1618). I have said that Harington is urbane, but it would be a mistake to think that he is therefore uprooted from his country of origin:

> 'Clowns, and not courtiers, use to go by clocks.'
> 'Courtiers by clocks,' said I, 'and clowns by cocks.'

And it is remarkable how close the Court was to the country: London in those days still retained traces of the market town and was surrounded by fields and farms. So one can say that the courtliest verse of the period is that which retains something of a proverbial pithiness. Here, for example, is Harington's epigram directed at his wife, who claimed that she was too old to dance:

> Well, Mall, if needs thou wilt be matron-like,
> Then trust to this, I will a matron like. . . .

But the wit gravitates to a moving treatment of married love:

> Be in my house as busy as a bee,
> Having a sting for everyone but me,
> Buzzing in every corner, gathering honey.
> Let nothing waste, that costs or yieldeth money.
> And when thou seest my heart to mirth incline,
> The tongue, wit, blood, warm with good cheer and wine,
>   Then of sweet sports let no occasion 'scape,
>   But be as wanton, toying as an ape.

Though smaller in scale, this is the same world as that of Jonson's 'Penshurst' and 'Inviting a Friend to Supper': the tone is witty and judicial, but the country is never far away.

Even the courtliest of Elizabethan poets never left folk-wisdom far behind him. Raleigh, in particular, delighted in matching poetic realism to courtly wit. Critics have, however, been curiously obtuse about this. Some have refused to ascribe the superb poem 'Walsingham' (c. 1592) to Raleigh, on the ground that it existed in one form or another before he came on the scene. It did: the poem we have in the Rawlinson manuscript is a deliberate reworking of an old folk-song—a means of mating Raleigh's adult disillusionment to the simple directness of the ballad. Similarly, the 'Passionate Man's Pilgrimage' (c. 1603) tends toward dramatic monologue: Raleigh uses the manner and approach of folklore to focus upon a faith which he could understand, could feel nostalgic about, even though it was one which he could not share.

Like Harington, Raleigh seems to draw his epigrams from the ancient form of the verse proverb, as in this grimly humorous warning to his scapegrace son (1600):

> Three things there be that prosper up apace
> And flourish, whilst they grow asunder far,
> But on a day they meet all in one place,
> And when they meet they one another mar;
> And they be these—the wood, the weed, the wag.
> The wood is that which makes the gallows-tree,
> The weed is that which strings the hangman's bag,
> The wag, my pretty knave, betokeneth thee.
> Mark well, dear boy, while these assemble not,
> Green springs the tree, hemp grows, the wag is wild;
> But when they meet, it makes the timber rot,
> It frets the halter, and it chokes the child.
> > Then bless thee, and beware, and let us pray
> > We part not with thee at this meeting day.

It is a tribute to Raleigh that few of those who have admired this poem seem to have noticed that it is in sonnet form; and, indeed, in this context, the world of the sonnet seems far away— vowed to formality through its dependence upon foreign models. But the sonnet is an overrated form. This epigram of Raleigh's draws rather upon proverbial speech; though it has advantages which such raw material cannot claim. Raleigh's alliterative strength, his wise and deliberate saws, are governed by a controlling wit. And the poem is none the less serious for being witty: 'It frets the halter, and it chokes the child' is a line which echoes beyond the immediate plot of the poem.

Raleigh was at his best in this vein of poetic realism. It was no accident that his one poem grounded in the pastoral convention, 'The Shepherd Ocean [i.e. Walter] to Cynthia' (1592), is a failure. No accident, either, that it was Raleigh who replied to Marlowe's ecstatic vision of nymphs and shepherds with chilling downrightness and the pointed wit of an adult (c. 1590):

> If all the world and love were young,
> And truth in every shepherd's tongue,
> These pretty pleasures might me move,
> To live with thee and be thy love. . . .

Marlowe died young, but Raleigh had grown up into a world of adult experience and disillusion.

The conventional picture of Raleigh as ideal soldier and courtier is very wide of the mark. Few of his expeditions were conspicuously successful, and some failed disastrously. And, after his spectacular entry into public life, he was frequently out of favour, if not in actual disgrace. So far from being a man of action with literary tastes, it would be more accurate to think of Raleigh as a man of letters whose financial necessities led him to undertake exploits for which he was temperamentally unsuited. His famous arrogance may well have been a mask to hide an inner insecurity. Certainly he was plagued with doubts and difficulties to which Sidney and Marlowe were strangers. This can be seen in his greatest single poem: 'The Lie' (c. 1595). Here the soul is sent through the world, from Court to Church, from King to Parliament, to show what seems to be a universal corruption. The opening is grave, even for Raleigh:

> Go soul, the body's guest,
>   upon a thankless arrant,
> Fear not to touch the best,
>   the truth shall be thy warrant:

Go, since I needs must die,
   and give the world the lie.

But it is a gravity informed with a characteristic wit. The court glows and shines, but so does rottenness; and rulers are powerless to move unless others move for them. The poem rises by stages to a furious climax, when it seems the whole social world is under indictment:

Tell zeal it wants devotion,
   tell love it is but lust,
Tell time it metes but motion,
   tell flesh it is but dust.
And wish them not reply
   for thou must give the lie. . . .

The poem ends with a dramatic reversal: although the soul's outspokenness challenges punishment, it can afford to speak out because it is indestructible. The poem, then, is a plea in favour of honesty—at all costs:

So when thou hast, as I
   commanded thee, done blabbing,
Because to give the lie
   deserves no less than stabbing,
Stab at thee he that will,
   no stab thy soul can kill.

It does not seem too much to class Raleigh as a major poet: as the author of 'Walsingham', 'The Passionate Man's Pilgrimage', 'To His Son', 'The Nymph's Reply', and this last masterpiece, 'The Lie'; as well as the reworkings of wholly traditional material such as 'What is our life?' and 'Now what is love?' and the epitaph, 'Even such is time'. It is remarkable that these can co-exist with poems of highly patterned rhetoric without needing any sharp realignment of the readers' sympathies in passing from one to the other.

Of comparable stature, and even more neglected, is Fulke Greville; who equally off-sets the court culture against the traditional ways of the countryside. But, more than Raleigh, he seems a visitor there:

> I, with whose colours Myra dressed her head,
> I, that ware posies of her own hand-making,
> I, that mine own name in the chimneys read
> By Myra finely wrought ere I was waking;
>   Must I look on, in hope time coming may
>   With change bring back my turn again to play?...
>   (*Caelica*, xxii, c. 1580)

Like Raleigh, Greville is capable of writing formally patterned
verse without relinquishing something of a popular tone. And,
like Raleigh, he can use this patterning—in this case, the repeated
'I..., I..., I...'—to build up to a climax of indignation:

> Was it for this that I might Myra see
> Washing the water with her beauties white?...

This has a packed density very far from the illusory 'plain
style' which Greville is supposed to share with Daniel and Drayton.
For instance, in the lines just quoted, there is a stunning concentration of meaning: the girl washes the water with her white
beauties; so white, indeed, that they actually whiten the water.
And in another Myra poem the girl actually becomes, through
her constancy this time, a basilisk or death-goddess. 'The world,
which all contains, is ever moving', plants fade, men die—

> Only like fate sweet Myra never varies,
> Yet in her eyes the doom of all change carries.
>   (*Caelica*, vii, c. 1577)

She is at once dooming (condemning to death), holding fixed
in doom, and so promising a 'doom' (fate) when everyone
shall be doomed (judged) and so doomed (cursed) to remain
constant, like herself, in doom.

Some of these concentrated effects have, indeed, drawn attention
away from the serious content of Greville's verse—content that
gives considerable evidence of original thought. It is easy enough
to put against Daniel's abstraction Greville's concreteness—

> The nurse-life wheat within his green husk growing
> Flatters our hope and tickles our desire . . .
>   (*Caelica*, xl, c. 1590)

—and one might also point to the colloquial touches in the phraseology. But how many critics have explained what these effects are for? Greville is in fact deprecating youth and praising maturity; the same theme as Donne's 'Autumnal' (c. 1607). The charms of youth are certainly appreciated, but they are at the same time criticised in words such as 'flatters' and 'tickles'. Greville takes this theme to a climax of resonant authority:

> Fair and sweet is the bud, more sweet and fair
> The rose, which proves that time is not destroying. . . .

And so he uses a proverbial emphasis to establish that time not only destroys but also brings to fruition.

Greville's depth of thought is even more manifest when he pins down his subtlety of reasoning to a particular referent. He does this characteristically in the choruses which intersperse his plays: for example, the great 'Chorus Sacerdotum' from *Mustapha* (c. 1609). This is Greville's one anthology-piece, and needs no especial emphasis here: other than to say that its scepticism is as pointed as that of Raleigh and even more intelligent:

> Yet, when each of us in his own heart looks,
> He finds the God there far unlike his books.

Equally pointed, and much less well-known, is the Chorus of the People, from *Alaham* (c. 1609). This is as remarkable for its political insight as for its proverbial wit:

> Kings, govern people—over-wrack them not:
> Fleece us, but do not clip us to the quick. . . .

The poem is arguing out Raleigh's apophthegm in 'The Lie', 'Tell potentates they live / acting by others' action', and the argument is put into the mouth of the people themselves, like a multiple dramatic monologue; a genuine chorus, in fact. It takes us almost as far as Lenin's dictum that the strongest government can be thrown off by a mere shrug of the people's shoulders:

> When we are all wronged, had we all one mind,
> Whom could you punish? what could you reserve?

But Greville does not need a play in which to set his drama:
he is also a fine religious poet—less self-torn than Donne, perhaps
with a more certain faith, but projecting as deep a feeling.
The tone in the choruses is predominantly public and social;
here it is inward and self-communing:

> Down in the depth of mine iniquity,
> That ugly centre of infernal spirits;
> Where each sin feels her own deformity,
> In those peculiar torments she inherits,
>   Deprived of human graces, and divine,
>   Even there appears this saving God of mine. . . .

It would be true to say that Philip Sidney was working through
to this tone towards the end of his life. And, in at least one
sonnet, he matches Greville in dignity of utterance:

> Leave me, O love, which reachest but to dust,
> And thou, my mind, aspire to higher things:
> Grow rich in that which never taketh rust,
> Whatever fades but fading pleasure brings. . . .

But the biblical allusion here has none of the urgency which
Greville was to bring to his transcriptions from the Liturgy—see,
for instance, Sonnet XCVIII ('Lord, I have sinned . . . yet Lord
deliver me'). And Sidney has not much work of this order
to set beside the writings by which he is generally known.
The formless prose of his fantasy *Arcadia* (1577–80) only occasionally gives way to a deft song-lyric or passing meditation;
the love-sonnets of the cycle *Astrophel and Stella* (c. 1580) seldom
rise beyond a skilled manipulation of existing conventions.

Still, it should be remembered that Sidney died young. He
produced his best work, small though it is in bulk, before Greville
reached his poetic prime. Sidney's influence must have counted
for a good deal with Greville; especially, I would say, the influence
of the religious sonnets. However, one must not judge a writer
by his influence but by what he achieves; and in such a judgment
Sidney would count for much less than Greville. No doubt,
as with Raleigh though in a different direction, the legend has
obscured the man.

There is no such excuse for the overrating of Spenser. Certainly

he and Sidney were highly thought of by the Elizabethans themselves, and one can trace their influence everywhere. But this
is equally true of Cowley and Cleveland in the later seventeenth
century; and nobody pretends that *their* poetic reputation is worth
very much today. One can, it is true, detect Sidney and Spenser
in Shakespeare's sonnets (c. 1593–96); but not in the best of
them:

> Tired with all these, for restful death I cry:
> As, to behold desert a beggar born,
> And needy nothing trimmed in jollity . . .

while even this lacks the personal emphasis of Shakespeare's dramatic poetry:

> For who would bear the whips and scorns of time,
> The oppressor's wrong, the proud man's contumely . . . .
> (Hamlet, 1602)

Verse of this order helps to explain why Shakespeare left the
constricting form of the sonnet, and the influence of Sidney
and Spenser along with it.

But Spenser cannot be criticised so easily as Sidney. It is
true that his minor poems are boring and repetitious and that
The Faerie Queene (1589–99) is a narrative with neither effective
plot nor inherent interest. But there are still times when the
aureate sophistication breaks down, and Spenser is nearer the
Middle Ages than he seems to wish. The allegorical presentation
of the seasons, for instance:

> Lastly came Winter clothed all in frieże,
> Chattering his teeth for cold that did him chill,
> Whil'st on his hoary beard his breath did freeze . . . .

But poetry of this order is only intermittent in Spenser. And,
when it occurs, it invariably contradicts that we can deduce
of his moral plan. Here, for example, Winter is presented as
being impotent; other seasons are 'full of lustyhed'. But this
local approval fights against Spenser's general condemnation of
lust; indeed, of passion of any sort.

That so few educated readers have got through *The Faerie Queene* is hardly a tribute either to Spenser's general plan or to the way he has carried it out. The usual tenor of the verse is languorous, and even soporific; and it belongs to a by-line that goes back to Surrey's translations of Virgil and Petrarch, and the consequent Italianisation of the English language. The line took some time to catch on, and it was not until *Astrophel and Stella* (c. 1580, published 1591) that it became popular. But Surrey, Sidney and Spenser were not only responsible for Constable, Drummond and the other Elizabethan sonneteers. The line continues in the weaker aspects of Milton, an admirer of Spenser, through Milton's own followers in the eighteenth century, themselves inclined to a Spenserianising bent, through the revised version of *The Prelude* and the earlier poems of Keats, up to Tennyson, the Pre-Raphaelites, and beyond. It is the substitution of mode for matter; of conventional literary form for precise utterance.

But the major Elizabethans belong to our time; that is their strength. And it is high time that we ceased to see the period as that of Sidney, Spenser, Daniel and Drayton; rather its key figures are Chapman, Jonson, Marston, Donne, Raleigh and Greville—together with the great translators, Stanyhurst, Golding and Harington. And that is to say nothing of those whose finest poetry is found in the drama.

As these names will show, we need have no recourse to the Petrarchans to see the period as an incredibly rich one. But the Elizabethans have been egregiously misunderstood. There are other sides to the Elizabethans than mock-simplicity, Petrarchan convention, and prosaic philosophising. The Elizabethan genius was for poetic realism, as one would expect in an age of nascent drama. Satire and translation were central to the age. At their best, the Elizabethans were very close to the Middle Ages of *Piers Plowman* and *Sir Gawain*, as well as to the metaphysical poetry of the seventeenth century.

4 Shakespeare's Handling of His Sources

Shakespeare never wrote if it was possible to rewrite. He had extraordinary powers of realising the implications latent in other people's plots. Indeed, he treated previous writing as raw material for his re-creation. It was seldom, however, that he worked from a single source. The conflation of different texts proved, as far as he was concerned, tantamount to original composition. So we find Virgil brought into partnership with the Psalms of the Geneva Bible, Italian *novelle* marching alongside Pliny's *Naturall Historie*, English folklore conjoining with reports from the new American plantations—and juxtapositions even more unlikely than these have been known to take place. Geoffrey Bullough's anthology of narrative and dramatic sources, brought to an impressive conclusion as recently as 1975, tells only part of the story. Many of the sources are to be found in material that is anything but dramatic: political theory, theology, lyric and elegaic poetry, both English and Latin.

The plays which result bear, to some extent, the impress of their originals. But this is no passive takeover. The quality of craftsmanship required is as much a matter of selecting details as of combining them into what may at last seem an inevitable form. This power to pick out the relevant idea involved the recognition of underlying affinities in works which, to a more superficial gaze, would seem highly disparate. Therefore the *oeuvre* of Shakespeare is the supreme example in English of the union of tradition with experiment.

In many instances, the finished Shakespeare play is an answer to its original source. Thomas Lodge has a pastoral romance, *Rosalynde* (1590), whose hero and heroine flee an oppressor and make their way, separately, to the forest. The girl, dressed in boy's clothes, conducts a courtship with her unwitting lover. Here, in summary, is the basic plot, not only of *Rosalynde*, but also of *As You Like It* (1599). But, in Lodge, the disguise of Rosalynde as Ganymede is meaningless—mystery for mystification's sake—while in Shakespeare it is a device to test out love. A prevailing theme in many of the plays is that passion should not be allowed too precipitate a development. The great courtship scene, IV i, uses classical allusion as a means of criticising the pastoral convention to which Lodge uncritically accedes. Before this scene, in III iii, we have been shown the Clown—one of Shakespeare's additions to the story—attempt to contract a fraudulent marriage with a young country girl in a dialogue echoing with remininscences of the cuckold's horn. Immediately after the courtship scene, in IV ii, we see Jaques, another of Shakespeare's additions to the plot, encourage a band of foresters who have just killed a deer to sing a chorus which also puns on cuckoldry. In this way, the celebration of young love, encapsulated in the lyric 'It was a lover and his lass', is surrounded by mocking commentary.

But the comedy does not rest there. The mockers themselves are mocked. In his famous speech on the ages of man, Jaques succeeds in leaving out of his account almost all that makes life worth living. The air of inclusiveness, so striking out of context, proves to be satire, not of life so much as of the satirist's view of life:

> All the world's a stage,
> And all the men and women merely players.
> They have their exits and their entrances,
> And one man in his time plays many parts,
> His acts being seven ages. . . .   (II vii)

One possible source, indicated by T. W. Baldwin (*Shakespere's Small Latine*, 1944), is the *Zodiacus Vitae* by Palingenius (1520–34):

> si recte aspicias, vita haec est fabula quaedam,
> scena autem mundus versatilis, histrio et actor
> quilibet est hominum . . .'.

This was translated (Googe, 1561) as

> Wherefore if thou dost well discern
>   thou shalt behold and see
> This mortal life that here you lead
>   a Pageant for to be . . .

But the words could derive from any of a score of *sententiae*, often set as exercises at school for the edification of the young. This is ironic, for Jaques's wisdom is illusory:

> And then the lover,
> Sighing like furnace, with a woeful ballad
> Made to his mistress' eyebrow. . . .   (II vii)

This is a reduction of love to idiotic terms. Sighing and ballad-making are precisely those activities which Rosalind does not allow to the passionate Orlando. Her disguise diversifies an otherwise too easy pattern of courtship. Behind it is a mind quite capable of outwitting the satirist. She, more than any other character, is the central voice of the play. The comedy may answer Lodge's idealised pastoral, but it refuses to precipitate itself into Jaques's cynicism. Both Scylla and Charybdis here are varieties of illusion. Rosalind's is a quest for sanity.

Twelfth Night (1601) even more than *As You Like It*, is a comedy about illusion. Almost every character is, in one sense or another, in disguise. Half of them imagine themselves to be in love and mistake the source or nature of their emotion. Guise, guile and beguilement are discussed incessantly. The question is ventilated especially by Viola:

> Conceal me what I am . . .   (I ii)
>
> I am not that I play   (I v)
>
> I am not what I am.   (III i)

She remains in disguise throughout the action and is not even given her true name until within 164 lines of the end.

Shakespeare in this picks up and enormously extends a theme prevalent in sixteenth-century fiction and drama. Over and over again we find a story which stems from the *Menaechmi* of Plautus.

For example, in *Gl'Inganni* (1547) by Nicolò Secchi we have a girl disguised as a page being sent by her master to woo a courtesan. She asks him to give up his suit on the grounds that there is a maiden lost in love for him. She hints repeatedly at the identity of the maiden, and even suggests her own proximity to the suffering wench. It is this 'so near, so far' technique that Shakespeare transformed into the elegaic verse of a crucial scene in *Twelfth Night*. Viola, disguised as the page Cesario, suggests to the Duke that, like him, she herself may be in love. Far more subtly than in Secchi, the girl describes, not herself, but the man she addresses:

> DUKE.   What kind of woman is't?
> VIOLA.   Of your complexion.
> DUKE.   She is not worth thee then. What years, i'faith?
> VIOLA.   About your years, my lord.   (II iv)

Throughout the scene, a connection is maintained between the image of a woman deeply but secretly in love and that of a flower fading. This deepens to its greatest intensity when Viola spells out her grief as far as she dare:

> she never told her love,
> But let concealment like a worm i' th' bud
> Feed on her damask cheek: she pined in thought,
> And with a green and yellow melancholy
> She sat like Patience on a monument,
> Smiling at grief. . . .   (II iv)

Here we have disguise within disguise; disguise acting as the delaying factor in the plot. A relationship is thus tested out. The disguise of the Duke, a romantic illusion that he was in love with Olivia, proved all too facile: 'That instant was I turned into a hart' (I i). Compare that easy pun with Viola's threnody of pain. But her masquerade is nearly carried too far: 'Disguise, I see thou art a wickedness' (II ii). *Twelfth Night* is a comedy of illusion; it reaches after, but never quite embraces, tragedy.

Troilus and Cressida (c. 1602), on the other hand, is a comedy of disillusion. The *Iliad* of Homer stands as a monument to bronze-age heroics, but the Middle Ages were concerned to humanise the epic. From being unimportant figures marginally concerned with the Trojan War, Troilus and Cressida (originally, Chryseis) become in Benoît's retelling (1160) star-crossed lovers and, as such, provide a kind of oasis in a narrative of martial arts. Boccaccio in *Il Filostrato* (1336) made them hero and heroine of a romance of their own. Chaucer, in his turn, built up Boccaccio's go-between, Pandaro, into an immense comic character and gave Criseyde a maturity and experience not found in earlier versions. In Shakespeare's time, *Troilus and Criseyde* was published with the Scottish poet Henryson's account of Cressida's death, *The Testament of Cresseid*, as a sort of extra book (see Speght, 1598 and many editions thereafter). It may have been the juxtaposition of Chaucer's romantic comedy with Henryson's biting condemnation that indicated to Shakespeare a way of satirising the plot.

Shakespeare's Troilus, in comparison with his prototypes, is callow and sensual. Pandarus is debased to a thing peering through bedroom windows and Cressida becomes a lady of the town. The trio represent in little the attitudes of a war itself debased and caricatured. The love between Troilus and Cressida is hollow and rotten; so is that of Helen and Paris; and the War of Troy is a cynical mockery:

> And look how many Grecian tents do stand
> Hollow upon this plain, so many hollow factions.
>
> (I iii)

No positive is to be found among the leaders of Greece and Troy. The Homeric heroes are brought low. Achilles becomes a gross *prima donna*; Agamemnon is shown as peevish and irresolute; Hector is well-meaning but ineffectual. The play oscillates between two great consults. The Trojans debate in terms of blind passion. In their turn, the Greeks are dominated by the great speech of Ulysses on Degree. There is a basic source for this in Chapman's version of the *Iliad* (1598)—'The rule of many is absurd'—but the speech is essentially sixteenth-century ideas of order rehandled. It owes much to Sir Thomas Elyot's *The Governour* (1531) and the 'Homily on Obedience' appointed to be read in churches, but most of all to Richard Hooker's *Laws of Ecclesiastical Polity* (1594):

if celestial spheres should forget their wonted motions and
by irregular volubilitie, turne themselves any way as it might
happen: if the prince of the lightes of heaven which now
as a Giant doth runne his unwearied course, should as it were
through a languishing faintnes begin to stand and to rest himselfe:
if the Moone should wander from her beaten way, the times
and seasons of the yeare blend themselves by disordered and
confused mixture . . . what would become of man himselfe,
whom these things now do all serve?

>   when the planets
>   In evil mixture to disorder wander,
>   What plagues, and what portents, what mutiny,
>   What raging of the sea? shaking of earth?
>   Commotion in the winds? frights, changes, horrors,
>   Divert and crack, rend and deracinate
>   The unity and married calm of states
>   Quite from their fixure? O, when degree is shaked,
>   (Which is the ladder to all high designs)
>   The enterprise is sick. (I iii)

This is superb poetry, though not of the kind it is generally
said to be. It is the language of Octavius, so to speak, rather
than Antony; the raging of the sea has only that place in the
passage allowed by an inexorably developing argument. The tone
is, to say the least, authoritative, but the authority of Tudor
political theory does not seem appropriate here. Neither Ulysses'
immediate remedy—obedience to the king—nor his plans concerning the cajolement of Achilles seem applicable to the problems
evinced in this version of the war against Troy. This is not
an adverse comment on the character of Ulysses: he is the one
Homeric hero who refuses to be debunked, and is ever the
voice of sanity. But sanity has no place in this whirling satire
of love and war. This in itself seems to place critically the
characters and the nature of the drama in which they perform.
Shakespeare found congenial raw material in the medieval rehandling of a legend which had already reduced considerably the
distance between Homer's demi-gods and his own sceptical
audience. But it took all his edge of caricature to turn this
comedy into the blackest of jokes, that which jeers at itself.
'All the argument is a whore and a cuckold'—Thersites' sum-

ming-up of the action stamps *Troilus and Cressida* as the most amoral of Shakespeare's plays.

Measure for Measure (1604), on the other hand, attempts to be a highly moral play, and, for the first two and a half acts, it succeeds. But it does not have, as *Troilus and Cressida* did, the help of its sources. The story, in fact, is a poor one to serve what promises, in earlier scenes, to be a drama of considerable grandeur. The Judge's Bargain, as it may be called, is told and retold through the sixteenth century. It is based upon a scandalous case written up in 1547 by Joseph Macarius which describes a bargain made by a judge with the wife of a convicted murderer. He had promised her that, if she committed adultery with him, he would release her husband. We owe to the researches of F. E. Budd (*Revue de Litterature Comparée*, 1931) a full knowledge of the development of this story. In the original version the judge, after the adultery, proceeds with the execution and is condemned to death by the governor of the province. Giraldi's later adaptation (*Hecatommithi*, 1565) makes the woman the prisoner's sister and causes her to plead successfully for the judge's life. Giraldi rewrote this in the form of a play (*Epitia*, 1573) in which the heroine's decision to plead for the judge is made more bearable by the (delayed) revelation that her brother is really alive. In these versions, and others, the heroine ends up marrying the judge. The original offence of murder, for which the prisoner was condemned, in later versions is altered to rape and then to the seduction of his betrothed.

In his turn, Shakespeare attempted to humanise the story still further. For the prisoner we read Claudio; for the sister we read Isabella; and for the judge, Angelo. Isabella is the first of the victims of the Judge's Bargain to refuse to be seduced by the judge. The refusal is supported by her novitiate: she is about to be dedicated as a nun. But Shakespeare's most remarkable extension of the source is the role of the governor or duke. In other plots, he is appealed to only at the very end; as the remote ruler of the province. In *Measure for Measure* he is not a *deus ex machina* but a *primum mobile*. This involves him as a character in an extraordinary complex of stratagems. He arranges a particularly unfeeling bed-trick and substitutes in Angelo's bed, for the hitherto dynamic Isabella, the passive Mariana. This character has been invented by the author to provide Angelo with a partner other than Isabella and so to protect her from the

(by now) mandatory intercourse with the judge. The effect however, is to bring in a shadowy figure devoid of articulacy or
credible antecedent. The Duke proceeds further to confuse the
issue in the last act by alternating his appearance in his own
person with an appearance as a friar; a disguise he has used
throughout the play. He is seized and unmasked; but, nothing
abashed, proceeds to a most singular series of judgements. Claudio
is revealed as alive and is given to his betrothed, Juliet; Angelo
is given to Mariana; and the Duke himself confers his hand
on Isabella. She does not react in any way either to this or
to her brother's resurrection. It is as though a leading character
had been snuffed out, and it must be a problem to produce
in the theatre.

All this is made the more extraordinary by the fact that the
Duke's secular bustle in the later scenes of the play has been
accompanied by a heavy access of gnomology in his utterance:

> There is scarce truth enough alive to make societies secure;
> but security enough to make fellowship accurst. Much upon
> this riddle runs the wisdom of the world.   (III ii)

This consorts ill with the Duke's sudden announcement of his
matrimonial intentions.

One must not deny that the later action is ingeniously managed,
but from this display of technique we turn to the poetry of
the earlier scenes:

>   man, proud man,
>   Dressed in a little brief authority,
>   Most ignorant of what he's most assured—
>   His glassy essence—like an angry ape
>   Plays such fantastic tricks before high heaven
>   As makes the angels weep; who, with our spleens,
>   Would all themselves laugh mortal.   (II ii)

This is a marvellous blend of Bible and proverb, old play and
theology. Even the Arden edition is unable to point out all
of the analogues:

> With what measure ye mete, it shall be measured to you
> againe   (Matthew 7)

Magistratum virum indicat   (Erasmus, *Adagia*, 1500)

Authority shows what a man is (Proverb)

Like a young ape, full of fantastic tricks
                    (Dekker, *Old Fortunatus*, 1599)

One compares an evill officer to an Ape on the top of a
house highly pearched   (Carew, *Sermons*, 1603)

> And as the Ape that counterfets, us doth to laughter
>   move,
> So we likewise doe cause and move the Saints to laugh
>   above
>   (Googe, *Zodiake*, 1561, after Palingenius)

> View but his picture in this tragic glass
>   (Marlowe, *Tamburlaine*, 1587)

God hath his influence into the very essence of all things,
without which influence of deitie supporting them their utter
annihilation could not choose but follow.
                    (Hooker, *Laws*, 1594, v 56)

What each of these has separately—authority, ape, glass, essence—
Shakespeare combines into the complex metaphor of the man
in authority as ape gesticulating before a glass; the glass itself,
a simulacrum of his fragile identity. The incisive rhythm, biting
down on the key words—'man', 'brief', 'ignorant', 'assured'—
carries enormous conviction. The smooth unfolding prose of the
Duke's schemes in Acts III and IV does not.

For all its fine qualities, *Measure for Measure* can be used as
a foil to greater plays. Some of these have very much the
same provenance. *Othello* (1604), for example, derives from a
source closely related to that of the Judge's Bargain. Giraldi,
in his *Hecatommithi* (1565), III 7, tells of a Moorish captain who
takes to wife a Venetian lady. He is greatly bewildered by
his ensign, who levels an accusation against her, saying that
she has committed adultery with a certain corporal, a family
friend. What the captain does not know is that the ensign himself
had attempted to seduce her and this accusation is an act of

revenge resultant upon his failure. The captain asks the ensign to kill this corporal, but he succeeds only in wounding him in the leg. He himself, helped by the ensign, batters his wife to death. But he misses her so much that, after a time, he turns upon the ensign, who has been the cause of his grief and loneliness. The ensign now enlists the aid of the crippled corporal to help him denounce the captain for the murder of his wife. The captain is arrested, but refuses to confess. However, he is under heavy suspicion and is sent into exile, where he is murdered by his wife's relations. The fate of the ensign is to die as a result of torture administered during an enquiry into some quite different crime.

What we have here is a sketch, and it may look at first sight as crude as the raw material that went into *Measure for Measure*. It is true that *Hecatommithi* III 7 is much more drawn out as a plot than *Othello*; it is also more dissipated in focus. Many features made familiar by Shakespeare are missing. The Desdemona figure appears not to know that she is suspected of adultery. The corporal comes to be demoted, as Cassio is in Shakespeare's play, but here it is by chance and not through the ensign's device. And in Giraldi the ensign's fate is not bound up with that of the captain as Iago's is with Othello. Nevertheless, the implications of tragedy are present. What must have seemed fascinating to a century hungry for fiction was the ascendancy the ensign was able to gain over the captain. It is a kind of object-lesson in vulnerability. The other interesting factor is the captain's colour—he is a Moor—which suggests a hint of miscegenation on the part of the Venetian lady. In a leap of imagination, Shakespeare linked these points together. The blackness of the Moor is the characteristic that left him open to the machinations of the ensign.

We are never allowed to forget for an instant that Othello is black. This occurs on one level as a series of quite friendly allusions to his alien antecedents, from the Duke, the Senate and the like—'brave Moor', 'the warlike Moor', and so forth. On another level he is discussed by Iago in terms of opprobrium: 'an old black ram / Is tupping your white ewe' (I i). This associates itself in Iago's mode of speech with a vein of sexual caricature:

the devil will make a grandsire of you. . . . you'll have your

nephews neigh to you; you'll have coursers for cousins and
gennets for germans.   (I i)

Giraldi's ensign is a two-dimensional figure who, we are told,
cloaks the villainy in his heart with high sounding and noble
words. In Shakespeare's play, these 'high-sounding' words are
spoken not by Iago but by Othello. He sustains a consistent
eloquence that marks him out as being different: an alien, a
traveller from an antique land, Othello the spaceman. He tells
the Venetian senate that he is rude of speech; characteristically,
he uses an elaborate vocabulary to do so:

> Wherein of antres vast, and deserts idle,
> Rough quarries, rocks and hills, whose heads touch heaven,
> It was my hint to speak, such was the process:
> And of the Cannibals that each other eat;
> The Anthropophagi, and men whose heads
> Do grow beneath their shoulders. . . .

And with what self-conscious grandeur does he protest to a
cynical Iago his singleness of purpose:

> Like to the Pontic sea,
> Whose icy current, and compulsive course,
> Ne'er feels retiring ebb, but keeps due on
> To the Propontic, and the Hellespont:
> Even so my bloody thoughts, with violent pace
> Shall ne'er look back, ne'er ebb to humble love,
> Till that a capable and wide revenge
> Swallow them up. . . .   (III iii)

The Othello music is drawn, as T. W. Baldwin has so ably
demonstrated (*Parrott Presentation Volume*, 1935), from Pliny's
Naturall Historie, translated in 1601 by Philemon Holland. The
way in which the style has been assimilated to Othello's utterance
indicates repeated frequentations of this work:

And the sea Pontus evermore floweth and runneth out into
Propontis, but the sea never retireth back againe within Pontus
(II 97)

the Firth is frozen and all an yce   (IV 2)

out of Pontus the sea alwaies floweth, and never ebbeth
again   (IV 13)

it sufficeth not . . . to have let Propontis gush through Hellespont,
and so to encroach upon the earth.   (VI 1)

Far-fetched and sonorous references are culled from Pliny to
form what amounts to the Grand Style. It is used not for its
own sake, to threaten the world in high astounding terms, but
to show a figure caught in his own rhetorical toils. A man
who compares himself with rivers and oceans, and who has
his gaze fixed resolutely on antres vast and deserts idle, is unlikely
to be aware of the mundane plotters excavating around his feet.

Some lineaments of Othello's character may derive, as Lois
Whitney suggested (*PMLA*, 1922), from an account of Leo Afri-
canus (*fl.* 1526) prefixed by John Pory to his translation of
The Geographical Historie of Africa (1600). Pory tells us that Leo
served Mahumet of Fez in his wars against Arzilla—a circumstance
that perhaps gives rise to 'I fetch my life and being / From
men of royal siege' (I ii). Leo himself gives an account of
jealousy among the Moors: 'they will rather leese their lives,
then put up any disgrace in the behalfe of their women'. Such
a comment associates itself with Othello's

> I had rather be a toad
> And live upon the vapour in a dungeon,
> Than keep a corner in the thing I love,
> For others' uses.   (III iii)

This is how Shakespeare builds upon the blueprint supplied by
Giraldi. Othello's language marks him out as an exotic. It is
his tragedy that he wants very much to be a citizen, as though
deeds could alter the circumstance of birth. He reproves the
quarrelling Venetians, Cassio and Roderigo, by demanding, 'Are
we turned Turks?' (II iii). The Turk, of course, is the enemy
of the State throughout the play: he is not only barbarous,
but coloured, too. This is the point of Othello's agonised

> one whose hand
> Like the base Indian, threw a pearl away
> Richer than all his tribe . . . .   (v ii)

He is at the end terrified that the letters back to Venice will show him to have been nothing better than a savage. Therefore he reverts—still in that sonorous verse—to one occasion in his life when he was ineluctably on the right side:

> in Aleppo once,
> Where a malignant and a turbaned Turk
> Beat a Venetian, and traduced the state,
> I took by the throat the circumcised dog,
> And smote him thus.   (v ii)

This is a tremendous *coup de théâtre*. Even in telling the story, Othello realises that he has changed sides—he has done the Turk's part upon a Venetian and slain Desdemona. His own sentence, therefore, must be death. And the only way to gain credibility is to execute that judgement upon himself. The irony is that, to do so, proves his own final condemnation.

Othello has been culpably open, against all reason and observation, to external prompting. He never understands what has happened to him; speaking, for example, of 'fate' and 'unlucky deeds' when, rather, he should have recognised his own credulity. A character so lacking in self-knowledge leaves himself vulnerable to any malign influences that come along. Iago here found a perfect subject. Like *King Lear* (1605), *Othello* is the tragedy of a man who but slenderly knew himself.

Like Othello, King Lear demands to know whether he is beloved. There is no decent answer to this question; affection cannot be proffered upon request. Lear's enquiry leads to his death, that of his family and the downfall of the kingdom.

No play in Shakespeare is richer in provenance. Some of this has been impressively set out by Wilfred Perrett (*Palaestra*, 1904). One thing he demonstrates beyond argument is that *King Lear* embodies a wealth of archetypes. The oldest of these is the Love Test, the sort of tale one associates with Cinderella. A whole clutch of versions centres upon the story of the king who drives out his daughter because she says she loves him like salt. A related group of folk tales deals with a father who throws himself on the mercy of his daughters in extreme old age. Such legends as these were drawn upon by Geoffrey of Monmouth, to flesh out his history of early British kings. In writing his Latin *Historia Regum Britanniae* (1135) he invented

King Lear, using the name of a Welsh sea-god whose analogues were associated with deposition and punishment. There was also a Norse Lir who ruled the storms and whose daughters were winds. It may have been connotations such as these that led Geoffrey to provide 'Leir' with a harrowing story conjoining the Love Test with a story of filial ingratitude. He set the resultant amalgam in the ninth century BC. It is the Lear story as we know it: the division of the kingdom, the driving out of the youngest daughter, the subsequent quarrel with the elder daughters. The main difference is that, in Geoffrey, Leir enlists the aid of 'Cordeilla' to invade his kingdom and reassume the throne. With minor variations, this is the story followed by the major chroniclers of British history.

Geoffrey goes on to relate that Leir reigned for three years and was succeeded at his death by Cordeilla. After five years she was deposed and imprisoned by his sisters' sons. In despair she killed herself. The great bulk of the chronicles follow this story too: notably Wace (1153), Matthew Paris (twelfth century), Layamon (c. 1205), Caxton (1480) and Fabyan (1483). This last formed the basis of Holinshed's *Historie* (1587 edition), itself, along with Geoffrey, the source of Shakespeare's play. Those who protest against the catastrophe of the play should first take issue with the chronicles. Where Shakespeare departs most strikingly from tradition is not in the death of Cordelia; it is in his refusal to restore King Lear.

Even for Geoffrey's purpose, the old folk-tale was over-simple. The love-test Leir put upon his daughters would be likely to bring some heavy consequences. It would not do to allow reconciliation to come about too easily. This would be to devalue the worth of the experience in the first place. Equally, ending the narrative with the old king's restoration would leave the story in suspense. Geoffrey therefore adds the fate of Cordelia by way of sequel and conclusion. To do less would be to remain in velleity.

There were homiletic works, notably the *Gesta Romanorum* (c. 1472), that did just this, mainly because they were concerned to draw a Christian moral out of a highly unChristian story. The old play of *King Leir* (1593) follows these anonymous moralists in seeking what is incompatible: Lear permanently on the throne and a Cordelia who is living and reconciled. This cuts across the sense of the plot, and the resultant distortions are disabling.

In the old play, the king is declared to be the pattern of all patience; he betakes himself to his prayers and his beads; he is seldom without a pious sentiment in his mouth. Such a figure would never have inspired five centuries of chroniclers. Essentially, this king is feeble:

> The world of me, I of the world am weary,
> And I would fayne resigne these earthly cares,
> And think upon the welfare of my soul. . . .

In his reinterpretation of the plot, Shakespeare advances a creed sterner that that of homiletic Christianity. He often seems in detail to answer points raised by the old play; a characteristic procedure with him. His Lear puts off sovereignty, true, but with a fierce zest:

> 'tis our fast intent
> To shake all cares and business from our age,
> Conferring them on younger strengths while we
> Unburthened crawl towards death. . . .   (I i)

Shakespeare's king is one whose will has known no check. He is a hunter and a fighter; essentially a pagan. He lives hard and swears hard: the characteristic is established early on: 'By the sacred radiance of the sun . . .', 'Now, by Apollo . . .', 'By Jupiter . . .' (all in I i). This is not only a trait of character. In the old play, the king is abused by his eldest daughter, but stumbles over an excuse for her:

> Poor soule, she breeds young bones,
> And that is it makes her so tutchy, sure.

But Lear, crossed by *his* daughter, spits out his spleen in terrible oaths:

> All the stored vengeances of Heaven fall
> On her ingrateful top! Strike her young bones,
> You taking airs, with lameness.   (II iv)

However, Lear himself suffers from the curses he calls down on Goneril: he swears his gods in vain. It is he, not Goneril, who is struck down by the elements:

> Rumble thy bellyful! Spit, fire! spout, rain! . . .
> But yet I call you servile ministers,
> That will with two pernicious daughters join
> Your high-engendered battles 'gainst a head
> So old and white as this. O, ho! 'tis foul.   (III iii)

Whenever Lear invokes the gods, his words are turned back on him. One cannot say that his prayers remain unanswered; rather, the answer is 'no'. It is he, not Goneril, who has had thankless children; it is he who, in old age, has become sterile. The process continues throughout the play: prayer, followed by a devastating answer—

> O let me not be mad, not mad, sweet heaven;
> Keep me in temper; I would not be mad.   (I v)

But he becomes so.

The answer to Lear's prayers devastates him; it also acts as purgation. The madness of Lear is Shakespeare's great extension to the chronicles. Previous authors make tentative gestures in that direction: 'Leir forment se dementa' (Wace), 'Thou yeeldest comfort to my crazed thoughts' (*King Leir*). But, in Shakespeare, the madness is the man, the logical outcome of Lear's rashness in the opening scenes. The extreme of passion it eventually gives rise to is also a way of bringing an extra dimension to both character and drama—Lear begins to see there are others suffering in the universe apart from himself:

> Poor naked wretches whereso'er you are,
> That bide the beating of this pitiless storm,
> How shall your houseless heads and unfed sides,
> Your looped and windowed raggedness, defend ye
> From seasons such as these? O! I have ta'en
> Too little care of this. . . .   (III iv)

Such utterance gives underlying purpose to the central portion of the play. It is as though Lear sees more clearly when he is mad. This is brought out by the complex and graphic imagery —'looped and windowed raggedness'. An image such as this gives new life to the concept of dilapidation. Man is his own ruined shelter in process of decay. Body, rags, and walls (in the semblance of 'unfed sides') are brought into relation here. The words play with the origin of 'window' as 'wind's eye', an eye to let in the wind. Protection has turned into vulnerability. The image associates, moreover, with the Fool's proleptic allusions to fathers that wear rags and are left in the storm (II iv) and to the cod-piece that housed before the head (III ii), itself an earthy way of showing how passion overcomes intelligence. Furthermore, it anticipates the appearance of houseless poverty in the person of Poor Tom, and so, on repeated frequentation, assumes the role of prophecy.

The storm, again, is Shakespeare's own development of the source material. There is a pale antecedent in Sidney's *Arcadia* (II x) 1577–80, and in the old *Leir* thunder intervenes to prevent the princess's messenger from taking the old king's life. But, in Shakespeare's *Lear*, the king's madness and the storm are at one:

> Strives in his little world of man to out-storm
> The to-and-fro conflicting wind and rain.   (III i)

Both madness and tempest eventually blow themselves out. A pause transpires during which the sub-plot takes charge, and, after one wild encounter with the blinded Gloucester, Lear is allowed to sleep. When he awakes, it is to be reconciled with Cordelia. But this is no fairytale reconciliation, as in the folk stories, nor is it distanced in the remoteness of history, as in the chronicles. Nothing is more poignant than Shakespeare's power to bring this story of legendary creatures intimately near to us. This reconciliation has been earned through suffering and is suffused with humility. The ethic of the drama has moved from pagan invocation and revenge to the solemn obligations imposed by the Old Testament:

> Have I caught thee?
> He that parts us will bring a brand from heaven
> And fire us hence like foxes. Wipe thine eyes;
> The good years shall devour them, flesh and fell,
> Ere they shall make us weep: we'll see 'em starved first.
> Come.   (v iii)

The undercurrent of allusion is part and parcel of this resonant verse. As in the earlier acts of *Measure for Measure*, Shakespeare is using the Bible to enrich his meaning. 'Great men are not alway wise: neither do the aged all way understand judgment' (Job 32). Jephthah was compelled to sacrifice his daughter because of a vow made to God, and she herself begs him to keep it (Judges 11). Abraham was unable to find ten just men in the cities of the plain and the Lord sacrificed them in fire and brimstone (Genesis 18, 19). Samson fastened firebrands to the tails of foxes and drove them down into the standing corn of the Philistines (Judges 15). Pharaoh dreamed that seven fat cattle were devoured by seven lean cattle and that seven good ears of corn were devoured by seven withered ears—this, too is a representation of sacrifice and was interpreted by Joseph to mean that the seven years of plenty in Egypt would be paid for by seven years of famine (Genesis 41). Job and Jephthah amalgamate into Lear, who is reproached from a whirlwind; Sodom and Gomorrah stand for the evil world of Edmund, Goneril, Regan and Cornwall; the years of famine have already come upon Lear's realm. His death, together with that of his daughter, is a sacrifice to redeem the land.

By the end of the play, we have moved from the ethic of the Old Testament to something approaching a new dispensation. This is brought about through another superb *coup de théâtre*. Albany has taken on the mantle of King Lear by the time he is informed that Cordelia is in great danger. He exclaims, 'The gods defend her.' As he speaks, the old king re-enters, Cordelia dead in his arms: a terrible reply to his prayer. What follows next marks the third of three stages of redemption. The first was when Lear prayed for the houseless wretches in the storm; the second, in the 'walled prison' scene, when he acknowledged his love for his daughter; the third is when, at last, he finds that he loves another not as well as but better than himself. It is a moment of grace from which he is not allowed to lapse:

> This feather stirs; she lives! if it be so,
> It is a chance which does redeem all sorrows
> That ever I have felt.   (v iii)

There is no way that father and daughter can live together

in this world which has been revealed as cheerless, dark and deadly. Cordelia's part in the plot is to give Lear his chance of redemption. Hers is truly the role of the saint who sacrifices all and so shows that virtue must be its own reward; but it is Lear who is at the centre of the drama. A perspective wider than the immediate scene is hinted at in the rich ambiguity of his final lines:

> Do you see this? Look on her, look, her lips,
> Look there, look there. (v iii)

Lear may think Cordelia recovering and alive; he may see a vision of her in death, 'on the other side'; or he may now recognise that this sacrifice means that no sacrifice thereafter can part them. It should be played in such a manner as to suggest a repentant sinner welcoming an intercession. Lear dies pointing out of the play at a revelation not vouchsafed to the spectators who remain behind.

The catastrophe of *King Lear* focuses events which are widely dispersed in the chronicles. Lear's death and that of Cordelia in the original sources belong to essentially different plots. In Shakespeare, one is made consequent upon the other. It is a line of action that flows from the first error, when Lear demands to know whether he is beloved, to the final revelation of the play, when his question is at last answered.

This richness of provenance makes for a complexity that reinforces *King Lear* as a structure both in the study and the theatre. We possess a library of distinguished *Lear* criticism; the century has seen a score of fine performances. *Macbeth* (1606), on the other hand, is notoriously difficult to produce. No one can doubt its entirety as dramatic poem, yet it seems to lack the due proportion of a play.

Most of what can be known about the background of this work occurs in a book by Henry Paul, *The Royal Play of Macbeth* (1950). The basic *Macbeth* plot occurs in a history by John of Fordun (c. 1385) and was rehandled through the centuries by successive chroniclers until it was brought to a high degree of polish in the Latin prose of Hector Boece or Boyce (1527). This was the basis of Shakespeare's primary source, the 1587 edition of Holinshed's *Chronicles*, which incorporates an English adaption by William Harrison of Boece's Scots translator. It retains the graphic qualities of the original:

> It fortuned as Makbeth and Banquho journied towards Fores, where the king then laie, they went sporting by the waie togither without other companie, save onelie themselves, passing thorough the woods and fields, when suddenlie in the middest of a laund, there met them three women in strange and wild apparell, resembling creatures of elder world, whome when they attentivelie beheld, woondering much at the sight, the first of them spake and said; All haile Makbeth, thane of Glammis (for he had latelie entered into that dignitie and office by the death of his father Sinell). The second of them said; Haile Makbeth thane of Cawder. But the third said; All haile Makbeth that heereafter shalt be king of Scotland. . . .

It can be seen that the old chronicle played into Shakespeare's hand. What he does is realise the implications of the drama and cast the narrative—for example, the description of the witches— into dialogue.

> BANQUO.   How far is't called to Forres?—What are these,
> So withered and so wild in their attire,
> That look not like th'inhabitants o'th'earth,
> And yet are on't? Live you? or are you aught
> That man may question? You seem to
>   understand me,
> By each at once her choppy finger laying
> Upon her skinny lips: you should be women,
> And yet your beards forbid me to interpret
> That you are so.
> MACBETH.   Speak, if you can:—what are you?
> 1 WITCH.   All hail, Macbeth! hail to thee, Thane of Glamis!
> 2 WITCH.   All hail, Macbeth! hail to thee, Thane of
>   Cawdor!
> 3 WITCH.   All hail, Macbeth! that shalt be King hereafter!
>
>   (I iii)

This is in essence a simple dramatic device, since obviously the playwright knows the story and can arrange a prophecy to match it. But what is peculiar about *Macbeth* is the precision with which the details are aligned. Hard upon the witches' heels enter

Rosse and Angus, the first of whom initially addresses Macbeth by his name, but goes on with a message from the king:

> And for an earnest of a greater honour,
> He bade me, from him, call thee Thane of
> Cawdor . . . .
>
> (ɪ iii)

These names echo through the play: 'Glamis and Thane of Cawdor' (ɪ iii); 'Glamis thou art, and Cawdor' (ɪ v); 'Thou hast it now, King, Cawdor, Glamis, all' (ɪɪɪ i). Such echoes are a linking device. So, too, is a distinctive form of serial imagery. Macbeth responds thus to Rosse's salutation:

> The Thane of Cawdor lives; why do you dress me
> In borrowed robes? (ɪ iii)

The clothes imagery is vivid and exact throughout:

> New honours come upon him,
> Like our strange garments, cleave not to their mould,
> But with the aid of use (ɪ iii)

> I have bought
> Golden opinions from all sorts of people,
> Which would be worn now in their newest gloss,
> Not cast aside so soon (ɪ vii)

> now does he feel his title
> Hang loose about him, like a giant's robe
> Upon a dwarfish thief. (v ii)

The plot is composite. Shakespeare has adapted details from other Scottish reigns and brought them in to give depth and atmosphere to this one. Kenneth II murdered the son of King Duff in order to protect his own heirs, but was sorely troubled in his conscience thereafter. The version of George Buchanan in *Rerum Scoticarum Historia* (1582) reads,

Tamen *animus, conscientia sceleris inquietus,* nullum *solidum* & sincerum ei *gaudium esse permittebat,* sed *intercursantibus per otium* cogitationibus sceleris foedissimi interdiu vexabatur; & per somnum *observantia visa horroris* plena quietem interpellabant. Tandem sive vere, quod quidam tradunt, *vox coelo edita est, sive turbatus animus* eam sibi ipse speciem finxerat. . . .

('His soul, disturbed by a consciousness of his crime, permitted him to enjoy no solid or sincere pleasure; in retirement the thoughts of his unholy deeds rushing upon his recollection, tormented him, and, in sleep, visions full of horror drove repose from his pillow. At last, whether in truth an audible voice from heaven addressed him, or whether it were the suggestion of his own guilty mind, he seemed thus to be admonished. . . .' Translated J. Aikman, 1827)

The italicised phrases point to a verbal correspondence between the torments of Kenneth and those of Macbeth.

> For Banquo's issue *have I filed my mind* . . .
> Put *rancours in the vessel of my peace*
>
> 'Tis safer to be that which we destroy,
> Than by destruction *dwell in doubtful joy*. . . .
> But let the frame of things disjoint, both the worlds suffer,
> Ere we will eat our meal in fear, and sleep
> In the affliction of *these terrible dreams*,
> That shake us nightly. Better be with *the dead*,
> *Whom we, to gain our peace, have sent to peace*,
> Than *on the torture of the mind to lie*
> *In restless ecstasy*. . . .
> O *full of scorpions is my mind*, dear wife   (III ii)
>
> Canst thou not minister to *a mind diseased* . . . ?   (v iii)

It is with the incursion of the 'vox coelo' that Shakespeare departs abruptly from Buchanan. In his original, he found no more than a straight accusation of infamy and a threat of divine punishment. Shakespeare, however, prefigures the pangs of conscience indicated in the passage quoted above by making the 'voice' prophesy the terrible dreams and restless ecstasies which are to persecute Macbeth throughout the remainder of the play:

> Methought, I heard a voice cry, 'Sleep no more!
> Macbeth does murther Sleep,'—the innocent Sleep;

> Sleep, that knits up the ravelled sleave of care,
> The death of each day's life, sore labour's bath,
> Balm of hurt minds, great Nature's second course,
> Chief nourisher in life's feast. . . .
> Still it cried, 'Sleep no more!' to all the house:
> 'Glamis hath murthered Sleep, and therefore Cawdor
> Shall sleep no more, Macbeth shall sleep no more!'
>
> (II ii)

In substituting this for the original accusation and threat, Shakespeare draws upon an entire literature of deprivation. Ovid in his *Metamorphoses*, XI 624, has

> pax animi, quen cura fugit, qui corpora duris
> fessa ministeriis mulces reparasque labori . . . .

Seneca in *Hercules Furens* (1067–7) has

> tuque, o domitor
> somne malorum, requies animi,
> pars humanae melior vitae . . . .

These have vigorous sixteenth-century translations, by Golding (1567) and Heywood (1566) respectively:

> O sleep, quoth she, the rest of things, O gentlest of
>   the gods,
> Sweet sleep, the peace of mind, with whom crook'd care
>   is aye at odds. . . .

and

> And then, O tamer best,
> O sleep of toils, the quietness of mind,
> Of all the life of man the better part. . . .

And there is a haunting invocation to sleep by Statius:

> Crimine quo merui, iuvenis placidissime divum,
> quove errore miser, donis ut solus egerem,
> Somne, tuis . . . ?

This last was widely imitated—by Sidney and Daniel, among others:

> Care-charmer Sleep, son of the sable night,
> Brother to Death, in silent darkness born,
> Relieve my anguish and restore the light;
> With dark forgetting of my care, return. . . .
>
> (Daniel, *ante* 1592)

And it is certain that Shakespeare knew these imitations, as well as the original. In this way, he brings into the barbaric world of Kenneth and Macbeth a civilised range of reference.

Macbeth himself goes through three stages: the ambitious general of Act I, the guilt-ridden murderer of Acts II and III, and the reckless tyrant of acts IV and V. His utterance, too, is most remarkable. The firstlings of his heart are certainly those of his imagination, and speech also. He no sooner thinks in practical terms of killing Duncan when he sees a vividly imagined dagger (II i). No sooner does he call for the dead Banquo at his banquet than he sees him as he must have looked at the instant of his murder:

> let the earth hide thee!
> Thy bones are marrowless, thy blood is cold;
> Thou hast no speculation in those eyes,
> Which thou dost glare with.   (III iv)

This scene is perhaps Shakespeare's most notable contribution to the Scottish source-material. It has an antecedent in a story in De Loier's *Treatise of Spectres* (1586, tr. Z. Jones, 1605). but the psychological insight here is manifestly superior. The Murderer has just informed Macbeth that Banquo lies in a ditch

> With twenty trenched gashes in his head;
> The least a death to nature.   (III iv)

But Macbeth's genius is to realise concretely from statement to inference. What he is told becomes for him an overwhelmingly present fact:

> now they rise again
> With twenty mortal murthers on their crowns
> And push us from our stools.   (III iv)

This psychological trait Macbeth shares with his creator. Over and over again, one has to say of Shakespeare that a hint in a chronicle or travel book or old play gives rise to all manner of images associated together with a richness that has no parallel in English literature. However, in this instance there seems to be not quite enough distinction between Shakespeare's basic technique and the poetry spoken by Macbeth. The character in performance, therefore, is liable to seem less individualised than the plot would require; even, perhaps, too sympathetic. There is not the distance that exists between ourselves and Othello, whose Plinyesque imagery and exotic trappings imply a personalised clarity of outline. Othello is further protected from false identification on our part by the counteracting presence of Iago: it puts him squarely in a play. In comparison, the Macbeths are exposed, with neither friends nor accomplices. We are confronted with their crimes, but we are also vulnerable to their suffering. It comes across with great force. There is, for example, no scene in Shakespeare more poignant than Lady Macbeth's sleepwalking; we cannot help, to a considerable extent, entering into Macbeth's 'terrible dreams'. Because of this, the treachery that underlies the hell Macbeth and his Lady have created for themselves is liable to recede somewhat into the background. It is as though the murder of Desdemona has been plotted in Act I and executed in Act II, with the rest of the drama to serve as an arena for the protagonist's dismay. In the study one reads, conditioned by previous frequentations of the work; one is one's own interpreter. A kind of critical attention is therefore possible that favours the serial techniques used in *Macbeth*. The imagery of blood, of night, of sleeplessness—all this interconnects, and we possess, in this way, an inalienable poem. But, in the theatre, the same work interposes extraordinary difficulties between actor and audience. I would not go so far as to say that a good production of *Macbeth* is impossible. But certainly it is in order to ask the reader whether he has ever seen one.

Antony and Cleopatra (1606), in comparison, is soundly buttressed. The central figure has a mode of speech that is highly characteristic. Nobody is likely to mistake Antony's viewpoint for that of the author:

> Let Rome in Tiber melt, and the wide arch
> Of the ranged empire fall. . . .   (I i)

This takes a step further the self-aggrandising diction we associate with Othello. It is impossible to talk sense in such a rhetoric:

> The shirt of Nessus is upon me, teach me,
> Alcides, thou mine ancestor, thy rage.
> Let me lodge Lichas on the horns o' the moon,
> And with those hands that grasped the heaviest club,
> Subdue my worthiest self. . . .   (IV xii)

Basically, the mode derives from Seneca, but it is Seneca heard through the adaptation of several Elizabethan rhetoricians. The present instance derives ultimately from *Hercules Oetaeus*:

> in astra missus fertur et nubes vago
> spargit cruore . . . .

> ('With Lycas thus his labours end, thrown up to heaven
> they say/That with his dropping blood the clouds he stained
> all the way . . .' translated J. Studley, 1581)

The page Lichas is flung to the stars because he brings Hercules—as a present from the hero's jealous wife, Deianira—the poisoned shirt of Nessus. Antony himself is seared by the treachery of Cleopatra, but his immediate reaction is verbal; the trajection, symbolic. And the speech, for all its extravagance, is prevented from detaching itself from context by its relationship with other references identifying Antony with Hercules. Shakespeare had read in Plutarch (translated Thomas North, 1579), his basic source, that Antony claimed the Greek demi-god as his mythical ancestor. In I iii Cleopatra terms him 'Herculean', and in IV iii mysterious music is heard and is said to signify that Hercules is deserting him. With all this, however, the level of extravaganza remains high. When Antony is not posing as Hercules, he is attitudinising as Mars. This means that he uses his rhetoric to prevent himself from recognising that his fortunes are on the wane. Therefore, this Antony-language, as A. L. French calls it (*Shakespeare and the Critics,* 1972), predominates in the later scenes of the play. Addressing the absent Cleopatra, whom he thinks dead, Antony says,

> Stay for me,
> Where souls do couch on flowers, we'll hand in hand,
> And with our sprightly port make the ghosts gaze:
> Dido and her Æneas, shall want troops,
> And all the haunt be ours.   (IV xiv)

This comes from Virgil, but it is seen through the eyes of the old play *Nero* (printed 1624; dating from well before that):

> Mingled with that fair company shall we
> On banks of Violets and of Hiacinths
> Of loves devising, sit and gently sport.

In *Aeneid* VI, Virgil himself makes the ghost of Dido turn away from her dead lover, Aeneas. But Antony's speech is Virgil transmuted by Ovid and by Elizabethan fantasy, and a vision of the underworld is conjured up where great lovers consort together for all eternity. Faced with the presumption of Cleopatra's death, what else is Antony to imagine? He certainly cannot bear very much reality.

At each setback, Antony takes refuge in intoxicating draughts of language. One does not have to be the critical Cæsar to see that he is doomed. His own lieutenant, the clear-sighted Enobarbus, remarks,

> I see still
> A diminution in our captain's brain
> Restores his heart. . . .   (III xiii)

The part that Enobarbus plays in the management of the play is out of all proportion to his significance as a character, considerable though that is. Plutarch mentions him only in passing, though with a good word for his persuasive qualities. But Shakespeare puts upon him the weight of Plutarch's history, particularly that which tends towards the evaluation of Cleopatra. What is straight narrative in North's Plutarch becomes evocative monologue in the mouth of Enobarbus:

She disdained to set forward otherwise, but to take her barge
in the river of Cydnus, the poope whereof was of gold, the
sailes of purple, and the owers of silver, which kept stroke
in rowing after the sounde of the musicke of flutes, howboys,
citherns, violls, and such other instruments as they played upon
in the barge. And now for the person of her selfe . . . .

> The barge she sat in, like a burnished throne
> Burned on the water: the poop was beaten gold;
> Purple the sails, and so perfumed that
> The winds were love-sick with them; the oars were silver,
> Which to the tune of flutes kept stroke, and made
> The water which they beat to follow faster,
> As amorous of their strokes. . . .   (II ii)

Even before he reaches 'her own person', Shakespeare has infused
Plutarch's narrative with amorous implication. The word 'barge'
is related to the royal presence in 'throne'—a 'burnished' throne,
moreover, that 'burned'; words which suggest the heat of South-
ern passion. The sails, 'purple' in Plutarch, are in Shakespeare
'perfumed' as well—so perfumed that 'the winds were love-sick
with them'. Sense is piled upon sense. Cleopatra is the Queen of
Love: her very appurtenances seduce the elements. Her oars are
silver, as in Plutarch, but they beat the water and so cause
the waves to follow faster 'as amorous of their strokes'. Thus
it goes throughout the entire speech. The details in Plutarch
are heightened and extended to one end: to show Cleopatra
as seductive and tantalising. She surpasses that picture of Venus
painted by Apelles where his art, in its turn, had surpassed
nature. In this way, Shakespeare transforms a description of a
river progress into the definitive account, in *Antony and Cleopatra*,
of the Egyptian queen. The speech occurs in an episode when
Antony has left Alexandria for Rome in order to confer with
his fellow generals. The imaginative presence of Egypt is therefore
established at the very heart of the Empire. This clearly shows
how futile any composition between Cæsar and Antony would
be if it were to exclude Cleopatra from its calculations. The
commentary is historically accurate, as a transcript from Plutarch,
but it has a dramatic authority that counts for far more. After
all, it is spoken by a character who has already established himself

as a trustworthy witness, and no friend to the Egyptian queen. Glamorous though Cleopatra and her entourage are made to seem in Enobarbus's description, the verse contains no trace of Antony-language. In its attention to detail, it is far more like the lucid verse spoken by Cæsar. It has, without losing the sense of character, qualities that are similarly choric. In this way, the extravagant story of Antony and Cleopatra is contained within a framework that is made all the more secure in that it is composed of recognisable characters who have the standing of eye-witnesses. It is inconceivable that the production difficulties attendant upon performances of *Macbeth* could arise with this play. The main problem would be to find an Antony and Cleopatra capable of projecting a powerful sense of romance. There is a protective device here, however. Cleopatra never in the earlier acts lives up to the charm attributed to her by Enobarbus. There is, in other words, a gap between Enobarbus's speeches and the actual presentation of Cleopatra. Yet this is turned to account, for it suggests that a degree of propinquity is necessary to find Cleopatra irresistibly attractive. The audience, through most of the play, is made to keep its distance. This is essential if the playwright is to avoid a distortion of sympathies. Because of this, moreover, we are able to maintain a judgement more detached than that of Cæsar. The latter, indeed, roundly calls Cleopatra 'whore'; but that is before he at length comes to meet her, in Act v. It is in this last act that Cleopatra reaches her greatest heights; here she certainly fulfils all prior report. The audience can now be allowed a closer emotional approach, because she is under her own sentence. First Antony, then Cleopatra, realises that the extremity of their behaviour has brought them on to an inevitable fate. Once· there is no return, each meets death unflinchingly. They rise to the level of their fantasies: they become, respectively, Mars and Venus. Our sympathy, therefore, is gained in the end without the necessity of forfeiting our judgement. It is salutary to reflect that *Antony and Cleopatra*, sometimes thought the most passionate of Shakespeare's tragedies, is in fact a critique of passion.

Passion of another kind is the motivating force of *Coriolanus* (1608). The play continues the choric techniques used to such remarkable effect in *Antony and Cleopatra*. The chief commentator is Cominius. He is a recognisable figure in the play—a former consul, a leading general—but his role is to interpret the events that happen before the spectators' eyes or to describe those that it is not convenient to set there:

> From face to foot
> He was a thing of blood, whose every motion
> Was timed with dying cries,   (II ii)

> He is their god. He leads them like a thing
> Made by some other deity than nature . . . .   (IV vi)

The speeches of Cominius bear to no small extent the weight of the source material of Coriolanus. This, like *Antony and Cleopatra*, derives from Plutarch, though the subject is one of narrower scope. The equivalent matter in Plutarch is straight history:

> When they sawe him at his first comming, all bloody, and in a swet, and but with a fewe men following him: some thereupon beganne to be afeard. . . .

> Hereupon his fame ranne though all Italie, and every one praised him for a valliant captaine.

Plutarch is factual, and North's translation is workmanlike English. But Shakespeare sharpens their details, and sharpens them after a definite mode. The imagery of Coriolanus tends to a consistent end, and that is the representation of the central character as one who has willed himself almost out of humanity. 'A thing of blood', 'a thing made by some other deity'—this comes with suggestive force from Cominius, who, after all, is one of the hero's allies. Aufidius, his erstwhile enemy, addresses Coriolanus as 'thou noble thing' (IV v). Menenius, his closest friend, describes him among the Volsces as 'a thing made for Alexander' and as an 'engine' (V iv). He also refers to him as 'a male tiger' (V iv), while Coriolanus calls himself, and is called, a 'dragon' (IV i, V iv) and an 'eagle' (V vi). The poetry he speaks is a tissue of references to war, couched in terms at once violent and abstract. Predominantly, the obsession is with blood, but it is not particularised with any visual immediacy. It is blood dropped (I v), shed, smeared, painted (I vi), masking (I vii), shed in 'drops' and drawn by 'tuns' (IV v). This marches along with a series of disease images, much more specific, aimed in denunciation at the common people. They are at one time or another called 'scabs' (I i), 'boils', 'plagues' (I iv), 'tettered measles' (III i) and 'curs' with 'rotten breaths' (III iii). Even this gives little idea of the willed and perverted power of this verse:

> Therefore beseech you—
> You that will be less fearful than discreet,
> That love the fundamental part of state
> More than you doubt the change on't; that prefer
> A noble life before a long, and wish
> To jump a body with a dangerous physic
> That's sure of death without it—at once pluck out
> The multitudinous tongue: let them not lick
> The sweet which is their poison. . . .   (III i)

A good deal of the force comes from the tension generated between the violent vocabulary—'pluck out the . . . tongue' and the like—and the measured advance of the syntax. In the second line quoted, the personal pronoun 'you' controls no less than four adjectival clauses, the second of which has its own adverbial clause of comparison and the fourth an adjectival clause dependent upon the noun 'body'. This section is a parenthesis within a main clause starting at the first line quoted and ultimately leading to a double noun clause dependent upon the verb 'beseech'. Such syntactical elaboration is characteristic of Coriolanus, and makes one feel that his anger is a deliberated extrusion rather than a spontaneous overflow. Coriolanus has allowed his passion to pervert him until he is not a man but a thing. Like Shakespeare's other tragic heroes, he falls victim to a doom of extremes.

The verse, as has been seen, borders on caricature. It reminds us how near to Jonsonian comedy the tragedy of Shakespeare is. This is true even of the transition period when Shakespeare was changing down from drama of the kind we have just looked at to what has been termed the 'serene comedy' of his final years. One finds grotesque touches of detail in *Timon of Athens* (1607–8)—

> Crack the lawyer's voice,
> That he may never more false title plead,
> Nor sound his quillets shrilly   (IV iii)

in *Cymbeline* (c. 1610)—

> The cloyed will—
> That satiate yet unsatisfied desire, that tub
> Both filled and running—ravening first the lamb,
> Longs after for the garbage   (I vi)

in *The Winter's Tale* (c.1611)—

> holds his wife by th'arm
> That little thinks she has been sluiced in's absence,
> And his pond fished by his next neighbour, by
> Sir Smile, his neighbour   (I ii)

and in *The Two Noble Kinsmen* (? 1611)—

> the aged cramp
> Had screwed his square foot round,
> The gout had knit his fingers into knots,
> Torturing convulsions from his globy eyes,
> Had almost drawn their spheres . . . .   (v i)

Perhaps *The Tempest* (1611) is not as serene as all that:

> I'll rack thee with old cramps,
> Fill all thy bones with aches, make thee roar,
> That beasts shall tremble at thy din.   (I ii)

This is the wise Prospero talking. It is not so unusual a mode of utterance as one might suppose:

> I'll manacle thy neck and feet together:
> Sea-water shalt thou drink; thy food shall be
> The fresh-brook mussels, withered roots, and husks
> Wherein the acorn cradled.   (I ii)

Here he is addressing, not his slave, as might be imagined, but a Prince of Naples and his future son-in-law. This is sorcerer as poet, as apparent designer of his own plot; authoritative, masterful.

Critics have had trouble settling upon the dramatic core of
The Tempest and so have found difficulty in adducing its roots.
Surely this is the crucial scene: the scene where Prospero confronts
Ferdinand, who is courting his daughter:

MIRANDA.   . . . This
               Is the third man that e'er I saw; the first
               That e'er I sighed for: pity move my father
               To be inclined my way!
FERDINAND.   O, if a virgin,
               And your affection not gone forth, I'll make
                  you
               The Queen of Naples.
PROSPERO.   Soft, sir! one word more. . . .
               I charge thee
               That thou attend me: thou dost here usurp
               The name thou ow'st not; and has put thyself
               Upon this island as a spy, to win it
               From me, the lord on't.   (I ii)

Ferdinand is arrested by Prospero and put to work piling up
logs. All Ferdinand's vexations are Prospero's trials of his love.
He stands up to them impressively. I ii, III i, IV i and V i
carry the weight of this plot, and they are the spine of the
play.
    The theme is that of the lover serving an apprenticeship to
his love's parent:

               this swift business
     I must uneasy make, lest too light winning
     Make the prize light.   (I ii)

It is archetypal: the story of Jacob and Rachel in Genesis 29.
Other instances of the story include 'Lady Featherflight' (see
W. W. Newell, *Journal of American Folk-lore*, 1913). The daughter
of a cannibal giant is courted by a youth seeking his fortune.
He is discovered at the giant's castle and is set to work thatching
a barn with feathers and weaving a rope out of sand. An Italian
version adds the idea of the hero being rooted to the ground
and having to split a vast number of logs. The tales on this
theme, in fact, are legion, and it is impossible to know which

particular one Shakespeare picked up for *The Tempest.* There is, moreover, a distinct association with the myth of Jason, who had to tame bulls, sow serpents' teeth and slay a dragon in order to gain from Aetes, King of Colchis, the Golden Fleece. It will be remembered that the King had a daughter, Medea, who fell in love with the hero; it will be further remembered that she was a magician. And she, certainly, is an unmistakable presence in Shakespeare's play, though many of her properties have been transferred to the central figure.

There was in 1471 a historical ruler of Genoa called Prospero Adorno, who was a deputy of the Duke of Milan. He had an alliance with Ferdinando, King of Naples, but was deposed circa 1488 and his brother Antony was made governor in his stead. Shakespeare could very well have found this story in Thomas's *History of Italy* (1549), which was reprinted in 1561. But the important point is that he does not here, as he did in *Measure for Measure*, stay within its conventions; neither does he develop them against the sense of the story. Prospero is sustained by resources far beyond those of Renaissance history. He designs the effectual plot of *The Tempest,* it is true, but he is given the power to do it. It is not for incidental lyricism that he speaks in the accents of the sorceress, Medea; the Medea not only of Ovid's *Metamorphoses,* but also of Arthur Golding's attractive English rendering:

> Ye airs and winds: ye elves of hills, of brooks, of woods
>   alone,
> Of standing lakes, and of the night approach ye everyone. ...
> By charms I make the calm seas rough, and make the
>   rough seas plain,
> And cover all the sky with clouds, and chase them thence
>   again.
> By charms I raise and lay the winds . . . .

Shakespeare in his blank verse gets rid of the sing-song utterance in an invocation that echoes pantheistically through literature as far as Wordsworth's magical invocation in the JJ manuscript (1798–99) that eventually became the first book of *The Prelude* (1805, 1850) In Shakespeare it comes out as

Ye elves of hills, brooks, standing lakes, and groves;
And ye that on the sands with printless foot
Do chase the ebbing Neptune, and do fly him
When he comes back . . .
            by whose aid
Weak masters though ye be—I have bedimmed
The noontide sun, called forth the mutinous winds,
And 'twixt the green sea and the azured vault
Set roaring war. . . .   (v i)

Unlike the Duke in *Measure for Measure*, Prospero has no need to lose dignity in disguise and probity in prevarication. He is coloured by the elements and extended through his spells. He is, moreover, flanked by dramatically effective agents. Ariel, derived from the Cabala, successfully carries out Prospero's schemes; Caliban, based on the Indians described by the Virginian colonists, vainly tries to thwart them. Both these figures—amazing creations in their own right—give Prospero's figure at the centre of the play credibility.

Apart from the central theme of the Love Test, the story is slight. The usurper, Antonio, urges the heir-presumptive to the throne of Naples to kill his brother. Caliban suborns two disaffected servants to start a mutiny. All this is easily foiled by Prospero, who stands against the barbarians as the representative of a civilisation more deeply-rooted than anything found in Naples.

It has proved impossible to avoid the suggestion of autobiography in all this. The figure of the sorcerer is a splendid means of allegorising the role of the poet:

            to the dread rattling thunder
Have I given fire, and rifted Jove's stout oak
With his own bolt; the strong-based promontory
Have I made shake, and by the spurs plucked up
The pine and cedar: graves at my command
Have waked their sleepers, oped, and let 'em forth
By my so potent Art . . . .   (v i)

One cannot help feeling a recapitulatory quality in this speech. It recalls the storm in *King Lear*, the march of Birnam Wood to Dunsinane, the ghostly patrols of Banquo and the elder Hamlet; it is, in fact, a celebration of Shakespeare's art. *The Tempest* is his last completed play, and it carries a sense of valediction. The association of Prospero's magic with books and study compel us further in that direction. But such, indeed, is the potency of the art, that Prospero still functions as a character within the dramatic framework of the play. He passes judgement on his purgatorial isle, and, in abjuring his rough magic, perhaps he passes a form of judgement on himself. It is touching that almost his last word is a signal of release to the muse that made his art possible. It is impressive, too, that in the end the wicked are left to the pinches, not of Ariel, but of their own consciences. As Wilson Knight says in *The Crown of Life* (1947), in poetic creation all is forgiven.

Most writers are more derivative than the public imagines, but few have played so wholeheartedly as this the role of adapter. One has to get rid of the notion of the self-made genius and child of fancy in contemplating the work of Shakespeare. He grafted on to a substratum of classical and biblical reading the chronicles and *novelle* necessary to the organisation of his plays. His various sources, as we have seen, are not cobbled into anthologies but fused into works that are recognisably wholes. This is not a matter of seeking after a language that is homogenous. Rather the process resembles that of an organist mixing various registers to mark out the contrasting divisions of a fugue or a partita. The mighty diapason of Othello derives from Pliny, and pitted against this is the proverbial utterance most sinisterly given to Iago. The objurgations of Lear draw heavily on the Old Testament, while the scrannel pipe of the Fool owes most to English folk-tradition. Antony's *basso cantate* is an adaptation of Seneca; the choric accompaniment supplied by Enobarbus is rearranged from Plutarch. To be intelligently traditional is to explore the best available sources: selecting, conflating and developing material as the nature of the theme demands. To be intelligently experimental is to be alive to the needs and interests of the time, incorporating new material as Shakespeare did the accounts of Popish superstitions into *King Lear* or of the Virginian plantations into *The Tempest*. That this synthesis of tradition and experiment has happened so rarely indicates how difficult it is to find a balance in the process. English poetry has swung through the ages from passive acceptance of precedent to Romantic loss of cultural memory. That Shakespeare can now be classified among Old Books or placed among the

Special Options is no slight evidence of this. An advance in writing may have to be an advance in rewriting, too. The reader, as well as the author, needs to realise the implications latent in the past.

5 Ben Jonson in the Seventeenth Century

Ben Jonson was not only witty in himself but also the cause of wit in other men. One does not know which to admire most, his classic sense of tradition or his pioneer originality. On to the medieval stock of English poetry he grafted the sophistication of the Latin classics. He made Catullus, Horace, Tibullus, Ovid, Propertius and Martial native to our language. The elegy and the ode, in the sense that we understand them today, were his adaptations. He developed the formal lyric that dominated the seventeenth century. He acclimatised to English the familiar epistle. Lastly, English comedy as an art-form is his creation: at once a refinement and a strengthening of Plautus and Terence. It was an aspect of drama which thinned out gradually through the Caroline and Restoration comedy of manners until it expired—still dominating English theatre—in the 1950s and 1960s. One cannot imagine literary history without Jonson as a central figure. His fertility is as extraordinary as his power of initiation. And, manifold though the forms were with which he inspired his successors, it is a matter of fact that he excelled in them all.

One remarkable phenomenon of seventeenth-century verse is the way in which content and form match, and, moreover, remain constant in relation to one another. George Saintsbury made the point in his edition of the Caroline poets when he quoted a stanza by Katherine Philips:

I did not live until this time
  Crowned my felicity,
When I could say without a crime
  I am not thine but thee.
                ('To My Excellent Lucasia, on Our Friendship')

'How did Donne or Jonson (for it was apparently one or the
other) discover this ineffable cadence? How did they manage
to teach it to (all but) all and sundry, for half a century?
How did it get utterly lost; and how has it only occasionally
and uncertainly recovered?' The cadence is tinkly enough by
the time it reaches Katherine Philips, the 'matchless Orinda',
whose poems came out in 1678. Yet her work is recognisably
in the line of the Ben Jonson, who invented the Caroline lyric—
such a poem as this:

Oh do not wanton with those eyes:
  Lest I be sick with seeing;
Nor cast them down, but let them rise,
  Lest shame destroy their being:
O, be not angry with those fires,
  For then their threats will kill me;
Nor look too kind on my desires,
  For then my hopes will spill me;
O, do not steep them in thy Tears,
  For so will sorrow slay me;
Nor spread them as distract with fears,
  Mine own enough betray me.
                ('Oh do not wanton . . .', early 17th century)

Jonson here catches the anxiety of new love which feels itself
threatened by kindness, as well as by unkindness. It is a mature
poet feigning the tentative quality of first passion. The basic
feel of the lyric derives from Horace or Propertius, but perhaps
Tibullus is the poet most closely adapted. He (i ii) has a passage
that begins,

Parcite luminibus, seu vir seu femina fias
  obvia: celari vult sua furta Venus . . . .

('Be not busy with your eyes, be you man or woman
that we meet. Love's goddess wills her theft should not
be seen . . .')

This is matched to a cadence drawn from the medieval ballads which were still sung in Jonson's day, and indeed for centuries after. I think that a reference to Jonson's Border descent is as relevant here as one to his education at Westminster. At any rate, we may see the origins of this influential verse form in

> O I forbid you, maidens a',
>   That wear gowd on your hair,
> To come or gae by Carterhaugh,
>   For young Tam Lin is there. . . . ('Tam Lin', c. 1549)

That is the ballad, with regard to later efforts, in an *ur*-formation. It eventually refined itself into such writing as this:

> The wind doth blow today, my love,
>   And a few small drops of rain;
> I never had but one true love,
>   In cold grave she was lain. . . .
>   ('The Unquiet Grave', ? 18th century)

Somewhere between 'Tam Lin' and this came the rhythm that stimulated Jonson to urbanise ballad metre and match it to the accents of the ancient Romans. There had been attempts at the form before Jonson: 'Madame, withouten many words' is a bold shot by Wyatt at the rhythm that was to become the Caroline lyric. But this earlier master lacked Jonson's certainty in English metre. 'And would you see my mistress' face' by Campion comes near the mark, but the presence of music made it possible for that lyricist—Jonson's immediate precursor in many respects—to indulge in a genial looseness that the younger poet never affected.

The assured example of Jonson made for certainty in those who came after him. In Jonson, the stance is that of tentative love; the beloved is required to give less than she wishes, whether it be love or disdain, and behind the verse is an attitude of stoic propriety. Thomas Carew stands the attitude on its head: his verse extends the urbane cadence of Jonson and acts as a kind of comment on 'Oh do not wanton'.

> Give me more love, or more disdain;
>   The Torrid, or the Frozen Zone,

Bring equal ease unto my pain;
  The temperate affords me none . . . .
                ('Mediocrity in Love Rejected', c. 1619)

Sidney Godolphin was perhaps nearest to Jonson in spirit—so
near that Dr Leavis in *Revaluation* attributed to the older poet
what is now taken to be one of Godolphin's own poems. In
his verse the cadence—still stoical, still gently admonitory—comes
out as this:

No more unto my thoughts appear,
  At least appear less fair,
For crazy tempers justly fear
  The goodness of the air. . . .
                ('No more unto . . .', *ante* 1643)

Almost the same effect, rather more deep-toned, in earnest behind
its courtly air is found in a poem often attributed to Henry
King:

Tell me no more how fair she is,
  I have no mind to hear
The story of that distant bliss
  I never shall come near. . . .   ('Sonnet', *ante* 1657)

It may be King, or it may equally be Godolphin, Strode or
any of a score of fine poets whose works are scattered under
the generic attribution of 'Anon.'. This poem, more than most,
shows how much the Jonson cadence was in the air, though
it cannot be a coincidence that the poets I have mentioned,
and many others of like distinction, were all educated at Westminster School under Camden and, later, Jordan. As the seventeenth
century wore on, the cadence became more and more associated
with the Cavalier—the gallant soldier who was a courtier and
wrote poetry in the intervals of battle. Robert Herrick gave
the form sufficient momentum to take it through the Civil War:

Bid me to live, and I will live
  Thy Protestant to be:
Or bid me love, and I will give
  A loving heart to thee. . . .
('To Anthea, Who May Command Him Anything', *ante* 1648)

Herrick, as far as we know, was a non-combatant. But his variation upon Jonson's form provides a vehicle for the attitude of many brave men. Sir Richard Lovelace took over one of Herrick's names, Anthea, and gave it a greater significance by rendering it as Althea—the loving mother who killed her son. This lends the poem a gloomy menace at a time of civil war:

> When love with unconfined wings
>   Hovers within my gates;
> And my divine Althea brings
>   To whisper at the grates:
> When I lie tangled in her hair,
>   And fettered to her eye,
> The gods that wanton in the air
>   Know no such liberty. . . .
>
> ('To Althea, from Prison', 1642)

There is here a compounding of love and war into an assured statement of the attitude very much to the fore in Jonson's poetry; the attitude of stoicism. It is a pity that Lovelace's poetry has been so subject to the vagaries of fashion.

> Stone walls do not a prison make,
>   Nor iron bars a cage;
> Minds innocent and quiet take
>   That for an hermitage;
> If I have freedom in my love,
>   And in my soul am free;
> Angels alone, that soar above,
>   Enjoy such liberty.

'Non possidentem multa vocaveris / recte beatum', indeed. ('Not him who possesses much would one rightly call the happy man'). This is one of the finest expressions of Horace's sentiment (Odes, IV ix) in English.

Along with the mode adopted by Herrick, this poem helped to set the tone of men who had need of all the stoicism they could muster. The Marquis of Montrose, for example, has this:

> My dear and only Love, I pray
>   This noble World of thee,

Be governed by no other Sway
 But purest Monarchy.
For if Confusion have a part
 Which vertuous Souls abhor,
And hold a Synod in thy Heart,
 I'll never love thee more
      ('My dear and only Love . . .', 1650)

or again—perhaps his most famous stanza:

 . . . He either fears his Fate too much,
  Or his Deserts are small,
 That puts it not unto the Touch,
  To win or lose it all.

That stoic confidence sounds the note of Cavalier poetry. I think
of Sir John Suckling:

 I prithee send me back my heart,
  Since I cannot have thine:
 For if from yours you will not part,
  Why then shouldst thou have mine? . . .
            ('Song', c. 1630)

and of Thomas Stanley:

 I prithee let my heart alone,
  Since now 'tis raised above thee,
 Not all the beauty thou dost own,
  Again can make me love thee. . . . ('Song', *ante* 1651)

 After the Civil War, it thinned out—in the work of Katherine
Philips, as we have seen, and in that of 'the mob of gentlemen
who wrote with ease': Sedley (by far the best of them), Dorset,
Sheffield, Roscommon, Halifax, among others. Two of these
later poets managed to give the Caroline lyric their own subtle
intonation. One was that strangest of Puritans, Andrew Marvell:

 My Love is of a birth as rare
 As 'tis for object strange and high:
 It was begotten by despair
 Upon Impossibility. . . .
      ('The Definition of Love', late 1640s)

Another was that most raffish of Restoration wits, the Earl of
Rochester:

> Absent from thee I languish still,
>   Then ask me not, when I return?
> The straying Fool 'twill plainly kill
>   To wish all Day, all Night to Mourn. . . .
>
>   ('A Song', c. 1670)

The acceptance of a darker world than even Jonson knew goes
along with the intricate variation of a cadence which was by
now time-honoured. Its rhythm had so definitely imprinted itself
upon people's minds that it was possible to develop the basic
stanza form by means of delicate rubato and syncopation. The
modes of adapting the classics, too, were so established that
it was possible to get very close to the Roman masters without
sacrificing individuality. Rochester here is perhaps recalling passages from Ovid's *Heroides*, possibly the epistle from Acontius
to Cydippe.

But the darkness overhanging the Civil War and its aftermath
lifted in the interests of the Peace of the Augustans; the eighteenth
century feared to be harrowed. And so the Ineffable Cadence,
as Saintsbury called the Caroline stanza, deteriorated into the
mechanical tinklings of Prior, Parnell and Gay, except in so
far as the last-named was able to revive the ballad form in
The Beggar's Opera (1728).

The indebtedness of the seventeenth century to Jonson is seen
in so many developments that it is hard to characterise them
without losing the reader in detail. For example, it was Jonson's
adaptations from Catullus, especially 'Vivamus, mea Lesbia', that
started off an especially successful series of poems in the line
of 'carpe diem'. 'Come, my Celia' (early 17th century) equals
its great original, and gave the theme an urgency and crispness
of Jonson's own:

> Spend not then his gifts in vain.
> Suns, that set, may rise again:
> But if once we loose this light,
> 'Tis, with us, perpetual night. . . .

Carew's 'Persuasions to Enjoy' and 'Persuasions to Love' give
the Jonson cadences a characteristically Cavalier polish:

For that lovely face will fail,
Beauty's sweet, but beauty's frail;
'Tis sooner past, 'tis sooner done
Than Summer's rain, or winter's Sun. . . .

('To A. L. Persuasions to Love', c. 1619)

But it was Herrick who deepened it into a resonance with
which he is not usually credited, in (among other poems) his
'Corinna Going a-Maying' (*ante* 1648). Like Lovelace, Herrick
has suffered from nineteenth-century over-exposure and twentieth-
century neglect. His advantage over Jonson—albeit his only one—is
the thorough knowledge of a rural terrain. In this great poem
the stylised beauty of 'Tu ne quaesieris' is adapted into a spring
ritual older than Christianity, or than the Romans. In spite of
its variegation of metre, the spine of the poem is the crisp
tetrameter of Jonson, now used to convey gathering gloom:

So when or you or I are made
A fable, song, or fleeting shade;
All love, all liking, all delight
Lies drowned with us in endless night.

Those same tetrameters run through the seventeenth century,
that time of poetry, pestilence and Civil War. Thus Edmund
Waller:

Beauty like a shadow flies,
And our youth before us dies.
Or would youth and beauty stay,
Love hath wings and will away. . . .

('To Phyllis', c. 1635)

That metre reaches out to the eternal verities in Marvell's urbane,
passionate 'To His Coy Mistress' (late 1640s):

Thy Beauty shall no more be found;
Nor, in thy marble Vault, shall sound
My echoing Song: then Worms shall try
That long preserved Virginity:
And your quaint Honour turn to dust;
And into ashes all my Lust . . . .

Jonson himself could not excel that. But it is still Jonson's cadence and Jonson's version of the theme which had so obsessed Horace and Catullus, though slowed down, deepened, and put into the Aeolian mode. In the finest poems of Marvell, as in those of Jonson and Herrick, we find the encounter of the sophisticated townsman with the grim reality of things as they are.

Where Jonson scores most heavily is in his adaptation of the heroic couplet, presumably from the Latin distich, into a major form of English poetry. One may feel that this would have happened anyway, but Chaucer's metre was misunderstood after its own time and Chapman's *Odyssey* did not rival in prestige his septametric *Iliad*. And the couplets of Donne's satires have more in common with dramatic verse than with later developments. So it can be said that Jonson was the first poet to make effective use of this central and enduring medium. Here, as with Caroline lyric, form is at one with content. Jonson saw the couplet as a vehicle for satire, epistolary verse and elegiac poetry. In this, to a great extent, poets at large have followed him.

The couplet form is one curiously suitable for acting as a restraint to powerful emotion. The poetry of Jonson is passionate, but under stoic control. One deciding factor here is a kind of ellipsis learned especially from Catullus, Horace and Martial. If one takes an apparently simple work, Catullus's epigram on his brother's grave (ci), one finds the poem shaped by the pressure of implication. In his fine analysis of the poem (in *Tradition and Originality in Roman Poetry*, 1968), Gordon Williams shows how the simple phrases make for particularity: this is no ordinary grave but one a great distance away, and the poet's presence there is no ordinary event but a single, unrepeatable occasion. This conveys, without stating the matter explicitly, a sense of loss. In a similar way, Jonson uses allusion as a mode at once controlling and rendering precise his emotion on the death of his first son.

> Farewell, thou child of my right hand, and joy;
> My sin was too much hope of thee, loved boy,
> Seven years thou wert lent to me, and I thee pay,
> Exacted by thy fate, on the just day.
> O, could I loose all father, now. For why
> Will man lament the state he should envy?

To have so soon scaped world's, and flesh's rage,
And, if no other misery, yet age?
Rest in soft peace, and, asked, say here doth lie
Ben. Jonson his best piece of poetry.
For whose sake, henceforth, all his vows be such
As what he loves may never like too much.

('On My First Son', 1603)

'Child of my right hand' is an exact translation of the Hebrew word Benjamin; a fact which Jonson may have picked up from the list of Christian names compiled by his old teacher (see Camden's *Remains*). Seven years is, in common law, the time after which a debt lapses. Therefore the day on which the boy dies is just, for it is exact, designed by God, and within the period during which payment of his life could be required. However it is only just within that period, and therefore the phrase, 'the just day', assumes a dual character. 'O could I loose all father now'—'loose', like 'just', is a controlled ambiguity. It refers both to a wish to unleash emotion in grief and also a wish not to be a father—punning on the word 'loose' in the sense of 'let go' and also in the sense of 'lose'. 'The state he should envy': the boy is static, unable to move, in a state; in state, being taken to God; therefore his state, both of immortality and of exaltation, is enviable. He has escaped the miseries of the world and now is with God. The last line, drawn from Martial, VI xxix, balances the second in expressing a stoic reaction: one should treasure nothing too highly on this earth if one wishes to escape the agony of grief when it is taken away. It is worth pointing out that the classically trained Augustine defined hell as the ultimate feeling of deprivation.

One can seldom mistake Ben Jonson's elegies for his epistles, even though they are for the most part in the same measure. In the epistles, the tone is that of celebration. The compliments are formal, the language draws a degree of attention to itself, the technique resembles that of the series of addresses to great men with which Horace began his first book of Odes. But there is a distinction to be made. Horace's second Ode calls upon various gods to help the State, and suggests that one of them may be already at hand in disguise. In context, this is an elliptical way of identifying Augustus with Mercury. Jonson's nearest equivalent was Sir Robert Cecil, and to do any such thing with this prosaic figure would have been ridiculous. So Jonson adopts a device that was to become familiar in English poetry, that of praising the subject indirectly. One of his Cecil poems declares that no poet could see such worth without celebrating it; but it is a poem about the need for verse to be celebratory, not a poem celebrating Cecil's virtue. On the whole, Jonson is happier on familiar ground: praising a patron, say, who is also a friend. One of the poems to the Countess of Bedford plays with her Christian name, Lucy, and its derivation from *lux*. The poem begins much as it ends—

> Lucy, you brightness of our sphere, who are
> Life of the Muses' day, their morning-star! . . .
> ('To Lucy, Countess of Bedford,
>   with Mr Donne's Satires', c. 1597)

—and it works through images of grace, rarity and excellence, all of which, by virtue of the opening and closing lines of the poem, derive from a light which is intellectual and spiritual and which watches over the poet's day. It is none the less distinguished for drawing upon Martial's i xxxix ('se quis erit raros'—'if there be any rare friends') and Tibullus's iii xix ('tu nocte vel atra / lumen'—'light even in night's darkness').

The middle ground that Jonson occupies is that of the great central feelings rather than those of the extremes. He writes of friendship, affection, the normal course of the day's events. It is this that makes him so strong in that area we have relinquished, the familiar epistle celebrating the pursuits which have been lost in the agonies and ecstasies of post-Romantic poetry. He says of himself,

> Well, with mine owne frail Pitcher, what to do
> I have decreed; keep it from waves, and press;
> Lest it be justled, cracked, made nought or less:
> Live to that point I will, for which I am man,
> And dwell as in my Centre, as I can . . . .
> ('An Epistle Answering to One that
> Asked to be Sealed of the Tribe of Ben', c. 1623)

Of friendship, he says that he chose to avoid 'fevery heats,

nor colds' in favour of those 'led by reason's flame'. Ben Jonson
is a great poet of friendship, and in the poem quoted here
he is answering one who asked to be regarded as a disciple.
The poem is usually thought to be addressed to Thomas Randolph,
and Randolph was only one of the young poets who marvellously
picked up their master's easy tone. In the following, the argument
derives from the Prologue to Persius's satires, but the voice
is that of Jonson:

> I was not born to Helicon, nor dare
> Presume to think myself a Muse's heir.
> I have no title to Parnassus Hill
> Nor any area of it by the will
> Of a dead ancestor, nor could I be
> Ought but a tenant unto poetry.
> But thy adoption quits me of all fear,
> And makes me challenge a child's portion there. . . .
>
> ('A Gratulatory to Mr Ben Jonson for
> his Adopting of Him to be His Son', c. 1625)

It is noticeable, however, that most of these disciples use Jonson's
epistolary accents with equal ease when eulogising the dead.
There is no sense of anguish beneath the structure of these occasional poems. So, though Jonson himself collected a remarkable
array of elegies—by Habington, Herrick, Waller, King, Falkland,
Cartwright and Cleveland, among others—they come over as
genial epistles, from one friend to another. Most of these poets,
even so, seem very well to have understood the change that
Jonson wrought in English. Here is Sir John Beaumont, Jr, on
the subject:

> Since then, he made our language pure and good,
> To teach us speak, but what we understood,
> We owe this praise to him, that should we join
> To pay him, he were paid but with the coin
> Himself hath minted, which we know by this
> That no words pass for current now, but his. . . .
>
> ('To the Memory of him who can never
> be forgotten, Master Ben Jonson', 1638)

The poem as a whole posits a view of literature—cool, perspicu-

ous—close to that of the humanist Vives, who was one of
Jonson's heroes. And, in more familiar terms, it differs very
little from Jonson's generous encomia on his living friends, many
of them wits and scholars, and from the elegies others of his
'sons' bestowed upon him. As Lucius Cary, Lord Falkland, says,

> I then but ask fit Time to smooth my Lays,
> (And imitate in this the Pen I praise) . . . .
>
> ('An Eglogue', 1638)

But these elegies could easily be paralleled by epistles. There
is no distinction between the two forms among Jonson's successors.
The tone of Carew's epistle 'To My Worthy Friend Master
George Sandys' (1636) is virtually identical with that of his
'Elegy upon the Death of . . . Donne' (1631):

> I press not to the Choir, nor dare I greet
> The holy place with my unhallowed feet;
> My unwashed Muse pollutes not things Divine,
> Nor mingles her profaner notes with thine;
> Here, humbly at the porch, she listening stays,
> And with glad ears sucks in thy sacred lays. . . .

> Can we not force from widowed Poetry
> Now thou art dead (great Donne) one elegy
> To crown thy Hearse? Why yet dare we not trust
> Though with unkneaded, dough-baked prose thy dust,
> Such as the unscissored Churchman from the flower
> Of fading Rhetoric, short lived as his hour,
> Dry as the sand that measures it, should lay
> Upon my ashes, on the funeral day? . . .

This certainly was the age of the great formal elegy, and there
is no doubt that Jonson's epistles, as much as his own elegies,
showed the seventeenth century the way. One thinks, perhaps
especially, of Abraham Cowley's elegies on Crashaw and on
Jordan, his old schoolmaster at Westminster; of his former school-
fellow William Cartwright upon Stafford and Greville; of Henry
King, yet another Westminster alumnus, on Lady Anne Rich,
Edward Holt and Donne; of Cleveland on Laud; and of Stanley
on Sandys, Hammond, Shirley, Hall, Isham and Lovelace (also

the subject of an elegy by Charles Cotton). Out of this line
came both the epistolary and the elegaic work of Dryden: his
epistle to Congreve and his elegy on Oldham show a common
tone. Whether written to a living friend or commemorating
a dead one, the language of these poems is at once conversational
and formal, admiring and distanced:

> Fabius might joy in Scipio, when he saw
> A beardless Consul made against the Law,
> And join his Suffrage to the Votes of Rome,
> Though he with Hannibal was overcome.
> Thus old Romano bowed to Raphael's Fame,
> And Scholar to the Youth he taught became. . . .
>
> ('Epistle to Mr Congreve', 1694)

> To the same Goal did both our Studies drive:
> The last set out the soonest did arrive.
> Thus Nisus fell upon the slippery place,
> While his young friend performed and won the Race. . . .
>
> ('To the Memory of Mr Oldham', 1683)

But Jonson, the originating master of this line, excelled even
Dryden in his acquaintance with the facts retailed. Without the
need to sacrifice formal distance, his poems are indeed familiar
epistles. When he writes to a friend—even if that friend is unnamed
in the poem—the verse becomes instinct with his personality.
Point after point is made, sharply and precisely, and the whole
built up into a revelation of the writer's personality, that of
the recipient, and the way of life they jointly share:

> It is the fair acceptance, Sir, creates
> The entertainment perfect: not the cates.
> Yet shall you have, to rectify your palate,
> An olive, capers, or some better salad
> Ushering the mutton; with a short-legged hen,
> If we can get her, full of eggs, and then,
> Lemons, and wine for sauce . . . .
>
> ('Inviting a Friend to Supper', early 17th century)

The tone of this, and indeed the whole poem, approximates
to Martial's v lxxviii, x xlviii and xi lii, with their detailing

of viands; and also to Horace's delightful ode to Maecenas,
III xxix, where the poet offers a simple meal beneath a poor
man's roof as pleasant change to the rich man satiated with
luxurious robes and tapestries (cf. also his Epistle I v). But Jonson's
details are more homely, and he has created for us a highly
particular sense of place, a feeling of life going on. The even
greater poem 'To Penshurst' (*ante* 1616) may well have been
conceived as a familiar letter—perhaps, as Thom Gunn suggests
in his excellent selection, of thanks; but it has far outgrown
its original conception. It links up with 'Inviting a Friend to
Supper' in that both are based on certain Horatian themes;
but 'To Penshurst' explores these themes in a manner redolent
at once of grandeur and intimacy. Perhaps most of all it resembles
not Horace but Martial in his encomium on Cæsar's tree (IX lxi)
and his description of Faustinus's villa (III lviii). The farm in
Martial is at once fertile and functional: generous without being
extravagant, attractive without being merely decorative. In Jonson's
English it comes out thus:

> The lower land, that to the river bends,
> Thy sheep, thy bullocks, kine and calves do feed:
> The middle grounds thy mares and horses breed.
> Each bank doth yield thee coneys; and the tops
> Fertile of wood, Ashore, and Sydney's copse,
> To crown thy open table, doth provide
> The purpled pheasant with the speckled side:
> The painted partrich lies in every field,
> And, for thy mess, is willing to be killed. . . .

What is 'picta perdix' in Martial becomes 'painted partrich'
in Jonson; and the original's 'impiorum phasiana Colchorum'
becomes 'purpled pheasant with the speckled side'. This latter
removes a needless allusion (to the sorceries of Medea) and supplies
a pictorial detail that is characteristic of the zest and particularity
of the description. It is through such touches that Penshurst
becomes an actual place. Such actuality is essential, for Jonson
is not only describing a manor but also celebrating a way of
life. It says a good deal for him that he can put this baronial
splendour across to our age which imagines that it is classless.
Much of the effect comes through concession: the first and last
lines of the poem assure us—what, in fact, is manifest throughout—

that Penshurst is not built for show, but for use; it is a place lived in, not merely wondered at.

Herrick rehandles this in his characteristic fashion. He has country matters, so to speak, retold in the tone of a sophisticate entering into the spirit of the occasion:

> The Pheasant, Partridge, Gotwit, Reeve, Ruff, Rail,
>   The Cock, the Curlew, and the Quail;
> These, and thy choicest viands do extend
>   Their taste unto the lower end
> Of thy glad table: not a dish more known
>   To thee, then unto any one . . . .
>   ('A Panegyric to Sir Lewis Pemberton', *ante* 1648)

Herrick stands to Jonson as Jonson to Martial. He can, of course, adapt from the original—the last two lines quoted relate to Martial's III lx—but he does so in Jonson's terms. And this was true of topographical poetry throughout the seventeenth century.

A close imitation of 'To Penshurst' is Carew's 'To Saxham' (c. 1620). Here, Horace and Martial are subsumed in the delicate play of post-Jonsonian conceit:

> The Pheasant, Partridge, and the Lark,
> Flew to thy house as to the Ark.
> The willing Ox, of himself came
> Home to the slaughter, with the Lamb,
> And every beast did thither bring
> Himself, to be an offering. . . .

As the century advances, more care is taken about the elegances of language. Along with this rise in decorum goes a playing down of magnificence in favour of good husbandry; a sign, no doubt, of the darkening politics of the time. Marvell makes a virtue of the austerity vouchsafed in Appleton House:

> Humility alone designs
> Those short but admirable Lines,
> By which, ungirt and unconstrained,
> Things greater are in less contained.
> Let others vainly strive t'immure
> The Circle in the Quadrature!

These holy Mathematics can
In every Figure equal Man.

('Upon Appleton House', c. 1650)

Order is in the ascendant here. It dominates Waller's view, written after the Restoration, of St James's Park:

Instead of rivers rolling by the side
Of Eden's garden, here flows in the tide;
The sea, which always served his empire, now
Pays tribute to our Prince's pleasure too.
Of famous cities we the founders know;
But rivers, old as seas, to which they go,
Are Nature's bounty; 'tis of more renown
To make a river, than to build a town. . . .

('On St James's Park', 1661)

The young trees could not be better ordered, says Waller, and beneath the older trees Charles walks engaged in ordering his estates.

Dryden takes over the Horace–Martial–Penshurst theme and reinterprets it in terms of the relatively modest life of his kinsman John Driden:

No porter guards the Passage of your Door;
T'admit the Wealthy, and exclude the Poor:
For God, who gave the Riches, gave the Heart
To sanctify the Whole, by giving Part:
Heav'n, who foresaw the Will, the Means has wrought,
And to the Second Son, a Blessing brought:
The First-begotten had his Father's Share,
But you, like Jacob, are Rebecca's Heir. . . .

('To My Honoured Kinsman, John Driden', 1700)

The whole account is couched in terms suited to a justice of the peace; that traditional role of the squire that may be found at least as far back as the description of the knight in *Piers Plowman*. Beyond Dryden, though, it is difficult to trace the country-house poems into the eighteenth century. Pope, indeed, put the whole conception of the manor on its head by satirising mercilessly the Duke of Chandos's country seat. But, by that time, aristocrats were once again building to impress. Interestingly enough, Pope's 'Epistle to Burlington' (1730–3) is a great expansion of that part of the Martial epigram on the Faustinian villa not used by Jonson and his successors. Martial does not only celebrate the unstudied plenty of Faustinus's villa; he also satirises the elegant starvation of the suburban house belonging to the addressee of his epistle, Bassus.

The genre evidently gave rise to some very fine poetry. But, in all this array of compliment, topography and architecture, it is Jonson who seems most inward with his subject. He supplies in 'To Penshurst' the unexpected but authentic detail—the pheasant with the speckled side, the woolly peach, the story of King James's surprise visit, the subtle fusion of landscape with people. In relating Jonson to his successors, moreover, we are drawing a chart of the major tradition of the seventeenth century.

It is in drama that Jonson bulks largest. If his lyric poetry is dedicated to experiences that are central, his comedy is concerned to ridicule the extremes in life. The language of Jonson's plays is, in a positive sense, a distorting medium. Sir Epicure Mammon in *The Alchemist* (1610) strives to imagine unlimited wealth, but the imagery of his speeches, though romantic and fantastic, is, as his name would suggest, a caricature of grossness:

> I will have all my beds blown up, not stuffed:
> Down is too hard: and then, mine oval room
> Filled with such pictures as Tiberius took
> From Elephantis, and dull Aretine
> But coldly imitated. Then, my glasses
> Cut in more subtle angles, to disperse
> And multiply the figures as I walk
> Naked between my succubae. My mists
> I'll have of perfume, vapoured 'bout the room,
> To lose ourselves in; and my baths, like pits
> To fall into; from whence we will come forth,
> And roll us dry in gossamer and roses. . . .

In this poetry, everything is at a slant—pneumatic beds, an oval room, pictures ingenious but obscene, mirrors that do not reflect so much as caricature. There is a deeper meaning, too. One loses oneself in those mists of perfume, one falls into the baths as into a pit—into *the* pit, one may infer. So the caricature exists, with all its extravagance, for a serious and moral purpose.

This speech fascinated the seventeenth century. William Strode has a morality play called *The Floating Island* (1636) in which the throne of Prudentius is usurped by Fancy. Her speech at the zenith of her fortunes picks up the romantic aspect of Jonson's dramatic poetry:

> Why have not I my Beds stuffed all with wind,
> Baths filled with Maydew? . . .

Jasper Mayne, like Strode and Jonson an alumnus of Westminster School, has a citizen comedy called *The City–Match* (1638) which, in some aspects, resembles Jonson's *Epicoene*. Here, an elderly merchant is tricked into a false marriage with a woman who pretends to be a whore. But it is upon the great speech of Mammon that he draws when a picture arrives as a gift for this 'wife' of his. Again, it is the moralistic aspect that is implied:

> It should be Mars and Venus in a net;
> Aretine's postures, or a naked nymph
> Lying asleep, and some lascivious satyr
> Taking her lineaments. . . .

Shackerley Marmion's play *A Fine Companion* (1633) owes a good deal to *Cymbeline*. But it is Jonson rather than Iachimo who is called upon to flesh out the character of Spruce, a great seducer of fine ladies. He glories in his specious rhetoric. Though linguistically thinner, this speech, too, may remind us that we have not travelled far from Sir Epicure Mammon:

> My several garbs, and postures of the body,
> My rules for banqueting, and entertainment:
> And for the titillation of my laughter
> Buffoons and parasites . . . .

In *The Lady of Pleasure* (1635) by James Shirley we have a conflict between the virtues of a sober country life and the libidinous pleasures of town. Celestina, a new widow, defies her cautious steward:

> I'll have
> My house the academy of wits, who shall
> Exalt their genius with rich sack and sturgeon,
> Write panegyrics of my feasts, and praise
> The method of my witty superfluities. . . .

And this is only one example from many in this play of the swelling Jonsonian eloquence that mocks the various characters' aspirations.

But it was Richard Brome who most of all absorbed Jonson and used his techniques dramatically. In *The Antipodes* (1638) he stages a play within a play, and that inner play spills out to the surrounding drama as a means of curing the various characters of their more extreme humours. Thus the jealous husband is made to overhear the wooing of his young wife by Letoy, the lord of fancy. This latter speaks, like other Caroline figures, in tones of true Jonsonian exuberance:

> Wouldst have gold?
> Mammon, nor Plutus' self should over-bid me,
> For I'd give all. First, let me rain a shower
> To out-vie that which overwhelmed Danaë;
> And after that another; a full river
> Shall from my chests perpetually flow
> Into thy store.

The play within a play is a form of psychotherapy conducted by one Doctor Hughball, who, with the aid of Letoy, has set up a feigned Antipodes, a world turned upside-down. As Hughball says,

> their Parrots teach
> Their Mistresses to talk. . . .
> They keep their Cats in cages
> From Mice that would devour them else; and birds
> Teach 'hem to whistle, and cry 'Beware the Rats, Puss.'
> But these are frivolous nothings. . . .

So Hughball takes his place among the other representatives of a great literary archetype whose peculiar qualities—to use Jonson's own phrase—have given English comedy its distinctive atmosphere. His immediate ancestor is Jonson's Alchemist, though there are obvious differences. For one thing, it is Jonson rather than the Alchemist who has control over the various situations. The victims come in to be cured, indeed, but the Alchemist is only an agent in the grand work of curbing their extravagances. To compensate for this apparent limitation, he has access to a far greater vocabulary than Hughball, or indeed any of Hughball's successors. His procedure may bear the semblance of reasoned logic but in fact it is the antithesis. The Alchemist's general air of decision is contradicted by a vocabulary at its most poetic when it borders on the nonsensical.

SUBTLE.   Look well to the register.
          And let your heat still lessen by degrees
          To the aludels.
FACE.   Yes, sir.
SUBTLE.   Did you look
          On the bolt's head yet?
FACE.   Which? on D, sir?
SUBTLE.   Aye;
          What's the complexion?
FACE.   Whitish.
SUBTLE.   Infuse vinegar,
          To draw his volatile substance and his tincture:
          And let the water in glass E be filtered,
          And put into the gripe's egg. Lute him well;
          And leave him closed in *balneo*.

Some of these terms are used in such a manner as to cause their secondary meanings to predominate. 'Bolt's head' and 'gripe's egg' are vessels used, respectively, for distillation and storage. Yet their names are metaphors which refer to the objects that they physically resemble. The denotation of 'bolt's head', in context, is that of a distilling-vessel; its connotation, though, is that of the head of a bolt. Thus the concept runs counter to the image and creates an effect of ambiguity. However, that ambiguity is controlled: the effect is to distract the reader's attention away from the ostensible science to an obviously false world of vain appearances. In other instances we have primary meanings of words lying a considerable distance away from immediate reference to the context; and this, too, serves as a distraction:

> Lute him well;
> And leave him closed in *balneo*.

'Lute' means to insulate with wet clay; '*balneo*' is a vapour bath. Here we do not have a visual metaphor to link object with word. In such cases, it would seem that the ambiguity borders on a degree of distraction so great as to make for incoherence. Yet this is not so: though the primary meanings in such instances as 'lute' and '*balneo*' are suppressed as far as the alchemist's laboratory is concerned, they have a bearing on the moral import of the play. '*Balneo*', after all, is primarily an obsolete version of 'bagnio', a brothel. The Alchemist's house is a place where science is prostituted to further greed and sensuality. Subtle may be talking nonsense; Jonson is not.

Most of the Alchemist's successors proved to be doctors of medicine; a comment on the social history of the time. Jargon rises to the level of poetry in Nabbes's *The Bride* (1638). Horten, a character who has little to do with the citizen comedy of the plot but who may be based on the physician Edward Jorden, extols his art:

> From my garden, sir,
> I can produce those simples, shall out-work
> All the compounds of drugs and show like miracles
> Compared with them. What needs the weapon salve,
> Condemned by some for witchcraft? when each dunghill
> Affords the *Persicaria*, that on wounds
> Works the like Magic. Panax Coloni
> Is known to every rustic, and Hipericon,
> And yet we must from Memphis and Judea
> Fetch Balsam, though sophisticate! . . .

This, as much as Shirley and Brome, has learned from the authentically swelling cadence of Jonson.

The treatment of charlatans after the Restoration lacks this kind of poetry, though it has something more of bite. Mopus, an astrologer, sets himself up as a physician in John Wilson's play *The Cheats* (1662), but his speeches are very much transcripts of the work of the Rosicrucian John Haydon: 'small, and yet great, earthly and yet watery, airy, and yet very fiery, invisible and yet easily found, soft as down, and yet hard above measure,

far off, and yet near at hand . . . .' Thinner still is the attempt
on the part of Thomas Shadwell to satirise the Royal Society.
Here we are dealing not with quacks and astrologers but with
the work of scientists such as Hooke, Boyle and Glanvill. Sir
Nicholas Gimcrack in Shadwell's *The Virtuoso* (1676) researches
into such matters as the fungus that attacks fruit, the possibility
of transfusing blood from animals to men; and this is meant
to excite the laughter of the audience. Such speculations will
seem less absurd in our own time than they may have done
in the seventeenth century, and so the satire has recoiled upon
the head of its author. Moreover, Shadwell has forgotten the
key point about Jonson's Alchemist: that his experiments exist
largely in specious rhetoric and are transacted for sordid gain.
He fails, not only morally, but linguistically as well:

> I assure you I have transfused into a human vein sixty-four
> ounces, avoirdupois weight, from one sheep. The emittent sheep
> died under the operation, but the recipient madman is still
> alive. . . .

As this suggests, there is little equivalent for Jonson's poetry
in the verse of the later Caroline dramatists; still less is there
any equivalent in the dramatic prose of the Restoration.

Not all of Jonson's language chooses to encompass this extent
of richness. Sometimes the vocabulary is pushed to an extreme
in one direction only. This is most often found in scenes of
straight invective. Such scenes are not infrequent in Jonson and
they are numerous in the plays of his successors. The archetypal
figure is Thorello, an earlier version of Kitely, in *Every Man
in His Humour* (1598). The archetypal scene is the one where
he raves in mistaken jealousy at his wife, Biancha:

> Out on thee, more than strumpet's impudency!
> Steal'st thou thus to thy haunts? and have I taken
> Thy bawd, and thee, and thy companion,
> This hoary-headed lecher, this old goat,
> Close at your villainy, and wouldst thou 'scuse it
> With this stale harlot's jest, accusing me? . . .

More powerfully, however, in *Volpone* (1605) we find:

> Be damned!
> Heart, I will drag thee hence, home, by the hair;
> Cry thee a strumpet through the streets; rip up
> Thy mouth unto thine ears; and slit thy nose,
> Like a raw rochet! . . .

This scene is an advance on the other, as *Volpone* itself is an advance upon *Every Man in His Humour*. The development can be characterised in terms of the greater physical force of the verse—'slit thy nose / Like a raw rochet'—and the energy with which this distorted emotion is projected. The author's judgement is present, however; not explicit, but implied by the context. Corvino threatens to proclaim his wife a strumpet, not because she prostitutes herself to Volpone, but because she refuses to do so.

The seventeenth century took its cue in this area from the earlier rather than the later Jonson. The husbands who denounce their wives through a whole succession of English comedies do so because they believe themselves to be cuckolded. In comparison with Jonson, however, the standpoint is simplified. The husband in Nathan Field's *Amends for Ladies* (1611) does, indeed, bring about his own suspicion by thrusting his wife on his friend; but the verse he speaks comes out more shrill than that of *Every Man in His Humour*:

> Z'oons, you are a whore, though I entreat him fair
> Before his face, in compliment, or so,
> I not esteem him truly as this rush. . . .

Thomas Randolph, though more of a poet than Field, does not rise much above the minimum required technically for the situation—a simple one, irrational jealousy—in *The Jealous Lovers* (1632):

> Tempt me not strumpet: you that have your hirelings,
> And can with jewels, rings, and other toys
> Purchase your journeymen-lechers. . . .

The willingness to distort, dictated by a character's extreme of passion, is exemplified rather than justified by the language of Henry Glapthorne in *The Hollander* (1635). Here Lady Yellow, confined to a nursing home, has proved chaste through numerous trials, but still the husband's jealousy recrudesces. In default of the Jonsonian range of vocabulary, however, Sir Martin Yellow's denunciation seems melodramatic:

> Viper, toad, out of my presence, ere my just waked
> Rage, get to its height. . . .

It is true that the prose in which comedies were couched after the Restoration avoids such stridencies. But it tends also to a considerable degree of conventionality. The jealous husband of Wycherley's *The Country Wife* (1675) is goaded by the woman's reluctance to write a letter dismissing her gallant, but his anger is two-dimensional and contains nothing that need surprise us:

> Once more write as I'd have you, and question it not, or I will spoil your writing with this. I will stab out those eyes that cause my mischief. . . .

In *The Old Bachelor* (1693), also, Congreve keeps well within the set convention of an old husband betrayed by a young wife, itself a set situation: 'Oh, thou salacious woman! am I then brutified?'

In spite of all these parallels, however, Jonson does not stand to the dramatic output of the later seventeenth century exactly in the same relation as he does to Caroline poetry. In non-dramatic verse he shares common interests with his successors. We find him excelling in the courtly lyric, in 'carpe diem', in the elegy, in the epistle, in the topographical poem. This is the centre ground of literature, and younger poets may equal Jonson in elegance but never in vigour. His dramatic concerns, on the other hand, are couched in extravagant verse even when they seem designed as a check upon extravagance. The attitudes to be condemned are social vices at an extreme: gross acquisitiveness, pseudo-scientific charlatanry, and the like. These are public attitudes, exposed to ridicule publicly, but such concerns were not the ones that the successors of Ben Jonson chose primarily to follow up.

It is true that Jonson's invention of the citizen comedy—for

that, among other things, is what *Every Man in His Humour*
is—provided such writers as Wycherley and Congreve with their
favourite situations, involving cuckolded citizens and effeminate
fops. But these are extravagances proffered for their own sake;
they form no part of a larger pattern. Nevertheless, Restoration
comedy was personalised in a way that that of Jonson was
not, to its advantage as well as to its disadvantage. Its preoccupation
with sexual romps limited the range of its social concerns, but
at the same time the later writers recognised the importance
of women.

Jonson's limitation as a dramatist is that he failed to develop
the Plautine comedy in any direction which would enhance the
status of the opposite sex. Characteristically, his female figures
are pawns to be utilised, and they come alive only in a vicarious
manner when rules are laid down for their conduct. Here is
the eccentric husband Fitzdottrel dictating to the eponymous hero
of *The Devil is an Ass* (1616) provisos designed to govern his
wife:

> you have heard and seen
> Something today, and by it you may gather
> Your mistress is a fruit that's worth the stealing,
> And therefore worth the watching. Be you sure, now,
> You have all your eyes about you; and let in
> No lace-woman, nor bawd that brings French masks,
> And cut-works; see you? nor old crones, with wafers,
> To convey letters; nor no youths, disguised
> Like country-wives, with cream and marrow-puddings.
> Much knavery may be vented in a pudding. . . .

It is plain how this looks forward, to *The Country Wife* of
Wycherley and to Congreve's bawds with baskets. And it is
fine poetry in itself: one notices the irony of this fallen Adam
instructing the devil to guard his wife as though she were herself
the apple of Eden. At the same time, however, one also notices
the passivity with which the wife is conceived—as a 'fruit' which
may be 'stolen'. She seems to have no volition in the matter.
The fact that this is the distorted view of a pathologically obsessed
mind, and is put forward in order to be criticised, does not
altogether redeem the matter. Nowhere in the play is Mistress

Frances, the wife, allowed to have her head as a dramatic character; any more than Biancha in *Every Man in His Humour* or Celia in *Volpone*. Of course this is only one element in a great play: there is no evidence that Jonson's successors could have handled its other themes, such as the corruptibility of mankind and the social inquity of vain speculation. And no doubt much of this was in the air at the time. Kathleen Lynch (*Philological Quarterly*, 1925) has pointed out a passage in *L'Astrée* (1608–24), a pastoral romance by Honoré d'Urfé, where Hylas is attracted to Stelle because, unlike the other shepherdesses, she can argue with him on his own terms. He therefore makes a covenant with her which has some points in common with that conceived by the contemporary *Devil is an Ass*. But there are two significant differences. The provisos in *L'Astrée* are not the outpourings of a sick mind; and they are mutual—as binding on the man as on the woman. For example:

> Que pour n'estre point menteurs, ny esclaues en effect, ny en parole, tous ces mots de fidelité, de seruitude, & d'eternelle affection ne seront jamais meslez parmy nos discours. . . .

> (That in order to avoid being slaves in reality or promise, none of the words of faithfulness, servitude and eternal love will be allowed to mingle with our conversation.)

It was the elegance of this, as well as the earthiness of Jonson, that strongly influenced the tone of subsequent comedy, at least in so far as it touched upon the social role of the female. Subsequent English attempts at what may be called the Marriage Bargain drew out of Jonson a particularity that d'Urfé's *L'Astrée* may be felt to lack. But where Jonson's successors out-distance him is in the human interest they give to their heroines.

There is little that is pastoral about the scene in John Fletcher's *Rule a Wife and Have a Wife* (1624) when the great heiress, Margarita, sets stern injunctions upon Leon, whom she has chosen to be her husband:

> you must not be saucy,
> No, nor at any time familiar with me . . . .

But this is the woman laying her commands upon the man: it has something of the sharpness of Jonson, but it is attached to the unJonsonian concept of the dominant female. This is true even of Jonson's closest disciples. The bounds of the relationship between man and woman are set up by Alice in Brome's *A Mad Couple Well Matched* (1636). She tells Saleware, her citizen husband, that they had covenanted 'that we should always be friends and call so, not after the silly manner of Citizen and Wife, but in the high courtly way'. A similar imprimis is found in Brome's earlier play *The Northern Lass* (1629) when the city widow, Mistress Fitchow, studies her remembrance for after marriage. The lady is still in the ascendant in Massinger's *The City Madam* (1632), and the laying down of provisos is taken as an index of Anne Frugal's vanity:

> In civil manners you must grant my will
> In all things whatsoever. . . .

All these attitudes, it must be remarked, are condemned by the playwrights concerned; by Fletcher, Brome, and Massinger. It is a lack of balance between the sexes that appears to be criticised.

After the Restoration, the balance of the sexes became more equitable. If the later comedy lacks Jonson's force, still it must be said that it shows up most strongly in that area where Jonson is least engaged; namely, recognition of the individuality of women. Dryden attempts the Marriage Bargain several times over: in *The Wild Gallant*, in *Marriage à la Mode*, in *Amphitryon* and, most successfully, in *Secret Love* (1667). The main plot demonstrates the sadness of Royalty, in that it may not marry as it will. As welcome light relief, there are a couple of wild flirts who, after some misunderstanding of each other, strike up their bargain. Here the man has a say as well as the woman. For example:

CELADON. Lastly, whereas the names of Husband and Wife hold forth nothing but clashing and cloying, and dulness and faintness in their signification; they shall be abolished for ever betwixt us.

FLORIMEL.   And instead of those, we will be married by the
more agreeable names of Mistress and Gallant. . . .

One of Dryden's brothers-in-law, James Howard, imitated this
in another tragi-comedy, *All Mistaken* (1667). Again we have
a solemn plot concerned with royal matrimony; again it is relieved
by a pair of wild lovers:

PHILIDOR.   Item, it may be I can love you but a week.
MIRIDA.   I don't care if it be but a day. . . .

Dryden's tone in these lighter passages is taken up even more
closely by Edward Ravenscroft in *The Careless Lovers* (1673).
The plot itself is adapted from Molière's *Monsieur de Pourceaugnac*
and recounts a young lover's discrediting of his unworthy rival.
The witty couple—as in Dryden, detached from the main plot—at
length, after some misunderstandings, draw uneasily together:

HILLARIA.   In Company, you shall never call me Wife, or
Dear, or Sweet-heart, but Madam.
CARELESS.   In Company you shall never call me Husband, or
by my Christian Name, but Mr. Careless. . . .

And Dryden is further imitated, albeit in a lower social register,
by Wycherley's comedy *The Gentleman Dancing Master* (1671)—a
parallel first pointed out by Ian Donaldson (in *The World Upside-
Down*, 1970). Monsieur Paris, disappointed of his cousin's hand,
proposes to Madam Flirt, a lady of the town, not a marriage
but a concubinage. She, in her turn, lays down a surprising
number of provisos. For example:

FLIRT.   . . . separate maintenance, in case you should take
a wife, or I a new friend.
MONSIEUR.   How! that too! then you are every whit as bad
as a wife. . . .

But the summation of the Marriage Bargain occurs in Congreve's *The Way of the World* (1700). Here we are back with
Jonson again—in some matters we never drifted far away—but
with a century's experimentation in dramatic character between.

In *The Devil is an Ass*, Fitzdottrell told Pug to keep a watch on Mistress Frances; but in *The Way of the World* Mirabell suggests to Mistress Millamant that she keep a watch upon herself: '*Item*, I shut my doors against all bawds with baskets, and pennyworths of muslin, china, fans, atlasses, etc.' Behind it all is indeed Jonson's attitude that subscription to marriage amounts to enslavement by conditions. The difference is that, in *The Way of the World*, the lady has a voice. It is one that has learned not only from Jonson but from d'Urfé and Dryden too.

MILLAMANT.   . . . d'ye hear, I won't be called names after I'm married; positively I won't be called names.
MIRABELL.   Names!
MILLAMANT.   Ay, as wife, spouse, my dear, joy, jewel, love, sweetheart, and the rest of that nauseous cant, in which men and their wives are so fulsomely familiar . . . .

Congreve was a connoisseur of that which had gone before him. Therefore he was able to take from his predecessors what pleased him most—in Fletcher and Wycherley, for example, as well as in Jonson, d'Urfé and Dryden. This accounts for the comparative richness of Congreve's texture, compared, at least, with other writers of prose comedy. But in his case it goes along with a centrifugal dispersion of plot. In this, indeed, he is inferior to several of his predecessors: Brome, shall we say, or Shirley. And later exponents, such as Vanbrugh or Farquhar, were essentially realists, and would best be discussed as precursors of the English picaresque novel.

Jonson, alone of the English comic writers, achieves tightness of form without sacrificing the range of language open to him. His poetry is, after all, linguistically more interesting than has been admitted until now. On the one hand his non-dramatic poetry maintains a serene surface, expressing the complexity of his attitudes through word-play and controlled allusiveness. On the other hand his dramatic verse goes in for surface caricature, grotesquerie, the exaggeration of already ridiculous postures. Between these two poles, his range is colossal. He has few rivals in the creation of character; fewer still in his variety of linguistic resource. In any serious reading he would be accounted one of the half-dozen supreme artists of our literature. And, as we have seen, this is endorsed by the attention paid to his work by the writers themselves. Ben Jonson has no rival at all in the quality, as well as the quantity, of influence he exerted over his successors.

6 The Poetry of Debate

Too much has been written about Milton's Grand Style. His apologists, from Arnold through Saintsbury to Christopher Ricks, deny this great poet one undoubted virtue: that of variety. Even so, the variety is mostly in what may be called the public sector. Milton can be statesmanlike, dogmatic, courtly, indignant, seductive, but he seldom appeals to the inner ear of the reader. This is not merely a personal characteristic. The temper of Milton's time was attuned to politics; and politics, moreover, spelt out loudly rather than—as in previous periods—whispered behind an arras. The governing tradition in poetry was declamatory, suited to the arena of debate. It is poetry where narrative structure, amongst other advantages, is likely to be sacrificed in the interests of argument.

This does not, however, mean that *Paradise Lost* (1667) can be reduced, even by the most admiring critic, to one undifferentiated surge and thunder. It requires no special ear to detect the various characters of the voices speaking in Milton's Great Consult (Book II):

> 'Thrones and imperial Powers, offspring of heaven,
> Ethereal Vertues; or these Titles now
> Must we renounce, and changing style be called
> Princes of Hell?'   (Beelzebub)

> 'My sentence is for open War: of Wiles
> More unexpert, I boast not'   (Moloch)

'I should be much for open War, O Peers,
As not behind in hate; if what was urged
Main reason to persuade immediate War,
Did not dissuade me most, and seem to cast
Ominous conjecture on the whole success:
When he who most excels in fact of Arms,
In what he counsels and in what excels
Mistrustful, grounds his courage on despair
And utter dissolution, as the scope
Of all his aim, after some dire revenge.'   (Belial)

Here we have Milton in three of his characters: as statesman,
as dogmatist, as courtier—the last honey-tongued and a wooer
of assemblies. We must remember that Milton wrote in an age
which saw the Long Parliament, the trial of Strafford, the trial
of Charles I and Cromwell's Councils of State. The oratory
of such occasions seems to ring through the various voices that
debate and wrangle in *Paradise Lost*. For example, the courteous
parentheses we hear in Belial's speech can be paralleled by those
of a number of Cavaliers, not least the utterances of the arch-intri-
guer, George Digby. Here we have him speaking in the House
of Commons against the Bill of Attainder on Strafford (1641):

Yea some (I thank them for their plain dealing) have been
so free as to tell me, that I suffered much by the backwardness
I have shown in this Bill of Attainder of the Earl of Strafford,
against whom I had been formerly so keen and so active.

Mr Speaker, I beg of you and the rest but a suspension
of Judgment concerning me, till I have opened my heart unto
you freely and clearly in this business.

Truly Sirs, I am still the same in my Opinions and Affections,
as unto the Earl of Strafford, I confidently believe him the
most dangerous Minister, the most insupportable to free subjects
that can be charactered.

I believe his Practices in themselves have been as High,
as Tyrannical, as any subject ever ventured on, and the malignity
of them are hugely aggravated by those rare abilities of his,
whereof God hath given him the use, but the Devil the application (in a word) I believe him still that Grand Apostate
to the Commonwealth, who must not expect to be pardoned
in this World, till he be dispatched to the other. And yet

let me tell you Mr Speaker, my hand must not be to that
dispatch. I protest, as my Conscience stands informed, I had
rather it were off. . . .

And so on, through patterned asseverations and qualifications
which, in their ingenuity, resemble nothing so much as George
Digby's devious life. We need not be surprised to find that,
after all this, Digby himself formed one of the Committee for
Strafford's impeachment.

I am not suggesting anything so simple-minded as a one-to-one
relationship between Satan's Belial and Charles I's Digby. Rather,
this mode of speech was in the air at the time. More, it includes
a key constituent of the language—a Cavalier constituent, we
may call it. This is a quality seen in the calculated self-deprecation
characteristic of the apostrophe of Belial and that of the intriguing
statesman of Milton's day. It suggests that the poet understood
his political opponents well.

The Puritans, on the other hand, when they argued, did so
with a self-conscious simplicity that arose, perhaps, from an awareness that they had few arguments to deploy, and even fewer
patterns of rhetoric. The point can be adequately defined by
citing the Abdiel of Book v—the good angel who, among the
cohorts of Lucifer, was unshaken, unseduced, unterrified:

> 'O argument blasphemous, false and proud!
> Words which no ear ever to hear in Heaven
> Expected, least of all from thee, ingrate
> In place thy self so high above thy Peers.
> Canst thou with impious obloquy condemn
> The just Decree of God, pronounced and sworn,
> That to his only son by right endued
> With Regal Sceptre, every Soul in Heaven
> Shall bend the knee, and in that honour due
> Confess him rightful King? . . .'

The sentence is composed of terse phrases whose syntax is simple
to the point of austerity. That final question—'Canst thou . . . ?'—
works because its force and onrush of words compels a belief
in its sincerity. Such a speech pattern reminds us of the righteous
fervour of Pym indicting Strafford (1640):

It is the Cause of the Kingdom, It concerns not only the
Peace and Prosperity, but even the Being of the Kingdom.
We have that piercing Eloquence, the Cries and Groans, and
Tears and Prayers of all the Subjects assisting us. We have
the three Kingdoms, England, and Scotland, and Ireland, in
Travail and Agitation with us, bowing themselves, like the
Hinds spoken of in Job, to cast out their Sorrows.

Truth and Goodness (My Lords) they are the Beauty of
the Soul, they are the Perfection of all created Natures, they
are the Image and Character of God upon the Creatures.

This Beauty, Evil Spirits, and Evil Men, have lost; but yet
there are none so wicked, but they desire to march under
the show and shadow of it, though they hate the reality
of it . . . .

This refusal to temporise, even by so much as a parenthesis,
marks out the speech of Abdiel from that of Belial. It also
marks out the speech of the good angels from those of the
devils; and, farther still, demarcates the pattern of utterance characteristically adopted by the Puritan from that of the Cavalier.

In *Paradise Lost*, Book v, Satan's reply to the onslaught of
Abdiel is to request a precedent—'"strange point and new! / Doc-
trine which we would know whence learnt". . .'. And Satan's
response to the denunciation of Gabriel in Book IV is to demand
recognition—'"Not to know me argues your selves unknown . . .".' By such utterances, in form of argument no less
than in mode of speech, we are reminded of Charles I on
trial for his life (1648), demanding a precedent for his trial
and asserting his rights as an extraordinary individual:

I would know by what power I am called hither. . . . Now
I would know by what Authority, I mean, lawful: there are
many unlawful Authorities in the world, Thieves and Robbers
by the highways; but I would know by what Authority I
was brought from thence, and carried from place to place,
(and I know not what). . . . I see no House of Lords here
that may constitute a Parliament, and (the King too) should
have been. . . . show me one precedent. . . . I say, Sir, by
your favour, that the Commons of England was never a Court
of Judicature, I would know how they came to be so. . . .
Sir, I am not an ordinary prisoner. . . .

To the Puritan conscience, such arguments seemed negative and might well have been emanations from the Father of Lies. The difficulty is that matters were more complicated than the myth of *Paradise Lost* allows. To see Pym and (say) Holles as angels and the King and Strafford as devils is to produce a black-and-white simulacrum of a situation that in itself would have taxed the palette of the Post-Impressionists. There is little question that an inflexible operation of his Divine Right brought the King to the extremity from which he answered at his trial. But, equally, there is little question that the trial itself was illegal. At least, no reputable lawyer could be found to bear a part in it.

To this extent, it is a simplification that brings about the poetry of debate. And there is a built-in paradox here. The plot of *Paradise Lost* involves a rebellion of the devils against God. But this might equally well have been how the Cavaliers saw the commons' attempts to curb the power of the King. In many ways the idea of the King of Heaven putting down a dissident faction would suit the latter situation better. It is, perhaps, a Cavalier story rather than a Puritan one. It is certainly hierarchical, even monarchical. Milton's poetic sympathies, there-fore, drive against the pattern of his plot, and this makes for occasional confusion in his utterance.

The strain is seen most obviously in the speeches of God:

> 'Only begotten Son, seest thou what rage
> Transports our adversary, whom no bounds
> Prescribed, no bars of Hell, nor all the chains
> Heaped on him there, nor yet the main Abyss
> Wide interrupt can hold; so bent he seems
> On desperate revenge, that shall redound
> Upon his own rebellious head. . . .' (III)

So begins, in rather strident and over-adjectival tones, an argument somewhat dangerous for Milton's case—that of omnipotence in relation to free-will:

> 'they themselves decreed
> Their own revolt, not I: if I foreknew,
> Foreknowledge had no influence on their fault. . . .'

This is an argument better implied than spelt out, and it is certainly one impossible to present in dramatic terms. It is a strength of the poem, not a weakness, that the devils are presented as self-motivating rather than as implements from God's puppet-box. But the explicit statements show symptoms, conscious or unconscious, of the strain involved. The characteristic utterance of the Puritan when stating a Puritan case tends to hyperbole and melodrama, especially noticeable in the verbs:

> The same ill Councils which first raised that storm, and almost shipwrecked the Common-wealth, do still continue, they blow strong like the East wind, that brought the Locusts over the land; Is it not time then my Lords, that we should unite and concentrate our selves, and defeat the Counsels of these Achitophels, which would involve us, our Religion, our King, our Laws, our Liberties, all that can be near and clear unto an honest soul, in one universal and general desolation. . . .

Thus Denzil Holles, in a speech to the Long Parliament on 4 May 1640, demanding justice against the King's ministers. To hindsight it seems extraordinary that he calls them Achitophels. Yet it is not as extraordinary as all that, for the allegory that was to give life to Dryden's poem *Absalom and Achitophel* (1681) was current long before there was any very obvious proto-type to fill the role of Absalom. In a pioneer essay, Richard F. Jones (*Modern Language Notes*, 1931) points out the predecessors of the great Restoration attempt at public poetry. There was Nathanael Carpenter's *Achitophel, or Picture of a Wicked Politician*, which began as a group of sermons in Oxford and was published in 1627. There was a broadsheet ballad, *The Prentises Prophecie*, which in 1642 linked the corrupt politicians, the Achitophels, with the Royalist bishops. The Puritan divine Samuel Gibson, preaching to the House of Commons in 1645, already foreshadows Dryden's own words in Part II of his poem: 'all the enemies of the King and Parliament be as that young man Absalom and that old fox Ahithophel' (*The Ruin of the Authors and Fomentors of Civil Wars*). But this particular story could equally well serve the other side. It was a Royalist who wrote a tract, *Absalom's Rebellion* (1645), in which Absalom represented the Parliament. The Restoration furnished closer and closer parallels

(*God's Covenant of Free Grace*, 1660; *The Tragedy of Treason*, 1680) until we have the closest of them all, a king's actual son rebelling against his father, and, moreover, doing so at the instigation of a somewhat foxy elder statesman. All this happened in Dryden's time. It may have been Charles II who asked Dryden to write a satire upon the topic, or (as Wallace Maurer argues, *Philological Quarterly*, 1961) it may have been Edward Seymour, the 'Amiel' of the poem. He, in 1681, was one of a triumvirate of ministers whom the King kept closest to the throne. In this great age of debate, poetry was as near politics as that.

But, in Dryden as in Milton, the politics is simplified by the poetry. The obvious example is the weakest of the many parallels between the period of writing and the biblical epoch: I mean, of course, the one-to-one relationship of Charles II to David. Let us grant that Dryden represents the King as discerning, magnanimous and merciful, and that these may well be the attributes of a Christian hero. But I do not see how these attributes can be found in the Old Testament figure of David. Moreover, David had certain traits, such as energy and ambition, that separate him as far from Charles as Charles's voluptuousness and sloth separated him from being an ideal positive for Dryden's poem.

So the strength of the poem is unlikely to be in its positives. And it is true that 'David' is the least striking of its characters, even though his speech at the end is based upon the King's own Declaration of 1681. Perhaps this is as much as to say that the political utterances of Shaftesbury, the Achitophel of the poem, were more interesting. His speech to the admiring Crowd—an entity Dryden has no patience with—is a remarkable simulation of mob oratory. Even more effective is his temptation of Absalom. But, though this inevitably evokes the drama of Satan's temptation of Eve in *Paradise Lost*, it also serves to show that poetic argument had, since Milton's day, thinned in texture. Amidst the sliding logic and rhetorical patterns of Satan's speech, *Paradise Lost* has this:

> 'will God incense his ire
> For such a petty Trespass, and not praise
> Rather your dauntless virtue, whom the pain
> Of Death denounced, whatever thing Death be,
> Deterred not from achieving what might lead
> To happier life, knowledge of Good and Evil . . . ?' (IX)

The irresoluble paradoxes, the elusively deployed concepts, the parentheses which beg questions so glozed over as scarcely to be met—these amount to a sinuous process of related casuistries that might seduce a controversialist far more practised than Milton's Eve. In comparison, Achitophel in the Dryden poem seems quite forthright:

> 'Believe me, Royal Youth, thy Fruit must be,
> Or gathered Ripe, or rot upon the Tree.
> Heaven has to all allotted, soon or late,
> Some lucky Revolution of their Fate:
> Whose Motions, if we watch and guide with Skill,
> (For human Good depends on human Will,)
> Our Fortune rolls, as from a smooth Descent,
> And, from the first Impression, takes the Bent:
> But, if unseized, she glides away like wind;
> And leaves repenting Folly far behind. . . .'

The witty sententiousness of this associates itself with an authorial voice and reminds us of set speeches in those plays which did so much to train Dryden in his mastery of the heroic couplet. One thinks of Queen Isabel's 'Love's an heroic passion' in *The Conquest of Granada*, Leonidas's 'How precious are the hours of love in courts' in *Marriage à la Mode*, or the famous 'When I consider life' spoken by the hero of *Aureng-Zebe*. In every case, the decisiveness of the statement removes something from the individuality of the character; and this is true of *Absalom and Achitophel*. Dryden is less successful than Milton in taking over different public voices.

The younger poet was limited in his ability to present character directly; however, he excelled in writing about it. We find him in full play, not in dramatic speech, but in the expository statement of character. One should, perhaps, compare the temptation scene in *Absalom and Achitophel* not with that in *Paradise Lost* but with Dryden's characterisation of his chief malefactor. In the portrait of Achitophel the verse hisses, frets, spits and twists back upon itself. It is a brilliant acting out of the sense:

> Of these the false Achitophel was first:
> A Name to all succeeding Ages Curst.
> For close Designs, and crooked Counsels fit;

Sagacious, Bold, and Turbulent of wit:
Restless, unfixt in Principles and Place;
In Power unpleased, impatient of Disgrace.
A fiery Soul, which working out its way,
Fretted the Pigmy Body to decay:
And o'er informed the Tenement of Clay....

Unlike that of Milton, Dryden's argument is at its best when there is no contender. His strength is in the creation of set characters such as this one of Achitophel. The classical pioneer of this mode was the Greek writer Theophrastus, who left a collection of such types as the Arrogant Man, the Man with a Grievance, and so on. The mode itself was given sharpness and point by the Roman satirists Persius and Juvenal, both of whom Dryden translated superbly. Theophrastus was made native in English by Ben Jonson, Thomas Overbury, John Earle and, on one brilliant occasion, Shaftesbury himself in a character of a neighbouring squire, a Mr Hastings. 'Characters' abound, too, in the work of historians; in, especially, Burnet, Gardiner, Clarendon, and Roger North. This form of expression, like debate itself, was in the air. It seems to me, however, that Dryden took off directly from Juvenal, who has lightning sketches of Crispinus, Catullus, Censennia, Alexander (Pella) and Cretonius, among others. He also appears to have drawn upon the more scarifying portraits in Persius: Ventidius, Natta, Dama. Indeed, the last two look forward more than a little to the bad poets, Og and Doeg, in the Second Part of *Absalom and Achitophel* (1682). But the Roman satirists used their characters as illustrations to a developing argument. Dryden, on the other hand, like Pope, made the argument a line on which to hang the various characters. The effect is to simplify.

It would be impossible, at the present time, to reconstruct the Popish Plot, the Exclusionist Party and the Monmouth Rebellion from *Absalom and Achitophel* alone. To that extent, the poem exists only in its parts. Still less can we take an interest in the arguments of Pope. Productions such as *An Essay on Man* (1730–2), very much after Bolingbroke and the younger Shaftesbury, were certainly applauded in their time. If we find them hard to struggle through now, it may be because they are wanting in a sense of felt life. Passages such as the following are, on a technical level, certainly impressive:

Go, wond'rous creature! mount where Science guides,
Go, measure earth, weigh air, and state the tides;
Instruct the planets in what orbs to run,
Correct old Time, and regulate the Sun;
Go, soar with Plato to th'empyreal sphere,
To the first good, first perfect, and first fair;
Or tread the mazy round his followers trod,
And quitting sense call imitating God;.
As Eastern priests in giddy circles run,
And turn their heads to imitate the Sun,
Go, teach Eternal Wisdom how to rule—
Then drop into thyself, and be a fool!

One admires the clinching effect of the couplets. But, at the same time, it is possible to hear each as too self-contained, too self-assured. What follows from this is that the reader feels uneasy about the attitude conveyed, in content as well as in expression. Can anyone really be allowed to dogmatise in this fashion without some kind of backing evidence? In the end, the very assertiveness of *An Essay on Man* makes for doubt in the reader. Such over-assurance of statement suggests that, beneath the glittering surface, is mere vacancy.

The trouble with this kind of poem, at least so far as the English language is concerned, is that the absence of concrete detail renders the form itself rather arbitrary. Without persuasive example or the pressure of implication, how can the argument be complete? In Latin or French there does not seem to be the same kind of problem. A statement in Racine frequently has the force of an English metaphor. This is true even of lesser writers. Boileau's *Art Poetique* was published in 1674 and was closely followed by the Soames and Dryden translation (1683), which gave it an extraordinary vogue in England. A succession of verse essays appeared—on Poetry (Sheffield), on Translated Verse (Roscommon), on Unnatural Flights in Poetry (Granville), on the Greatest English Poets (Addison), on the Different Styles in Poetry (Parnell), on Verbal Criticism (Mallet)—indeed, the vogue continued until well on in the eighteenth century. The best of these was undoubtedly Pope's *Essay on Criticism* (1709), much applauded in its time. If we find it hard to get through now, it is because, like *An Essay on Man*, it rests upon assertive argument rather than persuasive definition. When *An Essay on*

Criticism shows signs of coming alive, it is where, apparently to clinch an argument, Pope resorts to an example. This is best when it tends towards delineation of character. In other words, it is the character-sketch, not the didacticism, that enlivens the verse. One example is this character of a bad critic:

> Such shameless Bards we have: and yet 'tis true,
> There are as mad, abandoned Critics too.
> The Bookful Blockhead, ignorantly read,
> With Loads of Learned Lumber in his Head,
> With his own Tongue still edifies his Ears,
> And always Listening to Himself appears.
> All Books he reads, and all he reads assails,
> From Dryden's Fables down to Durfey's Tales.
> With him, most Authors steal their Works, or buy;
> Garth did not write his own Dispensary.
> Name a new Play, and he's the Poet's Friend,
> Nay showed his faults—but when would Poets mend?
> No place so sacred from such Fops is barred,
> Nor is Paul's Church more safe than Paul's Church-yard:
> Nay, fly to Altars: there they'll talk you dead;
> For Fools rush in where Angels fear to tread.

The texture here is certainly more actual than most of the *Essay*. Yet, in spite of the famous last line, we are conscious of a generalisation in the mode of this passage that still keeps it well removed from an existing scene. One way of marking Pope's extraordinary progress is to pay attention to the way in which his early stereotypes become sharper as they approach more closely the observation of a specific character. Compare the Dull Poet—

> What Crowds of these, impenitently bold,
> In Sounds and jingling Syllables grown old

—with the little-known 'Macer: A Character' (1715). This is, in fact, a caricature: not of dull poets in the aggregate, but of Ambrose Philips, the author of a set of pastorals Pope considered to be written in rivalry to his own.

When simple Macer, now of high Renown,
First sought a Poet's Fortune in the Town:
'Twas all th'Ambition his great Soul could feel,
To wear red Stockings, and to dine with Steele.
Some Ends of Verse his Betters might afford,
And gave the harmless Fellow a good Word.
Set up with these, he ventured on the Town,
And in a borrowed Play, out-did poor Crowne.
There he stopped short, nor since has writ a tittle,
But has the Wit to make the most of little:
Like stunted, hide-bound Trees, that just have got
Sufficient Sap, at once to bear and rot.
Now he begs Verse, and what he gets commends,
Not of the Wits his Foes, but Fools his Friends. . .

The original Macer was an obscure Roman poet, a friend of
Tibullus and Ovid, and his works are now lost. The implication
is that Philips, like his prototype, is a parasite upon more illustrious
men. When we consider that Philips was an intimate not only
of Steele but also of Addison, this sharpens both the name of
the character and the acerbity with which he is described. But
most readers will require a footnote to make them aware of
this. To that extent, 'Macer' fails to be as self-substantive as
the brilliant final version we find pointed up into the lines
that occur in the 'Epistle to Dr Arbuthnot' (1731–4):

The Bard whom pilfered Pastorals renown,
Who turns a Persian Tale for half a crown,
Just writes to make his barrenness appear,
And strains from hard-bound brains eight lines a year . . . .

There is a sense of drama here that we do not have in the
earlier version. That last line labours strenuously through its
collocation of 'b' sounds to get its sense out. The point of
the epistle in which it occurs is not its argument—who can
remember it?—but its set pieces, its character-sketches. Pre-eminent
among them is the portrait of Atticus. But this does not date
from the mid-1730s, when the epistle was finished and published.
Its first version appeared some twenty years previously, when
Addison backed a rival translation of the *Iliad* and so provoked
Pope into defending his own. The original 'Atticus' (1715) was
a savage characterisation:

> But were there One whom better stars conspire
> To bless, whom Titan touched with purer Fire,
> Who born with Talents, bred in Arts to please,
> Was formed to write, converse, and live, with ease . . . .

The years gave the poem more poise; yet, paradoxically, in the final revision the character is even more securely in focus:

> were there One whose fires
> True Genius kindles, and fair Fame inspires,
> Blest with each Talent and each Art to please,
> And born to write, converse, and live with ease:
> Should such a man, too fond to rule alone,
> Bear, like the Turk, no brother near the throne,
> View him with scornful, yet with jealous eyes,
> And hate for Arts that caused himself to rise;
> Damn with faint praise, assent with civil leer,
> And without sneering, teach the rest to sneer;
> Willing to wound, and yet afraid to strike,
> Just hint a fault, and hesitate dislike;
> Alike reserved to blame, or to commend,
> A timorous foe, and a suspicious friend,
> Dreading even fools, by Flatterers besieged,
> And so obliging that he ne'er obliged;
> Like Cato, give his little Senate laws,
> And sit attentive to his own applause;
> While Wits and Templers ev'ry sentence raise,
> And wonder with a foolish face of praise.
> Who but must laugh, if such a man there be?
> Who would not weep, if Atticus were he!

I have quoted this in full to make the point that it is a complete poem, superbly shaped. The opening is so dignified as to render ambiguous whether blame or praise is intended. The earlier lines depend on the conditional 'were' and 'should'. And yet, as that conditional dependence goes on, the indignation rises. It is held in bounds by ridicule: the public tone derides a man who has allowed himself to become self-important. This is seen in the famous simile,

> Like Cato, give his little Senate laws,
> And sit attentive to his own applause . . . .

The tone rises and sweeps towards what we may anticipate as a triumphant denunciation: 'Who but must laugh if such a man there be?' However, we are not allowed to laugh. The verse turns back on itself and hushes to the opening note of respect: 'Who would not weep, if Atticus were he!'

There is no sense that this has been wrenched from a context. The poem was conceived independently and would retain its marvellous poise, between satire and elegy, if all memory of Addison had been expunged from the records. This is one of a number of characters that are as dramatic as Milton's greatest speeches and as sharp as Dryden's most formidable set-pieces. They occur mostly in the *Moral Essays* and in the 'Epistle to Dr Arbuthnot'. I am thinking of Wharton in the epistle to Cobham; Flavia, Atossa and Chloe in the epistle to a Lady; Cotta, the Man of Ross, the Duke of Buckingham, Sir Balaam in the epistle to Bathurst; Timon in the epistle to Burlington; and Atticus, Bufo and Sporus in the 'Epistle to Dr Arbuthnot'. And each and every one of these characters is independent of its context. In the epistles to Bathurst and Burlington, it is true, the characters occupy the bulk of each poem and the argument appears to exist mainly as a linking factor. But in the memory they remain isolated sharp vignettes, obstinately unlinked. Even when a character is put forward to illustrate an argumentative trend, it is usually interchangeable with another character in an independent poem. Cotta, the miser, appears in an epistle on human riches, but would he be out of place in another, on the ruling passion? After all, we find another miser—Euclio—there. The fact of the matter is that the *Moral Essays* and the 'Epistle to Dr Arbuthnot' are less interesting as didactic wholes than are the individual characters which—somewhat arbitrarily—crop up in them. A pointed example, after all, is worth a great deal of assertion. And if one has a good enough example, very likely the assertion was unnecessary in the first place.

What we have in Milton, Dryden and Pope is a poetry which takes off from an imitation of the Ancients. But this was to embody only a part of the tradition, that part which could be made native to English—in the cases we have looked at, mainly the telling examples. It was also to limit the possible range of the poet; mostly, to what was decorous in a classical sense. Again, this leaves out a good deal which is possible in the English language. The concept of heroism, for example, is not only primitive but simplistic. Homer's bronze-age heroes settle arguments with a thrust of the spear, and subsequent epics have stylised human relations in much the same way. The concept of Good versus Evil expressed in terms of physical violence can be seen in the *Aeneid*, in *The Faerie Queene*, even in *Paradise Lost*—*vide* the absurdities of the War in Heaven. It is the incidentals of these poems that work in English verse. As civilisation wears on, the cult of the Noble Hero becomes increasingly trivialised. It is now fit only for children in the form of cowboy films or space-fiction epics. The heroic mode had a function, probably a patriotic one, once upon a time. But even among epics there are gradations. The *Chansons de Geste* are a particularly dreary extension of the genre. *La Chanson de Roland* (12th century), indeed, has its incidental felicities. But its verse is characteristically languorous and its plot is based upon an absurdity. When beleaguered by the wicked Saracens (originally, Basques), Roland refuses to sound his horn, even though that would have brought Charlemagne to the rescue. There might be some merit in Roland giving up his own life to a feeling of pride, though I doubt it, but it is a poor officer who will in this way sacrifice his men. The *Chanson* praised this as an act of heroism, but, when the jongleurs carried French romance into Italy, this chivalric world was seen more critically. In the *Morgante Maggiore* (*ante* 1487), Charlemagne becomes a foil and Orlando (Roland) a pawn. Most of the activity is ascribed to the less conventional figure of Rinaldo. The author, Pulci, plays for comedy rather than straight narrative. There is, for example, a good deal of deliberate digression. The Margutte episode of Canto XVIII exhibits a sympathetic rogue who mocks at the events that surround him.

The chief imitators of Pulci in the sixteenth century were Boiardo, Ariosto and Berni. Boiardo's poem (*ante* 1494) is chiefly important for inspiring its successors. One of them, the *Orlando Furioso* (1532), is a farrago of stories interspersed with episodes and diversions which prove to be the most arresting part of Ariosto's work. Perhaps even more influential among later poets was the *Rifacimento* of Berni (*ante* 1535) which recast Boiardo's original in a livelier and more popular mode.

It did not take long for this kind of spontaneous-seeming comedy to reach England. Harington's Elizabethan version of Ariosto (1591) is a masterpiece in its own right. It is full of witty, irreverent and irrelevant buffoonery. This poem has much the same relation to the sober heroics of Spenser as Ariosto himself has to *La Chanson de Roland*. To that extent, Harington acclimatised the Italian comedy to English. The mode was taken up by a number of Caroline poets. Let us grant that theirs was an age of dogmatism, when Charles I and Oliver Cromwell, though saying different things, both knew that they were right. It was also, however, an age of lesser fry, for whom the only thing certain was uncertainty. The *Leoline and Sydanis* of Francis Kynaston is equally post-Pulci and anti-Spenser. Here, as early as 1642, is a tone of intimacy with the reader, sanctioning the occasional asides into digression:

> Favours are oft, unhappily, by chance
> Bestowed: for 'mongst those courtiers that did wear
> The Prince's points, a Marquess was of France,
> Who for some heinous fact he had done there,
> Hanged in effigy, fled from France for fear,
> And so for refuge to Carleon came,
> *Monsieur Marquis Jean Foutre* was his name. . . .

This villain's very name is an affront to our intelligence! He seeks to make love to Sydanis and, in order to do this, blights her husband's virility:

> The sad events whereof to set before ye,
> Is as the dire Praeludium of our story. . . .

Kynaston was by no means alone in this period. More assaults upon the understanding of the reader may be found in Nathaniel Whiting's mock-heroic poem *Albion and Bellarma* (1637). Here is another ridiculous villain, this time called Count Fuco, and the hero starts as a virginal monk but eventually impregnates an entire convent. He elopes with one of the nuns and treats her to a honeymoon feast too outrageous to be annotated even by Saintsbury in his edition of the poem. In spite of that, and its virtual irrelevance to the plot, it is the best thing Whiting did. Taking leave of his lovers in mid-story, the author impudently tells us

> For having screwed them into firm embraces
> I will not waken hate or rouse disgraces.

The mode went on, though in slighter and more occasional poems. There is more than a hint of it in the raffish confidences of Suckling and Sedley. Prior adapts it—not too sensitively—to anapaestic metres which amble through the eighteenth century in verses by Walter Pope, John Collins, Hugh Kelly and Christopher Anstey; which stumble, at length, into the nineteenth century by courtesy of Thomas Moore (*The Fudge Family in Paris*, 1818) and Winthrop Mackworth Praed; and which become classicised into hexameters by A. H. Clough. Another line led to the tedious tetrameters of *Hudibras* (1663–78) and the lively tetrameters of Jonathan Swift; this mode ran through the eighteenth century via Gay, Green and Dyer. But neither anapaests nor tetrameters offer the variety of rhythm necessary to what is essentially, however subversive, a mode of comedy.

The times became once more attuned to the mode when the Regency poets found themselves possessed of the attitudes which had passed current in the Caroline era. In their period, as in that of the Charleses, there was an underlying disrespect for established order. It compelled the wits of the early nineteenth century into a truly Carolingian affection for attributes of the Italian mock-heroic. This took the form of rhymes that thumbed their way past decorum, of narrative which abdicated the responsibility of telling a story, of digression which turned out to be the main point of the poem. Throughout, whether by chance or design, there was an exuberant quality of improvisation.

No doubt irreverence and irrelevance, the anti-heroic anti-norm, was in the air. But the factor precipitating it in the early nineteenth century was quite a scholarly movement to bring the Italian romances before the reading public. Between May 1806 and June 1807, John Herman Merivale wrote about Pulci, and illustrated his articles with copious translations, in the influential *Monthly Magazine*. William Stewart Rose translated Casti, an eighteenth-century straggler after the great Florentines: his translation of *Animali Parlanti* (*ante* 1803) came out in 1816. He also translated Ariosto (1823). Both Merivale and Rose took over the easy and colloquial stanzas of the Italians, their absurd rhymes, comic digressions and all. Thus Rose, in his Dedication to *The Court of Beasts*, says to Ugo Foscolo,

> To whom so well can I inscribe my fable,
> As thee? since I, upon good proof, may sing thee
> *Doctum sermones utriusque linguae.* . . .

The mode was effective enough to arouse, quite independently, an obscure Scottish professor and an English diplomat in London. Dr William Tennant of St Andrews began his *Anster Fair* (1812) with a mock-heroic address to the reader:

> While some of Troy and pettish heroes sing,
>   And some of Rome and chiefs of pious fame,
> And some of men that thought it harmless thing
>   To smite off heads in Mary's bloody game,
> And some of Eden's garden gay with spring,
>   And Hell's dominions terrible to name—
> I sing a theme far brighter, happier, gladder,
> I sing of Anster Fair, and bonny Maggie Lauder. . . .

The diplomat, John Hookham Frere, likewise—though more suavely—indicates the paradoxical gap between (feignedly) humble means and (feignedly) great aspirations. *The Monks and the Giants* (1817) begins,

> I've often wished that I could write a book,
>   Such as all English people might peruse;
> I never should regret the pains it took,
>   That's just the sort of fame that I should choose:
> To sail about the world like Captain Cook,
>   I'd sling a cot up for my favourite Muse,
> And we'd take verses out to Demerara,
> To New South Wales, and up to Niagara.
>
> Poets consume exciseable commodities,
>   They raise the nation's spirit when victorious,
> They drive an export trade in whims and oddities,
>   Making our commerce and revenue glorious;
> As an industrious painstaking body 'tis
>   That Poets should be reckoned meritorious:
> And therefore I submissively propose
> To erect one Board for Verse and one for Prose. . . .

By the time *The Monks and the Giants* came out, Byron had already, in a letter of January 1814, praised Merivale's imitation of Pulci, *Orlando in Roncesvalles*. He himself received, in September 1816, a letter from his publisher, Murray, mentioning Frere's poem-in-progress and was introduced to it by Rose in Venice, September 1817. Byron knew exactly whose sophistication sheltered behind the rustic pseudonym of 'Whistlecraft'. Not only did he greatly admire the poem; he immediately began to imitate it. 'I have since written a poem (of 84 octave Stanzas) humorous, in or after the excellent manner of Mr Whistlecraft (whom I take to be Frere), on a Venetian anecdote—which amused me' (12 October 1817).

This was *Beppo*. It is a sign of the community of vision among these late acquirers of a forgotten mode that Frere thought the poem was an anonymous work by William Stewart Rose, It certainly resembles Rose, as it does Frere, in its far-fetched irrelevances and improbable rhymes. But there the resemblance ends. If it were not for Byron, there would be little point in exploring this largely underground mode of humour. But Byron converted what in English is mostly a minor line into a major genre of comedy. In *Beppo*, his first attempt at the genre, the accent is unmistakable:

'Tis known, at least it should be, that throughout
    All countries of the Catholic persuasion,
Some weeks before Shrove Tuesday comes about,
    The people take their fill of recreation,
And buy repentance, ere they grow devout,
    However high their rank, or low their station,
With fiddling, feasting, dancing, drinking, masking,
And other things which may be had for asking. . . .

The mode was taken by Byron to its logical conclusion: notice the characteristically 'low' touch in the last line. A good deal of his work came to outrage the chaste sensibility of Frere. Yet Byron shows himself superior to his predecessors in acuity of wit, projection of personality, freedom of speech and rhythm in the handling of his stanza. He takes irrelevance to a new extreme, blaming himself by way of paradox for so doing:

            I find
    Digression is a sin, that by degrees
    Becomes exceeding tedious to my mind . . . .

The result is that, on a rough count, about half of Beppo's ninety-nine stanzas are digressive. And an even higher percentage is off the point in *Don Juan* (1818–24).

This must be the most arbitrary poem of any merit in the language. It is arbitrary in structure, in texture, in tone, in rhyme. But this arbitrariness is a special technique, a functional version of what we should now call 'imitative form'. Unlike the archetypal Hero, whose every move is determined by the chivalric code, Don Juan inhabits an arbitrary world. Further, he is weak, unmanly, and surrounded by cartoon figures. His mistresses are arbitrary: 'And whispering, "I will ne'er consent"— consented'. The narrative is arbitrary:

> Here my chaste Muse a liberty must take.
>   Start not, still chaster reader, she'll be nice hence-
> Forward, and there is no great cause to quake.
>   This liberty is a poetic licence. . . .

Nobody ever gets anything they want:

> Under the bed they searched, and there they found—
>   No matter what, it was not that they sought. . . .

That characteristic 'low' touch again! Even when the forsaken Donna Julia sends Juan a letter from the convent in which she is imprisoned, it is patterned in rhetoric as exquisite as the paper on which it is written:

> And so farewell—forgive me, love me—no,
>   That word is idle now, but let it go. . . .

Her delicate script pretends that it is written hastily, and in a scrawl. This is a world of vain appearances, whose very vanity is what makes them interesting.

Perhaps the greatest section of Don Juan is when the 'hero' finally reaches London. This is far on in the poem (Canto XIII), and so has been missed by many anthologists. The pretensions of the London scene gain colour through being looked at by the eye of exile. But the result is not satire, since there is no norm from which this 'world' can be satirised. The London scene is one more addition to the meaningless accumulation of appearances. The names alone would give the game away, except that there is no game, unless it be in the naming of these ridiculous characters. What follows is a concatenation of pseudo-references:

> The noble guests, assembled at the Abbey,
>   Consisted of—we give the sex the *pas*—
> The Duchess of Fitz-Fulke, The Countess Crabbey,
>   The Ladies Scilly, Busey, Miss Eclat,
> Miss Bombazeen, Miss Mackstay, Miss O'Tabbey,
>   And Mrs. Rabbi, the rich banker's squaw,
> Also the Honourable Mrs. Sleep,
> Who looked a white lamb, yet was a black sheep,
>
> With other Countesses of Blank—but rank,
>   At once the 'lee' and the élite of crowds,
> Who pass like water filtered in a tank,
>   All purged and pious from their native clouds;
> Or paper turned to money by the bank.
>   No matter how or why, the passport shrouds
> The passé and the passed, for good society
> Is no less famed for tolerance than piety;
>
> That is, up to a certain point, which point
>   Forms the most difficult in punctuation.
> Appearances appear to form the joint
>   On which it hinges in a higher station.
> And so that no explosion cry 'aroint
>   Thee, witch', or each Medea has her Jason,
> Or (to the point with Horace and with Pulci)
> *Omne tulit punctum, quae miscuit utile dulci.* . . .

('He has won every vote who has blended profit and pleasure'—Horace, *Ars Poetica*).

This, and writing like it, seems to me an extension of the anti-heroic mode, owing a good deal to the Calvinism indoctrinated into Byron during his Aberdeen childhood. Calvinist theology teaches at once that the world is predetermined by the will of God and that this will is inscrutable. It follows that, while events are pretty well bound to happen, there is no chance of anyone understanding them. We need not be surprised that the poem is unfinished, and stops when a monk, thought to be a ghost, turns out instead to be the frolicsome Duchess of Fitz-Fulke:

> He found, as people on most trials must,
>   That he had made at first a silly blunder
> And that in his confusion he had caught
> Only the wall, instead of what he sought. . . .

The verse is saved from being negative by the delight it takes in itself. The wild rhyming, for example, brings meanings into relation that, left to themselves, would have remained isolated for the ordinary reader. The tone of voice, too, is highly individual; very much that of a man speaking to men. This is the decadence of the poetry of debate, but it is a rich and colourful decadence. Every now and then, the master of ceremonies emerges from his scenery to tell us that his stage is bare, or, if it is furnished, then the scenery doesn't matter. The poetry of debate, in fact, reached in Byron a stage where the author argues persuasively that there is no argument. One can see why he so admired Milton, Dryden, Pope—'It is all Horace then, and Claudian now among us' (15 September 1817).

The refusal of debate to fit itself neatly into English verse imposed limitations on Byron, as it did on his masters. It is difficult to know how to recommend *Don Juan* as a whole. On the one hand the poem exhales an extraordinarily distinctive atmosphere; it really is a world unto itself. On the other, its determined digressiveness renders it difficult to see it in terms of form. One is tempted to excerpt from *Don Juan*, as one can from the eighteenth-century picaresques (*Joseph Andrews*, *Roderick Random*), to which it also owes some allegiance. The greater digressions certainly have a life of their own, even when detached from context. One remembers with affection the Dedication; the digression on First Love (Canto I); on Wellington (IX); on contemporary poetry, on time passing (XI); on money (XII); on London (XIII); on Bryon's own writing (XIV). But, no question, they gain by being put back *in situ*, even when they are most determined to wrest themselves away from the parent narrative.

If, then, *Don Juan* is a triumph, it is a triumph of a personal

and unrepeatable kind. Whatever the antecedents, the line ends
at Byron. His poem has the same relation to the central traditions
of literature as *Gargantua and Pantagruel*, *Tom Jones* or, indeed,
Orlando Furioso itself. As such, it stands away from the main
line as a magnificent folly, a Brighton Pavilion. The same can
be said for poems more overtly serious in their ambitions. Without
a tough plot, the 'poem of some length' cannot exist. We
think of Milton in terms of speeches, a few similes and some
muscular narration; of Dryden in terms of characters and a
few speeches; of Pope almost entirely in terms of characters.
The incidentals are superb enough to render these authors great
poets, and no one denies it. But to say that is not to pay
tribute as a genre to the poetry of debate.

7 The Essential Wordsworth

After Chaucer and Shakespeare, I regard Wordsworth as our greatest poet. This may seem to many too favourable a judgement; yet even those who dissent from it might be brought to agree that Wordsworth is widely respected, and even read.

This is a tribute to his genius, for no poet has been worse arranged or edited more clumsily. The standard editions follow an arbitrary system laid down by the author in sterile middle age, and are frankly repulsive. The poems are classified under heads in a manner which has ensured that we read them with regard neither to chronology nor to merit. Side by side, in the section entitled 'Poems founded upon the Affections', 'Michael' and 'The Idiot Boy' rub uneasy flanks—one a masterpiece, the other unmeaning drivel. And either of them, good or bad, might as appropriately be found under the heading of 'Poems Referring to the Period of Childhood', or, quite possibly, 'Poems of the Imagination'. When one considers that this confusion is typical of the arbitrary arrangement of the Collected Poems throughout, it is a wonder that anyone reads Wordsworth at all.

But it can safely be said that no one reads him entire. In Wordsworth's case, more than in most, it seems that the public has been content to rely upon the selection of critics and editors. So that what we mean when we speak of Wordsworth is what some nineteenth-century worthy has made of him.

The two most influential selections have been those of Tennyson and of Arnold respectively. When I refer to Tennyson, I mean, of course, *The Golden Treasury* (1861). This was compiled by Palgrave on Tennyson's advice, and nowhere is Tennyson's hand more evident in the anthology than in the pieces culled from Wordsworth. For Tennyson, Wordsworth was a master of simplicity; although, as Arnold said of him, Tennyson often confuses simplicity with *simplesse*. As a result, the enormous selection of Wordsworth in *The Golden Treasury* is flawed by jejune efforts such as 'Simon Lee, the Old Huntsman' (1798):

> Few months of life has he in store
> As he to you will tell,
> For still, the more he works, the more
> Do his weak ankles swell. . . .

This is the Wordsworth of *The Stuffed Owl*, the Wordsworth in whom intention remains at a great distance from achievement. One can see the attempt to reach compassion, but any understanding of the old man's predicament is baulked by the ludicrous details and the uneasy self-consciousness that the ballad manifests:

> My gentle reader, I perceive
> How patiently you've waited,
> And now I fear that you expect
> Some tale will be related. . . .

No, this is emphatically not a Wordsworth who is readable nowadays. Moreover, in company with 'Simon Lee' and the Matthew poems, we must also relegate the Miltonic sonnets which are the other—literary, rhetorical—side of Wordsworth's output. Most of them are a mixture of objurgation and clumsiness—notice the awkward rhyme in the fourth line here:

> The World is too much with us; late and soon,
> Getting and spending, we lay waste our powers;
> Little we see in Nature that is ours;
> We have given our hearts away, a sordid boon! . . .

Milton was certainly living at that hour, and it was Wordsworth who resuscitated him. Here we have all the worst part of Miltonic verse—the exhortation, the generalisation, the accepted phrasing.

So, reading Tennyson's selection, one would assume Wordsworth to have no approach between a crude imitation of rustic speech and a dithyrambic gesticulation around abstract universals.

But Arnold himself was equivocal about this selection of Wordsworth: it 'surprised many readers, and gave offence to not a few'. Arnold's own selection (1879) is far more intelligent, and has remained the characteristic line on Wordsworth ever since. We find, for example, the great Arnoldian of our own time, F. R. Leavis in *Revaluation* (1936), discounting Wordsworth's 'philosophy' and concentrating on the meditative side of his work. And there is some point in doing this: like Leavis, Arnold in his own time refused to be led astray by the moralistic aspects of *The Excursion*, or the declamation of the 'Ode on Intimations of Immortality'.

But, in spite of this, there is something tentative and minuscule in Arnold's approach, echoed as it has been by critics ever since. 'His best work is in his shorter pieces. . . . I have not ventured on detaching portions of poems. . . . The *Excursion* and the *Prelude*, his poems of greatest bulk, are by no means Wordsworth's best work'—this stressing of the exquisite, but essentially minor, has gone on until the present day. The Lucy poems, 'The Solitary Reaper', these are perfect of their kind; but how far is their kind capable of sustaining major poetry? These are fragments of perception, beautifully caught, but without a context:

> No motion has she now, no force,
>   She neither hears nor sees;
> Rolled round in earth's diurnal course,
>   With rocks, and stones, and trees
>
> ('A slumber did my spirit seal', 1799)

—it was possible for Hugh Sykes Davies to misread this most egregiously (*Essays in Criticism*, 1965). But, after one had mastered one's indignation, it was possible to see how the misunderstanding had come about. Of what validity is Wordsworth's elegy unless we know, within the terms of the poem, for whom it was composed? Where is the context in which this 'She' exists? One need not go along with Mr Sykes Davies in identifying the feminine pronoun with the mind in order to have problems with this poem that take one beyond the poem itself—rapt and beautiful though it certainly is.

It seems to me, then, that Wordsworth is a larger and more complex poet than either Arnold or his modern apologists have made him. There is a tendency now to mute his originality: to suggest that his roots were in the eighteenth-century. This is so: the poetic realism of Wordsworth had much to do with Langhorne's pioneering work (1774–77); he can be related to Goldsmith (1770) and to the Cowper of 'Crazy Kate' (1784); Southey's 'Hannah' (1799) may have been instrumental in his movement from narrative in couplets to narrative in blank verse. But none of this explains the genuine horror with which *Lyrical Ballads* (1798) was received by the critics. It was in the course of a review of Crabbe—very acceptable to his Augustan ear—that Francis Jeffrey turned aside, in 1808, to deal with Wordsworth and Coleridge:

> The gentlemen of the new school, on the other hand, scarcely ever condescend to take their subjects from any description of persons at all known to the common inhabitants of the world; but invent for themselves certain whimsical and un-heard-of beings, to whom they impute some fantastical combination of feelings, and then labour to excite our sympathy for them, either by placing them in incredible situations, or by some strained and exaggerated moralisation of a vague and tragical description. (*Edinburgh Review*)

Of course, *Lyrical Ballads*, as the Preface suggests, was conceived as something of a pioneering enterprise, and there are poems as exaggerated as the showpieces of any other new school of poetry; 'Simon Lee' and the Matthew poems among them. But the piece upon which Jeffrey particularly turns his outraged attention is the one with far more tenacious claims on our sympathy: the incomparable, lovely

> There was a Boy, ye knew him well, ye Cliffs
> And Islands of Winander! many a time
> At evening, when the stars had just begun
> To move along the edges of the hills,
> Rising or setting, would he stand alone
> Beneath the trees, or by the glimmering lake,
> And there, with fingers interwoven, both hands
> Pressed closely, palm to palm, and to his mouth

Uplifted, he, as through an instrument,
Blew mimic hootings to the silent owls
That they might answer him. And they would shout
Across the wat'ry Vale and shout again,
Responsive to his call, with quivering peals,
And long halloos, and screams . . . .

('There was a boy', 1798)

What impresses us about this passage is its rightness, its inevitability. It is therefore hard to remember that, in 1808, poetry such as this could upset a critic through being original. Jeffrey's expectations are outraged; and, in commenting upon the poem, he seems to be looking everywhere but in the right direction. In particular, he is obsessed by a passage I have not quoted, the death of the child.

> The sports of childhood, and the untimely death of promising youth, is also a common topic for poetry. Mr Wordsworth has made some blank verse about it; but, instead of the delightful and picturesque sketches with which so many authors of moderate talent have presented us on this inviting subject, all that he is pleased to communicate of *his* rustic child, is, that he used to amuse himself with shouting to the owls, and hearing them answer. To make amends for this brevity, the process of his mimicry is most accurately described . . . this is all we hear of him; and for the sake of this one accomplishment, we are told, that the author has frequently stood mute and gazed on his grave for half an hour together!

After the conventional portraits of eighteenth-century poetry, sketched plainly enough in Jeffrey's expectations, this piece evidently seemed *outré*, even arbitrary. But possibly there is an explanation for its failure to make him look in the right direction. Jeffrey is, for instance, badly worried by the way in which the description of the bird-calls leads on to the boy's death. But though the connection is made in the version that Jeffrey was reading and that is usually published, the first draft of the poem shows that the death is extraneous. In its original version, the poem is autobiographical—a straight recollection of Wordsworth's own childhood. The account of the child's death is therefore an addendum. Perhaps a case could be made out for it: the boy is, after all, received into the nature which he was imitating.

But, as Jeffrey's adverse reaction shows, the end of the poem has been a source of critical deflection, and certainly has no deep-rooted organic connection with the rest of it. It is just possible that, confronted with the original draft, Jeffrey would have had less to say about the piece's tendency towards dramatic inflation; though there is no evidence that he could have responded to its mythopoeia. For him—and this is clear from his comments on Crabbe as well—a succession of events can have no more than its literal significance. To do Jeffrey justice, he concedes that the mimicry is 'accurately described'; but he does not see there is more to it than that. Wordsworth is depicting a boy who is willing himself into the woodland, into the life of the trees; it is no accident that he is not merely disturbing the owls but actively—and successfully—imitating them, recreating something of their nature in himself. And, in the passage which Jeffrey ignores—

> a gentle shock of mild surprise
> Has carried far into his heart the voice
> Of mountain torrents, or the visible scene
> Would enter unawares into his mind . . .

—the boy becomes part of the lake and woodlands with which he is communing.

Even as it stands, the poem shows the astonishing mythopoeic power of Wordsworth when he began writing, as well as indicating the direction in which his greatness lies. No wonder that, in his own lifetime, some members of the public preferred Helen Maria Williams, Samuel Rogers, Thomas Campbell—to say nothing of the popular vogue of Byron, Scott and Moore. But Coleridge held out against the tide; recognising, as fine poets do their peers, the master-spirit of the age.

Yet, even granted his originality, Wordsworth had dreadful luck with the critics. There can be no doubt that the reviews of *The Excursion* caused him to suppress the remainder of his discursive work in blank verse. Some critics nowadays attempt to whitewash Jeffrey, who wrote the key review of *The Excursion* (1814). But consider his words:

The volume before us, if we were to describe it very shortly, we should characterize as a tissue of moral and devotional ravings, in which innumerable changes are rung upon a few very simple and familiar ideas: but with such accompaniment of long words, long sentences, and unwieldy phrases—and such a hubbub of strained raptures and fantastical sublimities, that it is often difficult for the most skilful and attentive student to obtain a glimpse of the author's meaning—and altogether impossible for the ordinary reader to conjecture what he is about. . . . (*Edinburgh Review*, 1814).

These strictures were occasioned by grave faults in the poem, but this cannot justify Jeffrey's brutality and insensitivity. He had used more measured terms in reviewing work that was far inferior to *The Excursion*. Clearly there was something in Wordsworth that outraged him; but his outrage brought about some heavy consequences. Wordsworth had been expecting great things of *The Excursion*, and there can be no doubt that he was shattered by the reception accorded to this first instalment of his life's work. There can be no doubt, either, that it was the failure of *The Excursion* that determined him to leave *The Prelude* (1805), a far greater poem, unpublished. After all, it was similar enough in mode to invite attack, and much more personal. Moreover, some portions of it, such as 'There was a Boy', had already been published separately and been jeered at. One cannot, therefore, blame Wordsworth for seeking to avoid a chorus of ridicule that might have had severe repercussions on his health and sanity.

However, although he never dared publish the poem, Wordsworth tinkered about with it for forty-five years; ironing out its early colloquialisms, strengthening its moralistic links, turning his youthful perceptions into the otiose Miltonicism that dogged his later poetry. And, by an irony as exquisite as it is poignant, it is this later version that has been promulgated.

Readers had difficulty with it even in the later nineteenth century. Arnold, as we have seen, avoided choosing passages from it for his selection and the editors of the Moxon edition of Wordsworth excluded it altogether—because of its manifest inferiority to the poet's other work! It was only gradually that it became current, and then only through an interest in the poet's life as distinct from his writings.

The promulgation of the 1850 text is a matter for keen regret. Professor de Selincourt claimed it as a much better composition than the 'A-text' of 1805; but the reasons he gives for his preferences are very odd. For instance, he seems to feel that, in some way, Wordsworth strengthened his poem by taking out the colloquialisms that 'suggest a man talking to his friend'. Instead, de Selincourt favours the later version's Miltonic inversion and heavy explicitness. And, less accountably, his preference has been followed by Dr Leavis: 'No one is likely to dispute that the later version is decidedly the more satisfactory' (*Revaluation*, 1936). This may be taken as a general judgement, though it should be said that the passage most immediately under discussion is the one in Book II beginning 'Blessed the infant Babe'. Dr Leavis's preference in this instance has been challenged by Donald Davie (*Articulate Energy*, 1957). But I hardly think the dissension worth taking up: the passage in question is discursive and meditative, and a comparison between its two existing versions is likely to be no more than a discrimination between contrasting modes of mediocrity. My case would rather be that Wordsworth was essentially a narrative poet, the greatest since Chaucer, and that therefore we should consider him at his best. Such a consideration would act as a means of differentiating between the two *Preludes* by way of analysing, with comparisons, the efficacy of the earlier one.

This should be done initially in terms of language. Wordsworth is not usually credited with exactness or precision in this field; still less with sensuous vitality. And yet if we consider one of the key episodes of the 1805 *Prelude*, and see how Wordsworth maltreated it in later years, we can give the lie to this presupposition.

A crucial example is the account of Wordsworth's expedition to Snowdon (Book XIII in the 1805 version; Book XIV in the 1850 version)—not, so far as I can gather, one of the most frequented parts of *The Prelude*. And yet, in the earlier version at least, it exhibits a preternatural keenness of eye and ear. It begins briskly enough—

> In one of these excursions, travelling then
> Through Wales on foot

–but, in the later version, 'Wales' is atrophied into 'the Northern tracts of Cambria', and to the simple word 'excursions' is added the pious hope 'May they ne'er / Fade from remembrance'.

There is a frankly tactile description of the evening—

> It was a summer's night, a close warm night,
> Wan, dull and glaring, with a dripping mist

—but the older Wordsworth mashes up the rhythm up into an unrelieved chain of adjectives: 'It was a close, warm, breezeless summer night . . . .' No wonder Wordsworth has a reputation for failure in sensuous detail!

But the real success of the earlier version, and it is tremendous, is the mystical illumination that flashes upon the poet in this scene—an illumination that seems to me greatly superior to the much-fêted 'Simplon Pass'. Here the concrete particulars of the summer night assume startling urgency as they impinge upon the young traveller's mind:

> and lo!
> The Moon stood naked in the heavens, at height
> Immense above my head . . .

> Far, far beyond, the vapours shot themselves,
> In headlands, tongues, and promontory shapes,
> Into the sea, the real sea . . .

> Meanwhile, the Moon looked down upon this show
> In single glory, and we stood, the mist
> Touching our very feet . . . .

But, *pace* Wordsworth's 'Immortality' ode, the things which he had seen, he now could see no more. In the later *Prelude*, the Moon does not stand naked in the heavens, but 'hung' in a 'firmament'; and we lose the sense of immense height in favour of a description of this same firmament—'azure without cloud'.

Again, the 'vapours' of the early version are in flux—they 'shot themselves / In headlands, tongues and promontory shapes'. But, in the later version, they appear as '*solid* vapours *stretched* / In headlands, tongues . . .'. Now this is a complete impossibility, since the vapours cannot be solid, and, if they were, could not be stretched—and, if they *could* be stretched, they would hardly stretch into forms as various as those of headlands, tongues and promontories. Such images as these could only be appropriate to something flexuous and evanescent.

But, worst of all, Wordsworth's stark simplicity—'the moon looked down upon this show'—is Miltonised into this cumbrous periphrasis:

> the full-orbed Moon,
> Who, from her sovereign elevation, gazed
> Upon the billowy ocean . . . .

All personality is drained off; we are left with received gestures, such as 'full-orbed', 'sovereign elevation'—which give us no idea of how things looked to the young Wordsworth—indeed, there is no sense of that passionate spectator at all!

These verbal points are not small ones, even in the local context of a single episode; and, multiplied as they are throughout the revised *Prelude*, they serve to blur and dissipate the sharp impressions of the original. I am not imputing deliberate falsification so much as a desire in the aging Wordsworth to restore the literary decorum which his younger self had so sharply outraged. These verbal changes, however, often produced an entire dislocation of narrative.

One of the finest narratives Wordsworth ever accomplished is the encounter, in Book IV of the *Prelude*, with the Discharged Soldier. His spectral figure is thrust at us with stark directness:

> He was of stature tall,
> A foot above man's common measure tall,
> Stiff in his form, and upright, lank and lean;
> A man more meagre, as it seemed to me,
> Was never seen abroad by night or day.
> His arms were long, and bare his hands; his mouth
> Showed ghastly in the moonlight: from behind
> A milestone propped him, and his figure seemed
> Half-sitting, and half-standing. I could mark
> That he was clad in military garb,
> Though faded, yet entire. He was alone,
> Had no attendant, neither dog, nor staff,
> Nor knapsack; in his very dress appeared
> A desolation, a simplicity

> That seemed akin to solitude. Long time
> Did I peruse him with a mingled sense
> Of fear and sorrow. From his lips, meanwhile,
> There issued murmuring sounds, as if of pain
> Or of uneasy thought; yet still his form
> Kept the same steadiness; and at his feet
> His shadow lay, and moved not. . . .

These sharp, detached details never lapse into catalogue: what fuses them together is the sense of the man's vulnerability and loneliness. And it is Wordsworth's greatness that he can make so static a mode as description—description, moreover, of a stationary object—develop in the manner of narrative. This effect of development is partly owing to the poet's sense of the beholder: we are keenly aware of Wordsworth himself watching the old man.

Unfortunately this awareness has faded out in revision, and, with it, half the significance of the events recorded:

> A man more meagre, as it seemed to me,
> Was never seen abroad by night or day

becomes merely assertion—

> a more meagre man
> Was never seen before by night or day.

This latter is no more than prosaic. Not only has the sense of observation been blunted, but also the keening 'e'-sounds of the original have been muffled by a change in word-order that reduces the key-word, 'meagre', to insignificance, and removes all expressiveness from the rhythm.

With the effect of ghostliness in the original goes the fear that the young Wordsworth has of the man—

> Long time
> Did I peruse him with a mingled sense
> Of fear and sorrow

—but this is omitted from the revision. In its stead, we have a moralistic reflection upon the contrast between the soldier and 'the trappings of a gaudy world'. This is an awkward dispersion of one faculty Wordsworth excelled in, the sense of place.

It could, of course, be argued that some contrast with the soldier is necessary, if only to set his lank figure in perspective. But this, in fact, is provided in the 1805 version:

> In a glen
> Hard by, a village stood, whose roofs and doors
> Were visible among the scattered trees,
> Scarce distant from the spot an arrow's flight

—which at once sets off the loneliness of the old soldier and also suggests that help is nearer than he supposes. Again, this is missing from the revised text, and is replaced by circumstantial detail—'we reached a cottage'—as though Wordsworth were no more acquainted with the country than the old soldier himself.

This narrative is more than its literal detail. For instance, the soldier at first sight appears wholly vulnerable, without a staff; but, after Wordsworth makes his approach, he picks his staff up out of the grass where it had lain neglected. The soldier himself has been at fault in giving way to self-pity; help was at hand. And the poet, seen as an instrument of that help, was himself mistaken in imagining the soldier to be utterly vulnerable—the staff may not have been immediately apparent, but it was there. The inference is that no man is entirely alone—the very word 'staff', coupled with the soldier's biblical diction, has an unmistakable echo of the psalmist.

One cannot quite call this symbolism. Rather, I should like to adopt a phrase suggested to me in another context by one of my students, Mrs Judith Hutchinson, and call the staff a 'significance' of 'significant object'—bearing a meaning, that is to say, beyond the immediate situation, without necessarily following a one-to-one pattern of symbolism.

This 'significance' is blurred by Wordsworth's changes in revision: in the suppression, for instance, of the fact that shelter was close at hand. This suppression leaves us with a sense of arbitrariness, as though the poet was able to offer help merely by accident. While in the original he appears an agent of providence.

And narrative of this order, the order of the earlier *Prelude*, was lost to writers of the time; partly through the stupidity of critics, partly through Wordsworth's own diffidence. The 1805 version stands as a pointer to all that narrative verse should have been able to accomplish in the nineteenth century. Its suppression was one of the great set-backs of literature; as great, in its way, as the premature deaths of Keats and Shelley, and those of the poets of the 1914–18 war. A vital link in a great tradition of literature was thereby missing; a crucial example was denied the poets of the rising generation. For *The Prelude* was a major advance in the handling of narrative: a decisive move forward from Goldsmith and Cowper; more far-reaching than Crabbe. It could have been the basis for a revival of narrative verse.

This, in fact, never took place. Since *The Prelude* was not published, writers had to turn elsewhere for their inspiration. Clearly Crabbe himself could offer little: though a great poet, he was at the end of a long tradition; as his eclipse, after his death, clearly shows. His perceptions were hard and particular, but his backward-looking technique prevented him from making the fullest use of them. And the other poets of the time were far more circumscribed in subject-matter: Keats, no escapist himself, gave rise to a curiously Parnassian school of poetry, which excluded the grittiness of fiction. No, if writers had to learn, they could learn only from the greatest poet of the age; and, since they could not go to *The Prelude*, they went to *The Excursion*.

Among Wordsworth's greatest disciples are John Stuart Mill and George Eliot. It is no coincidence that these are writers of prose; a political philosopher and a novelist, respectively. This suggests there is more in the sheer content of Wordsworth's verse than has generally been acknowledged: Mill, in his *Autobiography* (1860s) describes it as the very culture of the feelings; and his social concern, like that of Arnold, has a Wordsworthian root.

But the greatest disciple was George Eliot. The silent suffering of Maggie in *The Mill on the Floss* (1860), the deliberate stylisation of rustic simplicity in *Silas Marner* (1861), the massively heroic figures of Adam Bede and Caleb Garth—these owe much, in moral perception, to Wordsworth; to say nothing of the sheer technique of presentation. And if we agree with Dr Leavis (*The Great Tradition*, 1947) that these represent a foreshortening of George Eliot's art—moral fable rather than realistic narrative—this is only to say that the novel had to grow away from Wordsworth if it was ever to take account of the necessities of prose.

But such a growing away, while it increased the possibilities of 'naturalism', also brought in an unavoidable tendency towards disruption. One can say that Victorian novels carry up to half their bulk in waste matter—mostly by way of explanatory links between episodes or material relating to character which is imaginatively extraneous. George Eliot herself built up the realistic, circumstantial side of fiction, and achieved a masterpiece in this vein in *Middlemarch* (1871–2)—the poetic vision has gone, but the massive observation commands respect; all that can be done in the form of realistic fiction is done here. But any attempt to go beyond realism results in fragmentation. It is the attempt to include ideal characters in a naturalistic framework that brings about the disruption of *Felix Holt* (1866) and *Daniel Deronda* (1874–6)—novels whose interest lies away from their titular heroes. The form of *The Prelude* could accommodate heightened perception and short-cuts across narrative; but such advantages were not available to the novelists who were, in some sense, Wordsworth's successors.

It is, then, not too much to suggest that, had *The Prelude* been published when it was written, in 1805, these successors would not have used prose as the medium for their fictions. On the contrary, the weight of narrative would have rested upon verse—as, indeed, had been the case in all previous civilisations. The prose tale has usually been identified with light reading; its rise and decay during the last 150 years as the central medium for fiction has been a divagation. All its greatest achievements—*Wuthering Heights, Moby-Dick, Our Mutual Friend, The Rainbow*—aspire towards the condition of dramatic poetry. But dramatic poetry, for obvious reasons, is not readily accomplished in the form of prose. The failures usually occur at what should be climaxes—intensifications of reality when the prose tale reaches out after a concentration which is essentially unproselike. Ahab's pseudo-Shakespearian soliloquies, for example, coarsen the flexibility of the blank verse which they imitate. Or think of the celebrated Egdon Heath passage in *The Return of the Native* (1878). Prose encourages a plethora of description here: its otiosity has no parallel in the austere treatment of landscape in Hardy's verse. Even *The Rainbow* (1915), tremendous masterpiece though it is, has many pages which are highly patterned in rhythm and heavily charged in imagery, which strive after the power of poetry, and which, in so doing, present insoluble problems to the reader. Ultimately the difficulty is one of density: the eye travels too quickly over the prose to be able to take in the concentration of meaning; the work demands to be read aloud, and, being in prose, affords little guide or opportunity for the reader to do this.

The Prelude, on the other hand, was, so to speak, composed aloud—Wordsworth reciting it on his marches over the hills, dictating it to his sister, and ever afterwards insisting that it should be spoken to an audience. There is an insistent quality of rhythm in *The Prelude* that confirms our feeling that heightened narrative or dramatic poetry cannot be taken in through the eye alone. Consider the great scenes of the 1805 *Prelude*, such as the ones just discussed—these have at once a heightening of rhythm and intensification of vision that is impossible to prose. For prose is a medium where explanations are necessary and where the decisive patterning of rhythm is next to impossible without making heavy demands on the reader. Therefore attempts to go outside the limits of explanation and naturalism are bound to bring about lapses in execution, if not in imagination.

The great narrators of the nineteenth-century wrote prose because there was no way open to them in verse: the crucial documents were suppressed, and it is a credit to them that they used the available tradition as well as they did. But the tradition was, in fact, one near to prose: there are lapses in *Lyrical Ballads* not dissimilar to those which occur in George Eliot, Hardy and Lawrence. Jeffrey pointed out similar lapses in *The Excursion*—insensitively, because he could not put the faults of the poem in perspective. Faults it certainly has, however, and they are largely the faults of prose. For instance, it is noticeable that in *The Excursion* Jeffrey particularly objects to the detail spent upon exploring the character of the old pedlar in Book I, and to the moral drawn at the end of that book.

But it must be remarked that what Jeffrey was reviewing in itself was a revision—one of several attempts Wordsworth made to rewrite what seems to have been his first really great poem, 'The Ruined Cottage'. The earliest draft we have of this dates from January–February 1798, but an even earlier version was read to Coleridge in June 1797; and it seems to have been considerably shorter. One would give a good deal for this original draft, which inspired Coleridge with the conviction that his new friend was the greatest poet of the age; but I think that, to some extent, this can be reconstructed.

It is noticeable that, for all his animadversions upon the rest of *The Excursion*, Jeffrey was favourably disposed towards the account of Margaret and her desertion by her husband—'We must say that there is very considerable pathos in the telling of this simple story.' And there can be no doubt that this is the central core of the poem. My own belief is that the portions to which Jeffrey objected, the Wanderer and the moralising, are accretions upon the original story.

Even the earliest draft we have, that of 1798, has flaws: the story of the Wanderer's life disrupts the narrative. It is, for instance, noticeable that Wordsworth had trouble in inserting the passage which begins 'He from his native hills / Had wandered far'—there are two alternative entries, at l. 59 and l. 264 respectively. This alone would suggest some lack of imaginative connection. But the Wanderer's story also adds a great deal which is immaterial to the plot; and it operates at much lower pressure than the rest of the poem. It is therefore reasonable to suppose that lines 48 to 300, which explain the Wanderer's background and which represent the aspect of the poem which Jeffrey most disliked, are an addendum. Weight is given to this supposition by a textual variant in a transcript which Coleridge made of the end of the earliest draft in 1797. This has the Wanderer addressing Wordsworth as 'Stranger'—which suggests that the Wanderer was, in the first version of the poem, a person unknown to Wordsworth, who would not, therefore have been acquainted with his story. And this is supported by an apparent inconsistency in l. 41 of the 1798 draft—which states that Wordsworth had seen the old man for the first time only the day before. It would seem, then, that the Wanderer is an accretion upon an original which was exclusively concerned with the story of Margaret. Since the process of revision was largely a matter of expanding the moralistic side of the poem, it would seem that it was only from the second draft onward that Wordsworth felt the temptation to build the Wanderer up into a major figure with a story of his own. This is borne out by the fact that each successive revision, between 1798 and 1814, expands the story of the Wanderer and adds a further layer of moralising. A draft of 1799, reprinted by Jonathan Wordsworth in his *Music of Humanity* (1969), separates the two stories but retains a good deal of moralising in each of them and in many ways is verbally inferior. Later the stories were reunited. But certainly the version of 1798 is nearest to the original. Even as we have it, this

'Ruined Cottage' is free of much of the extraneous matter that later accumulated: there is, for instance, nothing to compare with the egregious passage in *The Excursion* which begins 'Oh! many are the poets that are sown / By nature'. And I suppose that the Wanderer (or pedlar, as he is in the earlier version) could be defended as providing a sort of moral equipoise to Margaret—he has wandered far from his home, like her husband, but to some purpose. But ultimately it is to the story of Margaret that we turn; and, if we omit the Wanderer's story from the 1798 draft, what we will be left with is the original 'Ruined Cottage' of 1797. And it is a very great poem indeed.

All the more pity, then, that its publication history has been more chequered even than that of *The Prelude*. The two versions most frequently referred to, both inferior, are Book 1 of *The Excursion*, with all its moralisings, and a sort of cento of various drafts prepared by Arnold for his selection from Wordsworth. Even the 1798 draft, which seems to me more satisfactory than either, is available only in the notes to Volume v of the edition of Wordsworth by Helen Darbishire—who says, grudgingly, that it seems worthwhile to reproduce it *in extenso*!

Successive revisions have made 'The Ruined Cottage' seem more prosaic than it is. It may not have the flash of vivid illumination that characterises *The Prelude*; but it does share with that poem the accurate observation of detail that is *more* than detail—description which reveals a moral vision. In a real sense, Margaret *is* her cottage: as her life is disrupted, her cottage, too, decays. There is nothing occult about this: the gradual deterioration can be accounted for naturalistically. And yet it is more than realistic description—so much more that, when we first encounter the cottage, there is something demoralised about it, almost to the point of anthropomorphism:

> It was a plot
> Of garden ground now wild, its matted weeds
> Marked with the steps of those whom as they passed
> The gooseberry trees that shot in long lank slips
> Or currants hanging from their leafless stems
> In scanty strings had tempted to o'erleap
> The broken wall. . . .

This is the characteristic reaction of an observer. The advantage

of having the poet himself viewing the landscape is that we
do not rest with commentary: the cottage impinges alarmingly
on his uninformed gaze. Margaret's story is all the richer by
being narrated through another dramatised consciousness: that
of the old pedlar, who knows, as the poet does not, the steps
that led to the ruin so vividly set before the spectator's eye;
and the remainder of the poem, after this initial confrontation,
is his retelling of these past circumstances.

The story is a simple one—a family falling upon hard times
and sickness, the woman being deserted by her husband, her
baby dying. But the poem gains in focus through the device
of narrating all this in terms of the cottage. Thus we see, before
the bad times come upon them, a thriving family whose husband
kept the cottage and its grounds in order:

> '. . . They who passed
> At evening from behind the garden fence
> Might hear his busy spade which he would ply
> After his daily work till the day-light
> Was gone, and every leaf and flower were lost
> In the dark hedges. . . .'

But the harvest fails, and the countryside is reduced to destitution
in time of war. In spite of this,

> '. . . Margaret
> Went struggling on through those calamitous years . . . .'

But a fever shatters her husband, and, during his sickness, their
savings are consumed. The husband's labours now assume a disordered, frenetic quality:

> . . . He blended where he might the various tasks
> Of summer, autumn, winter, and of spring. . . .'

From now on, the story acquires a seasonal pattern: we see
only intermittent glimpses of the cottage, on the old pedlar's
infrequent visits to the district. This, however, enables us to
judge the decay of the cottage, and of the family; we see the
various stages of dissolution. The pedlar next comes by in early
spring:

> '. . . . At the door arrived
> I knocked, and when I entered with the hope
> Of usual greeting Margaret looked at me
> A little while, then turned her head away
> Speechless, and sitting down upon a chair
> Wept bitterly. . . .'

The action is as graphic as that of a stage play. Her husband has deserted her; but she is courageous, and attempts to carry on his work as well as her own:

> '. . . We parted. It was then the early spring;
> I left her busy with her garden tools . . . .'

But a family deprived of its head cannot keep order for long; and, on his next visit, in the 'wane of summer', though all appears much the same, the pedlar notices signs of decay:

> '. . . Her cottage in its outward look appeared
> As cheerful as before; in any show
> Of neatness little changed, but that I thought
> The honeysuckle crowded round the door
> And from the wall hung down in heavier loads . . . .
> The unprofitable bindweed spread his bells
> From side to side, and with unwieldy wreaths
> Had dragged the rose from its sustaining wall
> And bent it down to earth. . . .'

The detail is not only sharp and accurate, but, in my sense of the term, 'significant'. Margaret herself is bowed with grief, now that she is unprotected. Just as her cottage and garden are neglected, out of order, so she spends her time wandering without purpose while her child cries, neglected in the cottage. The pedlar does what he can, but the case is hopeless:

> '. . . I left her then
> With the best hope and comfort I could give.
> She thanked me for my will, but for my hope
> It seemed she did not thank me. . . .'

The grim irony of the phrasing acts out the starkness of the facts: there is no future for this woman. And, indeed, when the pedlar next returns, on the earliest day of spring, the decay is far advanced:

> '. . . her house
> Bespoke a sleepy hand of negligence. . . .
>   Of her herbs and flowers
> It seemed the better part were gnawed away
> Or trampled on the earth; a chain of straw
> Which had been twisted round the tender stem
> Of a young apple-tree lay at its root,
> The bark was nibbled round by truant sheep.
> Margaret stood near, her infant in her arms
> And seeing that my eye was on the tree
> She said, "I fear it will be dead and gone
> Ere Robert come again!" . . .'

We hardly need the explicit identification of tree and child: both are deprived of the bond that might have sustained them, both are eroded by suffering. Except for her baby, and her little boy now apprenticed away from her, Margaret has no wish to live; and 'many seasons pass' before the pedlar returns to these parts. By that time, Margaret, who has been retreating as a character right through the poem, is dead; and we learn of her fate only through hearsay, without even the personal observation of the pedlar. Apparently, towards the end, she no longer even had the heart to wander:

> '. . . Master, I have heard,
> That in that broken arbour she would sit
> The idle length of half a sabbath day
> There—where you see the toadstool's lazy head . . . .
>   Seest thou that path?
> The greensward now has broken its grey line:
> There to and fro she paced through many a day
> Of the warm summer . . . .'

Margaret's life has been encroached upon, just as the fungus has reared its head in the garden or the path has been partly obliterated by the greensward:

> '. . . Meanwhile her poor hut
> Sank to decay, for he was gone, whose hand
> At the first nippings of October frost
> Closed up each chink, and with fresh bands of straw
> Chequered the green-grown thatch. . . .'

We have reached, in the history of the cottage, the point at which the poet first came across it—sapped by frost and rain, open to the wind:

> '. . . and, stranger, here
> In sickness she remained, and here she died,
> Last human tenant of these ruined walls.'

The graphic simplicity is characteristic and supreme: no embellishing metaphors are required here. The observed facts speak for themselves and beyond themselves, out to the human situation of which they are a dramatic summary.

'The Ruined Cottage' is, in one sense, richer than 'Michael', since it has the colouring of the intermediaries, Wordsworth and the pedlar: the narrative is seen through the dramatised consciousness of two spectators with varying degrees of dramatic involvement.

Nothing of this kind transmutes the austerity of 'Michael' (1800). This poem stands at the ultimate reach of Wordsworth's art, the reduction of all variousness of human experience to a stark simplicity. No further development could be imagined; and none came.

In plot, the poem is not dissimilar to 'The Ruined Cottage': a story of loss and desertion, no doubt drawing for its raw material upon what Wordsworth could envisage of the abandoned Annette Vallon, and feeding upon the root of his helpless remorse. At the same time, the situation in 'Michael' is set at a distance, and one might have guessed that an equipoise savouring of quietism was impending.

This is not to criticise the poem, though, which is surely the most flawless piece of work Wordsworth ever accomplished. It was certainly the most easily composed; alone among the great masterpieces it is not bedevilled with variant texts, endless revisions and needless addenda.

Like 'The Ruined Cottage', the poem begins, ends and is centred upon a 'significant object':

> Beside the brook
> There is a straggling heap of unhewn stones!
> And to that place a story appertains . . . .

The story is, massively, Michael's; and, in a sense, it is an example against what's thought to be Wordsworth's general belief in the fortifying influence of nature. This is a man superbly in tune with his environment:

> Hence had he learned the meaning of all winds,
> Of blasts of every tone . . . .
>   he had been alone
> Amid the heart of many thousand mists
> That came to him and left him on the heights. . . .

Unusual self-reliance, great bodily strength—these are the keynotes of Michael's presentation, struck again and again throughout. The poem, in other words, even more than 'The Ruined Cottage', is concerned to show what happens when phenomenal courage and physique are sapped by adversity.

And more even than with Margaret and her family is the positive cycle of Michael's life built up—his labouring with his young son, his helping his wife after the day's work in the field is over. The 'positive' is reinforced by the light from the cottage which beams out over the valley and gives the cottage its affectionate name, 'The Evening Star'. This is an emblem of regularity, constancy, industry:

> The light was famous in its neighbourhood,
> And was a public Symbol of the life
> The thrifty Pair had lived.

The integration which Michael has achieved did not come about by chance; it has been hard-won. We are told that the fields he owns were burdened with debt when they came to him, and that the root of his industry lay in his efforts to clear them.

But in old age disaster overtakes him. A surety which the

shepherd had given for his nephew has been broken, and the
forfeit amounts to half his substance:

> This unlooked-for claim
> At the first hearing, for a moment took
> More hope out of his life than he supposed
> That any old man ever could have lost.

It seems that some of the fields must be sold. But this he
cannot endure; and perhaps his sorrow is mistaken:

> '. . . yet if these fields of ours
> Should pass into a Stranger's hand, I think
> That I could not lie quiet in my grave. . . .'

So, in a sense, he sacrifices, instead of the fields, his son—who
is sent away to the city to make his fortune:

> '. . . Our Luke shall leave us, Isabel; the land
> Shall not go from us . . . .'

This is tenacity gone wrong; yet Michael is not merely miserly.
He is trying to leave the land to Luke as unencumbered 'as
is the wind / That passes over it'. And, in a kind of guarantee
of co-operation, the boy lays the first stone of a sheep·fold
which the old man had been intending to build with him.

Unluckily, the boy goes to the bad; the episode is treated
perfunctorily, as befits a report from 'the dissolute city'. Once
torn up from his environment, Luke has no real identity, and
eventually loses himself 'beyond the seas'.

As with Margaret, so with Michael: the body appears to endure
while the mind is broken. His routine, in outward appearance,
looks much the same:

> Among the rocks
> He went, and still looked up upon the sun,
> And listened to the wind . . . .

But the 'significant object' is the sheep fold, that emblem of
co-operation. He goes, indeed, to the fold; but it is never built:

> and 'tis believed by all
> That many and many a day he thither went,
> And never lifted up a single stone.

This justly admired master-stroke suggests the breaking of a spring: there is no purpose in the old man's life now his son has gone. His life, like that of Margaret, has been encroached upon; and, as in 'The Ruined Cottage', all that is left to the beholder is the wreck of Michael's hope:

> the remains
> Of the unfinished Sheep-fold may be seen
> Beside the boisterous brook of Green-head Gill.

The brook and the winds sweep through the poem: it is only humanity, anchored to its small inheritance and material possessions, that is beaten down; and human works along with it.

This lofty subject is matched by its style, which is very much that of the Authorised Version; indeed, as H. A. Mason has demonstrated (in *Delta*, 1963) a few alterations would serve to give one the exact rhythm and accent of the Bible. Mr Mason feels that behind the poem stands the Book of Ruth; for me the sustaining inspiration seems to be the Sacrifice of Isaac.

Just for once, however, Wordsworth was not impelled to alleviate the grimness of the poem with a patched-on moral. There are some verbal differences between the text as it appears in the Collected Poems and that first published in *Lyrical Ballads*—the latter is preferable. But, in the main, it seems that this was a poem Wordsworth was prepared to stand by.

However, it is not surprising that its influence has been mainly upon prose, since the austerity of the style derives from a prose inspiration. The same may be true of the influence of 'The Ruined Cottage'; though, since this was circulated only in adulterated versions, it is hard to be sure.

Influence apart, however, there can be no doubt that the poems I have discussed brought something new into literature. They show, for instance, a handling of narrative vastly superior to anything since Shakespeare and the medieval poets; and an aspect of narrative unknown even to these great narrators—the concentration upon a single experience until all its implications are drawn out of it. In many respects, these poems unite the virtues of prose and poetry—clarity and definition on the one hand, emotional heightening and dramatic rhythm on the other. The supremacy of these poems, however, should not be taken as a denial of the presence in Wordsworth's work of several other major works: 'The Leech Gatherer' (1802) and 'Tintern Abbey' (1798), for example. But the first is flawed by its discursive beginning and a jaunty moral at the end, not unlike that tacked on to 'The Ruined Cottage' in later versions. And 'Tintern Abbey' is rendered highly ambiguous by its absence of discernible plot. I should push F. W. Bateson's reading in his book on Wordsworth (1954) rather further than he does, and say that it is a love poem written to his sister Dorothy by Wordsworth—who, rather disquieteningly, identifies himself with the mountain winds blowing against her. But both 'The Leech Gatherer' and 'Tintern Abbey' are considerable works, even if they do not represent Wordsworth at his greatest.

There are, moreover, a fair number of really good secondary pieces—few of which have been given the attention they deserve. Some of them are overflows from other poems; and I should instance the passage about the three knots of fir-trees (1798), in rhythm and manner akin to *The Prelude*, which may be found in Volume V of de Selincourt's edition (Appendix B, No. III); or the enchanting account of a boy playing in the snow (1798), which may have been intended for 'Michael' (Vol. II, Notes, p. 480). More familiar will be the delicate nature-pieces, which are at their best when associated with Dorothy Wordsworth: 'Nutting' (1798), for example, and the 'Poems on the Naming of Places' (1800)—especially No. IV, with its unforgettable picture of the sick peasant. This last is one of many straight descriptions of rustic and vagrant life, such as 'Old Man Travelling' and 'The Old Cumberland Beggar' from *Lyrical Ballads*, and 'Beggars' from the far inferior *Poems* of 1807. These have a good deal in common with Crabbe and Clare, but would hardly convert one to Wordsworth without the backing of the greater poems.

It seems to me that a critic must put his cards on the table and say what the poet he is writing about has achieved and what his greatest poems are. It is an astonishing fact that, in all the work that has been produced on Wordsworth, no one has ever come out unequivocally and done this.

The anthologies assure us that it is the minor poems—especially those from the collection of 1807—that keep Wordsworth alive.

Let me, then, finish by reiterating my opening contention: Wordsworth is a narrative poet, more mythopoeic than Crabbe, more concentrated than Byron, with more human interest than Keats or Shelley, and fewer eccentricities than Coleridge. He has not the urbanity or deep insight of Chaucer, nor the dramatic power of Shakespeare; but his handling of narrative is manifestly superior to that of Milton and he is less fragmented than Dryden or Pope. His finest work reflects the focus of concentration upon a single situation so as to bring out all its implications. Work of this order may be found in the earlier version of *The Prelude*, especially in the episodes of the Stolen Boat, the Ice Skater, the Discharged Soldier, the Mouldered Gibbet, and the Ascent of Snowdon; in the earliest extant version of 'The Ruined Cottage'; and in 'Michael', as it appears in *Lyrical Ballads*.

In many ways, Wordsworth deserves to be termed the first modern poet; partly because he was the first to be badly out of step with his time, but mainly because he placed enormous reliance upon his perceptions as an individual. The arresting, static quality of his figures is paralleled only by the extraordinary way in which they seem to develop under his unwavering gaze. Wordsworth's power to create fictions such as these seems to me equal to that of any of the great novelists, and he is less flawed, in his actual narrative, than they are. He has access to a heightened speech which is impossible to prose. Because of this, Wordsworth seems to me, as no novelist is, indefinitely re-readable.

8 The Romantic Dichotomy

The critics show none of their usual caution in defining the romanticism of Romantic poets. On the contrary, we are liable to be overwhelmed by the consensus about the links that bind together poets as seemingly disparate as Blake, Coleridge, Shelley and Keats. 'The internal made external' says M. H. Abrams (*The Mirror and the Lamp*, 1953), following not so far behind A. W. Schlegel's definition of 1801 (*Vorlesungen über schöne Literatur*). It was, said Logan Pearsall Smith, a new conception of the artist as genius, above the law and given to strange fits of passion (*Words and Idioms*, 1921). By the time Edmund Wilson came to write *Axel's Castle* in 1931, the definition had become generally accepted: 'Romanticism, as everyone has heard, was a revolt of the individual.' But definitions have continued to pour in, monotonous in their congruity:

> The romantic principle asserts that form is an organic event, proceeding from the intuitive experience of the artist
> > (Herbert Read, *The True Voice of Feeling*, 1953)

> For the Romantics ... belief in the imagination was part of the contemporary belief in the individual self
> > (Maurice Bowra, *The Romantic Imagination*, 1950)

> The whole nature of 'romanticism' itself was determined by a stress on the individuality, the uniqueness, of an individual poet himself. (W. W. Robson, *Critical Essays*, 1967)

With the possible exception of Logan Pearsall Smith, the critics do not seem to realise how damaging to the poets their definitions are. If a writer is not to take account of tradition, society or his audience, he is cutting himself off from much that could usefully determine the growth of his individual sensibility. The words 'originality' and 'genius', which lope at the heels of the Romantic poet, suggest that he is expected to spin fictions out of his own intestines. Since this is impossible without some external help, the chances are that he will go to the first books to come to hand and imitate them, in haste, with little understanding and not much more technique.

In effect, this is what happened. No one is going to accuse the Romantics of disciplined reading or firm grasp of texts. Their fits of passion are characterised by improvisation, guesswork and incipient hysteria, often bordering on self-pity. This seems all the more damaging when one considers that, like many people whose reading is inadequate, the Romantics set themselves up as instructors of mankind. The situation seems even worse if we reflect that they forsook their own real lyric gifts in doing so.

Let us take as an instance a precursor of Romanticism with a mind more disciplined than most: Thomas Gray, elegist, melancholiac, and professor of Modern History at Cambridge. We shall not find in him many of the virtues of his predecessors. But one thing he shared in common with Milton and Dryden was a sound classical education, and to this we owe the 'Elegy Written in a Country Churchyard' (1746–50). Like many later Romantic productions, this is so far from being 'original' as to consist of a tissue of references, presumably to Gray's favourite books. And so far from being 'individual', it is a weak grasp on the actual that renders Gray capable from time to time of writing nonsense, though in a mellifluous way. Consider, for example, the most famous stanza in this very famous work:

> Full many a gem of purest ray serene
> The dark unfathomed caves of ocean bear:
> Full many a flower is born to blush unseen,
> And waste its sweetness on the desert air.

Successive editors of Gray, all the way up to the indefatigable Mr Lonsdale, have been sedulous in their search for sources. The following, at least, seem justified:

There is many a rich stone laid up in the bowels of the
earth, many a fair pearl in the bosom of the sea, that never
was seen, nor never shall be
                            (Joseph Hall, *Contemplations*, 1612–26)

    Like beauteous flowers which vainly waste the scent
    Of odours in unhaunted deserts
                            (William Chamberlayne, *Pharonnida*, c. 1644, IV v)

    There kept my Charms concealed from mortal Eye
    Like Roses that in Deserts bloom and die.
                            (Pope, *The Rape of the Lock*, 1711, II)

But the closest source, it seems to me, is an Italian canzone
by the sixteenth-century poet, Celio Magno:

    Ma (qual in parte ignota
    Ben ricca gemma altrui cela in suo pregio,
    O fior, ch'alta virtù ha in se riposta
    Visse in sen di castità nascosta,)
    In sua virtute e'n Dio contento visse,
    Lunge dal visco mondan, che l'alma intrica.
    ('Chi di l'agrime un fiurne a gli occhi presta', *ante* 1602)

    (But, as in an unknown place
    A very rich gem conceals its value from its neighbour,
    Or a Flower, which has great virtue reposed in it,
    Has lived hidden in the bosom of chastity,
    He lived content in his virtue and in God
    Far from the worldly birdlime which entangles the soul.)

Gray's version is more Romantic than any of these, and therein
lies his downfall. The Italian poet is concerned to keep a potentially
dangerous image at a distance. It exists not in its own right,
but as an illustration to a theme—in this case, an account of
an Horatian figure content to live with his virtues and his God
far away from the entanglements of the world. But Gray does
his best to bring the individual image into life; unfortunately,
he has neither the understanding nor the experience with which
to do this.

Full many a gem of purest ray serene
The dark unfathomed caves of ocean bear . . . .

How can a gem emit any kind of a ray if denied access to an original light-source? Where, in these 'dark unfathomed caves', is the light that it can reflect?

Full many a flower is born to blush unseen
And waste its sweetness on the desert air.

What kind of flower is it that blooms all by itself in the desert? How is it fertilised, how watered? The image dies for want of exact detail. We are reminded of the naturalist Gray, whose main researches consisted of annotating Linnaeus and who sent his friend Wharton reports upon the progress of the crops from the comparative comfort of his sickbed. The scholarship for which Gray was renowned, and which left so few tangible results, prefigured Coleridge's reputation for erudition and that of Shelley for scientific insight.

To rely upon such phantasms as genius and originality is to fall victim to any *ignis fatuus* that comes flickering through one's mind. But at least Gray had read systematically in his youth. The same cannot be said of Blake, who refused to go to school on the grounds that he couldn't stand the discipline. About the work of this poet—immensely gifted though he was—two theories are tenable. One is that, after the death of his brother Robert, his memory became dangerously out of control, so that, when he thought he was writing from intuition, he was in fact recalling the books of mystical philosophy he had ransacked in earlier years. The other theory is that, starved of experience, knowledge and subject-matter, Blake went in cold blood to these same philosophers and versified them, more or less clumsily, into what we now know as the prophetic books. I will leave the probabilities for the Intentionalists to sort out. What concerns the reader is that for most of his life Blake was producing masses of obscurity which generations of scholars have attempted, with varying degrees of success, to explain. We are all indebted to the researches of Foster Damon (*William Blake*, 1924) Kathleen Raine (*Blake and Tradition*, 1969) and George Mills Harper (*The Neoplatonism of William Blake*, 1961), but it is necessary to suggest that the discovery of a probable source is not identical with the interpretation of an achieved effect. Blake is the archetypal Romantic who let go of a lyric gift in favour of didacticism and pseudo-prophecy. The early lyrics are at once sombre and fresh, like those of Shakespeare, from whom the young Blake learned so much. Even when there is a source readily ascertainable for one of the *Songs of Experience* (1794), the arcane knowledge never drowns out the meaning:

> Ah, Sun-flower! weary of time,
> Who countest the steps of the Sun,
> Seeking after that sweet golden clime
> Where the traveller's journey is done:
>
> Where the Youth pined away with desire,
> And the pale Virgin shrouded in snow
> Arise from their graves, and aspire
> Where my Sun-flower wishes to go.

Desire is killed in this chilly world, and the sun-flower is an aspiration after a paradise where labour is ended and love can begin. It is a simple-minded attitude, fitted for a short lyric, and I do not see how it could be faulted. There is a sharpness in the verbs—'*pined away* with desire', '*shrouded* in snow'—which carries, as Gray's sand-flowers don't, a sense of immediacy. The fact that the poem has an ascertainable prose source does not damage it. It doesn't help us much either. What it shows is that the young Blake was capable of separating usable material from dross, and drawing an image from Proclus out of the convoluted prose of his translator, Thomas Taylor, and putting it into economical and rhythmically striking verse. In a massive quotation about similitude in nature, Blake hit upon this:

> For how shall we account for those plants called heliotropes, that is attendants on the sun, moving in correspondence with the revolution of its orb? ... Hence the sunflower, as far as it is able, moves in a circular dance towards the sun; so that if any one could hear the pulsation made by its circuit in the air, he would perceive something composed by a sound of this kind, in honour of its king, such as a plant is capable of framing.

(Thomas Taylor, Introduction to the *Hymns of Orpheus*, 1792)

The poem gives us the perception and spares us the mystical hypothesising and neo-Platonic cant of its source. This is adaptation, certainly, but creative adaptation by a mind in possession of its experience. Unfortunately, poems of this order are rare in Blake and come very early. To build upon a lyric gift, more than a good ear is necessary: more, even, than a sense of relevance. The poet requires an idea of tradition and an understanding of the craft he professes. Blake never underwent any course of study that could compensate for his lack of schooling. For a man so interested in the philosophy of the past his ignorance of Greek and Latin was limiting, to say the least of it. Blake's reading fell into three areas; one might almost say three periods, except that each came to overlie the other. At first he was an ardent disciple of Swedenborg; later he went to the Neo-Platonists as translated by Thomas Taylor; later still he took up with the writings of such crypto-alchemical philosophers as Paracelsus and Boehme—also in unsatisfactory translation. The result of seeking to absorb marginal and incompatible philosophies was an incoherence that grew in his work to the extremes of incomprehensibility.

It is certainly possible, if one is scholar enough, with the right books at one's elbow and some knowledge of the author's method of symbolism, to draw out a concept of Blake's intention in the prophetic book *Milton* (1804–8). Whether it is worth the effort is another matter. Basically, there are three elements of narrative competing for attention. One is the conflict between Blake and his patron, Hayley; another is the descent to earth of Milton in an attempt to rectify his errors about sexuality in *Paradise Lost*; a third consists of material incorporated from *The Four Zoas* (1795–1804) regarding Blake's vision of the universe and its creation. There is nothing much to bind these elements together, apart from a loose form resembling the rhythms adopted by James Macpherson for his spurious translations from the legendary poet Ossian (1765). The characters of the poem further confuse the issue by fluctuating in a fashion highly arbitrary. Thus Blake appears as Palambron (Pity) as well as in his own person; while Hayley appears as Satan and in the end—contradicting what of Blake's mythology can be deduced from the other prophetic books—is identified as Urizen, the rational god or demiurge. The poem, claims Blake, was written with great ease, from immediate dictation, twenty or thirty lines at a time. This may be, but the rhetoric of the verse creaks beneath a great weight of allusion. When Milton descends to earth he is condemning himself to death just as much as Persephone (cf. *The Book of Thel*, 1789) descending into the underworld. But he leaves his shadow, or finer being, with seven angels (Revelation 5:6) in the land of Beulah (see *Pilgrim's Progress*, 1676–8, towards the end of Part I):

> As when a man dreams he reflects not that his body
>   sleeps,
> Else he would wake, so seemed he entering his Shadow:
>   but
> With him the Spirits of the Seven Angels of the Presence
> Entering, they gave him still perceptions of his Sleeping
>   Body
> Which now rose and walked with them in Eden, as an
>   Eighth
> Image Divine though darkened and though walking as
>   one walks
> In sleep, and the Seven comforted him and supported
>   him. . . .

This derives in verbal formulation from a passage in Swedenborg, one of a series of experimental cases seeking to demonstrate that man is really a spirit. The translation—Blake never knew the original Latin—is by Thomas Hartley:

> A man is brought into a middle state betwixt sleeping and waking, during which he knows no other than that he is perfectly awake, forasmuch as all his senses are as lively as ever, his sight, his hearing, and what appears still more strange, even his feeling; nay, this last is at such a time more exquisite than at others. In this state I have seen angels and spirits to the life, have heard them speak, and, what would be thought still more wonderful, have touched them, though the material body then bore no part therein. . . .
>
> (*Heaven and Hell*, 1758, translated 1778, para. 440)

But I cannot see that Blake's verse is an advance on this prose, whether one takes it as Swedenborg or Hartley. The passage from *Milton* is cumbered with featureless monosyllables that are made to take an undue weight of explanation—'*else* would he

wait, *so* seemed he'—and this holds up the narrative while Blake
gets this particular meditation off his chest. Still less can *Milton*
be said to constitute an improvement on Beulah as seen by
John Bunyan:

> In this country the Sun shineth night and day; wherefore
> this was beyond the valley of the *Shadow of Death*, and also
> out of the reach of Giant *Despair*, neither could they from
> this place so much as see *Doubting-Castle*. . . .

The allegorical entities in Bunyan would be precise components
of a narrative, even if one had no prior acquaintance with Giant
Despair and Doubting-Castle. However, at the beginning of the
second and last book of *Milton*, Blake manages to draw a few
of his various threads together. He repeats, in an improved version,
his vision of Beulah:

> It is a pleasant lovely Shadow
> Where no dispute can come, Because of those who Sleep.
> Into this place the Sons and Daughters of Ololon descended
> With solemn mourning, into Beulah's moony shades and
>   hills
> Weeping for Milton . . . .

It is, still, more cumbered with abstractions than Bunyan, but
what becomes clear is that Milton has learned wisdom. Ololon
is an emanation of Milton's wives and daughters, and, in learning
about them, he has discovered the truth about the opposite sex.
Characteristically, for a Romantic poet, this takes form as a
vision of nature, and it certainly is the most striking passage
in the prophetic book, looked at as poetry:

> Thou hearest the Nightingale begin the Song of Spring.
> The Lark sitting upon his earthy bed, just as the morn
> Appears, listens silent; then springing from the waving
>   Cornfield, loud
> He leads the Choir of Day: trill, trill, trill, trill,
> Mounting upon the wings of light into the Great Expanse,
> Re-echoing against the lovely blue and shining heavenly
>   Shell,
> His little throat labours with inspiration . . . .

This shows that the young lyricist had not altogether died in the middle-aged prophet. But we may be puzzled to see how this ties in with the understanding of women that is to prove Milton's salvation. The passage would be effective, by itself, as a lyric—anticipating Whitman, let's say. But, as an integral part of the poem, it raises more difficulties than it resolves.

This is the trouble with the prophetic books if one attempts to take them as works of art. *The Four Zoas* is best read bearing in mind the story of Cupid and Psyche, as told by Apuleius and translated by Adlington (1566). But in fact it is an anthology of ruinous adaptations from Blake's early lyrics: one can trace lineaments of 'The Sick Rose', 'A Poison Tree', 'The Chapel of Gold', 'Auguries of Innocence' as one reads on. Moreover, this particular prophetic book has little independent existence, since Blake lifted entire portions of it to be reworked into *Milton* and *Jerusalem* (1804–20). That latter book occupied him until his death, and it is even more long-winded and arbitrary than the others. Even the place-names with which it is belarded relate not to geographical location but to private associations in Blake's mind. Whatever their merits—and there are some striking incidentals, especially in the earlier ones—the prophetic books represent nothing so much as a Pyrrhic victory of Blake's will over his talent.

Words like 'genius' and 'originality' have been freely applied to Blake. And it is true that he had little regard for logic and reason. Bacon, Locke and Newton, in particular, are explicitly denounced many times throughout his work. Yet on various occasions he found them a useful quarry. The inquisitive reader will find notable parallels between Locke's *Essay Concerning Human Understanding* (1671–89, II xxiii 13) and Bromion's speech about extrasensory perception in *Visions of the Daughters of Albion* (1793). And the angels' description in *Milton*, Book II, of those combined under the tyranny of Satan owes a good deal to the translation of the *Principia* (1687) as undertaken by Andrew Motte (1729, Book III, General Scholium). But the use made of these admirable sources is characteristically Romantic: an impressionist's lifting of the odd charismatic phrase rather than an attempt to understand the great empiricist philosophy that, almost as much as English poetry, is a glory of our letters. I cannot see how being unable to think clearly is an advantage. Repeatedly Blake claimed to write under inspiration. But what comes through is recollection, deliberate or haphazard, of philosophers, mostly bad, in translations mostly indifferent.

It is uncritical to take the Romantic afflatus on trust. As the researches of Anna von Helmholtz (*Bulletin of the University of Wisconsin*, 1907), Joseph Warren Beach (*ELH*, 1942), and, latterly, Norman Fruman (*The Damaged Archangel*, 1971) have shown, the inspiration of Coleridge was no more divine than that of Blake. 'No work of true genius dares want its appropriate form' proclaims Coleridge, defining an organicist theory of the arts. But that very statement is a straight lift from Schlegel's *Vorlesungen über dramatische Kunst und Literatur* (1811): 'Formlos zu sein darf also den Werken des Genius auf keine Weise gestattet werden' wrote this great critic, whom only English insularity prevents our seeing as a pioneer ('The works of genius cannot therefore be permitted to be without form; but of this there is no danger'). There is not much in the literary theory of Coleridge that cannot be found, better expressed, in Schlegel, Schelling, Fichte. Even while proclaiming his celebrated account of Imagination—a favourite word among Romantics—Coleridge drew upon another pioneer, Professor Arthur Browne of Trinity College, Dublin, whose essay 'Fancy and Imagination' appears in his *Miscellaneous Sketches* of 1798. Occasional poems such as 'Mutual Passion' or 'A Farewell to Love' prove to be not as occasional as all that, being recast from Ben Jonson and Fulke Greville. Even the anthology piece 'Lewti' was adapted from an early poem by Wordsworth, not noticeably to its advantage:

> As these two swans together ride
> Upon the gently swelling tide
> > ('Beauty and Moonlight', 1786)

> As these white swans together heave
> On the gently swelling wave.   ('Lewti', 1798)

Coleridge has been given the benefit of too many doubts. His flashing eyes and floating hair owe more to the lamp than to inward vision. I doubt whether much time would have been spent in reading 'Kubla Khan' (1798) if it had not been for the anecdote that supports it. Everyone knows, or thinks that he knows, how Coleridge fell asleep in a lonely farmhouse over a passage in *Purchas his Pilgrimage* (1617). It is common knowledge that the author composed 300 lines based upon this passage in his sleep. The fact that we have only fifty-four of them is explained by Coleridge being interrupted in the act of copying them out by a person on business from Porlock. The anecdote, all things considered, is nearly as remarkable as the poem. But Norman Fruman, in *The Damaged Archangel*, has raised some awkward questions. What was *Purchas his Pilgrimage*—a rare folio of some thousand pages—doing in a lonely farmhouse? Surely Coleridge hadn't carried it there under his arm? How did the person from Porlock know of Coleridge's presence in those parts? What business could it be that he came to discuss with Coleridge— Coleridge, the most unbusinesslike of people? In brief, the testimony on behalf of the genesis of 'Kubla Khan' derives from one source, Coleridge himself, and his notorious unreliability on other biographical matters hardly disposes us to credulity regarding this one.

Since that time, drafts of the poem—notably the Crewe manuscript—have been discovered, and its apparent spontaneity is one of the more agreeable aspects of its author's technique. But his technique is not sufficient to disguise the poem's jerkiness of form and exiguity of content. The main effect of the Porlock story is to allow the poem to be overrated by those who prefer biography to criticism. Extraordinary lines it certainly has:

> A savage place! as holy and enchanted
> As e'er beneath a waning moon was haunted
> By woman wailing for her demon-lover! . . .

However, they are very obscure. John Livingston Lowes in the energetic source-hunting of *The Road to Xanadu* (1927) showed us whence they derive; so did Norman Fruman:

> 'Strates,' said I . . . 'remember the water is inchanted . . .'
> (James Bruce, *Travels to Discover the Source of the Nile*, 1790)

> All Cashmere is holy land
>   (James Rennell, *Memoir of a Map of Hindoostan*, 1793)

> Where, near the fountain, something like despair
> Made, of that weeping willow, garlands for her hair.

. . . 'Why dost thou weep, thou gentle maid?'
(Lamb, 'A Vision of Repentance', 1797)

Or o'er some haunted stream with fond delay,
Round an holy calm diffusing
(Collins, 'The Passions', 1746)

They had not sailed a league, a league,
A league but barely three,
Until she espied his cloven hoof
And she wept right bitterly.
(Anon., 'The Demon Lover', ? 17th century)

On this showing, it would appear that 'Kubla Khan' was put
together from the books and poems Coleridge happened to have
around him—Lamb's manuscript arrived on 15 April 1797—and
put together not very coherently at that. Kubla disappears until
the end of the second section, and the third section has little
to do with anything that has gone before. The Abyssinian maid,
in particular, may come out of Bruce's *Travels to the Nile* or
Purchas his Pilgrimage itself, but has no necessary connection with
the overall narrative. Indeed, once we start looking at the poem
as narrative rather than opium dream, even the word 'narrative'
seems to be an overstatement. 'Kubla Khan' is best taken as
a by-product from Coleridge's real masterpiece, 'The Ancient
Mariner' (1797).

This poem seems to have been written in response to a challenge
from Wordsworth. At any rate, it was he who sent Coleridge
to Shelvocke's *Voyages* (1726), in which there was a fine description
of the albatross seen by sailors around Cape Horn. Wordsworth
also seems to have supplied Coleridge with the essentials of
his plot (Notes dictated to Isabella Fenwick, 1843, reprinted in
de Selincourt's edition of Wordsworth, 1940, Vol. V): all witnesses
agree he told his friend that one of the sailors had killed the
albatross and suggested that in the poem he should suffer from
the tutelary spirit of the region as a result. Even the persona
of the Ancient Mariner owes something to Wordsworth's preoccupation with loneliness and old age. One is reminded of such
characters as the old sailor of the 'Gothic Fragment' and the
aged man in 'Guilt and Sorrow'—both of which come very
early. Indeed, 'The Rime of the Ancient Mariner' was actually

begun as a joint venture on a walk over the Quantock Hills. But Wordsworth saw that his style and that of Coleridge would never match, and left Coleridge to complete the tale himself, rather to the latter's embarrassment. For this was a subject that, quite literally, Coleridge knew nothing about. He had never even been on board a ship, let alone made a voyage to the exotic climes of his poem. Neither did he know anything about the practice and superstition of mariners. As R. C. Bald suggests (*Nineteenth Century Studies*, 1940), the evidence of Coleridge's notebooks indicates that *Purchas his Pilgrimage*, Captain Cook, James Bruce and the *Philosophical Transactions of the Royal Society* were all pressed into service to fill the abyss from which the poem was born.

But the abyss was not infertile. For one thing, Coleridge had read Percy's *Reliques of Ancient English Poetry* (1765) with a more than ordinarily acute ear. The result was a version of the ballad form decidedly more varied than its original. For another, the situation of the chief character was in essentials, though not in incidentals, that of the author himself:

> O Wedding-Guest! this soul hath been
> Alone on a wide wide sea . . . .

Those who have had contact with depressive illness will experience a thrill of recognition. This is the sea as metaphor. The aspect of the theme that comes uppermost is the gap between a crime committed and a penalty exacted. No doubt the Ancient Mariner was wrong to kill the albatross, but does he deserve what follows: isolation from his fellow-men? In this figure, derived from the poems of Wordsworth though he be, Coleridge found a correlative for the guilt that he himself poured out in endless letters and notebooks. 'Intolerable images of horror,' he wrote to his brother three years before the Ancient Mariner set sail, 'they haunt my sleep—they enfever my dreams!' What we have in this poem is a dramatic presentation of guilt through the medium of the ballad form and the detail picked up from travel books. The detail, in a sense, pre-exists the poem:

> the sea thereby being replenished with severall sorts of gellies and forms of Serpents, Adders and Snakes, Greene, Yellow, Blacke, White, and some partie-coloured, whereof many had

life   (Purchas, 1617 quoting Sir Richard Hawkins, 1593)

when they swim in the Water they hold their Legs together, and so they row along
        (Martens, *Voyage to Spitzbergen and Greenland*, 1694)

some small sea animals were swimming about ... that had a white, or shining appearance   (Cook, *Voyages,* 1771)

sea [that] seemed covered with a kind of slime   (*ibid.*)

the Water of the Sea looked like Oil
        (Father Gorée, quoted in the *Philosophical Transactions of the Royal Society*, Jones's Abridgment, Vol. V, pt. ii)

—all of which gets synthesised into a scene of nauseating disgust:

> The very deep did rot: O Christ!
> That ever this should be!
> Yea, slimy things did crawl with legs
> Upon the slimy sea.
>
> About, about, in reel and rout
> The death-fires danced at night;
> The water, like a witch's oils,
> Burnt green, and blue and white.

This did not come from the deep well of the subconscious posited by Livingston Lowes; rather it is a result of a frenzied hunt through a miscellaneous range of books borrowed from friends and from the Bristol Library to enable a poem on an alien theme to get done in time. But the psychic need of the man was such as to isolate and pick out these images of colourful loathing. And yet, seeing the water-snakes:

> Within the shadow of the ship
> I watched their rich attire:
> Blue, glossy green, and velvet black,
> They coiled and swam; and every track
> Was a flash of golden fire.

> O happy living things! no tongue
> Their beauty might declare:
> A spring of love gushed from my heart,
> And I blessed them unaware:
> Sure my kind saint took pity on me,
> And I blessed them unaware.
>
> The self-same moment I could pray . . . .

In learning to appreciate the colour and life of the water-snakes, he learns to forgive himself; and his guilt—in the person of the albatross—falls off and sinks 'Like lead into the sea'.

The poem itself is a therapy: like the Mariner, Coleridge had a compulsive urge to tell *his* story, but was never able to write anything of this order again. The whole poem has a Romantic fortuitousness: what we are given is a dramatic presentation of guilt, not any real understanding. Because of this, Coleridge was unable to build upon the poem. There are many sharp images in the poetic fragments, the letters, the notebooks:

> The reed roofed village still bepatched with snow
> Smoked in the sun-thaw   (1798)

> Farmhouses that at anchor seemed—in the inland sky
> The fog-transfixing Spires   (1828)

> a hollow, unquiet and changeful between the waters/water with glassy wrinkles, water with a thousand wrinkles all lengthways, water all puckered and all over dimples (1803)

> such wild play with meteoric lights ... which they made rebound in sparkles or dispand in off-shoots and splinters and iridescent needle-shafts of keenest glitter (1819)

The first two quotations are verse fragments thirty years apart; the last two are culled at random from the notebooks and letters respectively. And I would far rather have those notebooks than the coldly Gothic 'Christabel' (1797) or the attractive but diffuse conversation poems, (1795, 1797–8). The fragmented sensibility they reveal is fascinating. Indeed, personal fascination is the stock-in-trade of the Romantic poet, but it hardly amounts to an *oeuvre*. Time and time again, when we should be discussing the work, we find ourselves grappling with the personality of the man.

This is very much the case with Shelley, whose reputation has been distorted by the uncritical encomia with which he has been showered. The sort of exaggeration I mean can be sampled in the following, often quoted, comment by Alfred North Whitehead:

> What the hills were to the youth of Wordsworth, a chemical laboratory was to Shelley. It is unfortunate that Shelley's literary critics have, in this respect, so little of Shelley in their own mentality. They tend to treat as a casual oddity of Shelley's nature what was, in fact, part of the main structure of his mind, permeating his poetry through and through. If Shelley had been born a hundred years later, the twentieth century would have seen a Newton among chemists. . . .
>
> (*Science and the Modern World*, 1925)

Why should a scientist, used to making deductions from evidence, advance so unlikely a hypothesis? Shelley's interest in chemistry, evidenced chiefly in the disorder of his room at University College, has come down to us on the testimony of Jefferson Hogg, one of those anecdotal friends with whom the Romantics were prone to surround themselves (*Life of Shelley*, 1858). It is true that Shelley uses much imagery that critics without Professor Whitehead's training have taken to be scientific; but a close reading of the verse would establish that the science used is odd in itself and often misapplied. Like Blake, like Coleridge, Shelley had a good ear and a natural lyric gift; like them, he forsook his natural talent in order to convert the world. Many of his miscellaneous poems were written on impulse and never returned to again. This kind of improvisation produced the hypnotic clarity of 'Evening: Ponte al Mare' (1821), the macabre imagining of 'The Waning Moon' (1820) or the felicitous song-rhythm of 'The keen stars were twinkling' (1822). It can also produce very great nonsense indeed. At his best, when he kept within his lyric abilities and took the trouble to revise a little, Shelley achieved 'The Ode to the West Wind' (1819), 'Ozymandias' (1817), 'England in 1819'—poems which, if they do not cut deep, are at least well constructed and precise in their execution.

But, of all the Romantics, Shelley's reputation seems most to rest upon legend. The archetypal poet—tameless and swift and proud—exists, for the most part, in the anecdotes that disciples, and disciples of disciples, tell about him. The erudite Shelley who, in the intervals of writing *A Refutation of Deism* (1814), spent the summer of 1812 translating Baron d'Holbach's *Le Système de la Nature* (1770)—this Shelley doesn't exist. Neither does the translation. The inquisitive will find such fragments as Shelley undertook to translate embedded in the notes to *Queen Mab* (1812), and these notes exude a confidence denied to that dreary and simplistic poem. Further, Shelley the scientific philosopher is just as much a wish-fulfilling creation. Carl Grabo's book *A Newton among Poets* (1930) followed up Whitehead in promulgating a Shelley who was a tireless research worker and analyst. It passes current that Shelley observed oceanography and meteorology and delved into the advanced phenomena of atmospheric electricity. The facts are more prosaic. Internal evidence assures us that Shelley at no time read profoundly in Tiberius Cavallo, Celsus, Trotter, Herschel and the highly technical Italian of Giambatista Beccaria. Rather, the author of 'The Cloud' picked up most of what he wanted to know about the atmosphere from a convenient summary of Father Beccaria's work in *Nicholson's Journal*, a magazine of popular science. Here (February 1813) he found that lightning navigated the clouds and decided their movements and direction! (Cf. Richard Kirwan, 'On Rain', *ibid*, June 1803). And from Erasmus Darwin (notes to *The Botanic Garden* 1789–91) he got the idea that it was the electricity in the rain that made the plants grow—'the electricity decomposes water into these two airs termed Oxygene and Hydrogene, there is a powerful analogy to induce us to believe that it accelerates or contributes to the growth of vegetation'! This is bad science and gave rise to abominable verse:

> I bring fresh showers for the thirsting flowers
> From the seas and the streams;
> I bear light shade for the leaves when laid
> In their noonday dreams.
> From my wings are shaken the dews that waken

The sweet buds every one,
When rocked to rest on their mother's breast,
As she dances about the sun. . . .

('The Cloud', 1820)

There is another, and more potent, influence here. It is that
of Shelley's old science teacher, Adam Walker, who—among
other things—wrote, 'Water rises through the air, flying on the
wings of electricity', *A System of Familiar Philosophy*, 2nd edition,
1771, rep. 1799, Lecture VII. It is clear that, like Erasmus Darwin,
Walker could not understand the difference between an analogy
and a concept. The result was that he passed on to his hopeful
pupils at Syon House and Eton ideas that at worst were
erroneous—he was entirely self-taught—and, at best, thirty years
out of date. In the age of Lavoisier and Davy, Adam Walker
was still going on about caloric and phlogiston; and Shelley
appears to have taken it all in uncritically. The researches of
Peter Butter (*Shelley's Idols of the Cave*, 1954) have shown the
close connection between the lectures of this remarkable eccentric
and the imagery of *Prometheus Unbound* (1818–19). What he has
not shown is that the influence was entirely to Shelley's disadvantage. Shelley had a leaning towards conversation poetry, but,
given a story in which the hero spends most of his time chained
to a rock, it would seem that the only possibilities of action
were in the mind. So the various friends and attendants of
Prometheus go on to no small extent about the phenomena
of the universe, very much according to the ideology of Adam
Walker, Erasmus Darwin and the latest popularisation of Beccaria.
Indeed, without close reference to their work, it would be hard
to make much sense of *Prometheus Unbound*. Given that Prometheus, now released, is resting in a cave with his acolytes
about him, what has the following scene to do with anything
actual?

IONE.   Sister, it is not earthly: how it glides
             Under the leaves! how on its head there burns
             A light, like a green star, whose emerald beams
             Are twined with its fair hair! how, as it moves,
             The splendour drops in flakes upon the grass!
             Knowest thou it?

PANTHEA.   It is the delicate spirit
            That guides the earth through heaven. From
               afar
            The populous constellation call that light
            The loveliest of the planets; and sometimes
            It floats along the spray of the salt sea,
            Or makes its chariot of a foggy cloud,
            Or walks through fields or cities while men
               sleep,
            Or o'er the mountain-tops, or down the rivers,
            Or through the green waste wilderness, as now,
            Wondering at all it sees. Before Jove reigned
            It loved our sister Asia, and it came
            Each leisure hour to drink the liquid light
            Out of her eyes, for which it said it thirsted
            As one bit by a dipsas . . . .

The idea of one creature drinking liquid out of another creature's eyes I find, like much of Shelley's ethereal imagery, rather disgusting. But this is because it derives, not from experience or observation, but from guesswork, and grotesque guesswork at that. Adam Walker asks, 'If the impulse of light be greater, on one half of the earth than on the other, may not this also account for its annual motion about the sun, to produce the seasons?' *A System of Familiar Philosophy*, 2nd edition, 1771, Introductory). The answer is, no; or rather, that the amount of energy afforded by light is as nothing to that derived from gravity. But one can see how this formulation produced Shelley's untenable image of 'the delicate spirit / That guides the earth through Heaven.'

Again: the light that burns about the Spirit of the Earth 'like a green star' owes a good deal to the science correspondent of *Nicholson's Journal*, 'R. B.' Referring to an experiment by Beccaria (February 1813), he says that the Father sent a sky-rocket through a fog and saw 'the star of electric light' denoting negative electricity. He adds, however, that Beccaria achieved this effect only once, and thought that his original observation was mistaken. But even a failed experiment is good enough for the Newton among poets, who uses it to obfuscate imagery already sufficiently obscure. An even closer source of this 'green star' may be a note of Erasmus Darwin's which speaks of a ship 'floating along' and—without identifying the phenomenon as phosphorescence—

relates that the sea seemed 'converted into little stars, every drop as it breaks emitting light'. With all this, we don't really need to invoke Adam Walker's theory of the earth as a giant magnet whose power attracts clouds down and condenses them into rain! We have quite enough nonsense going on in *Prometheus Unbound* itself.

Like so many of the Romantics, prophets without a creed, Shelley was anxious to teach before he had learned. One would never guess from his work that he lived in an age of serious scientific experiment. Why, at the time of the mature Davy and the young Faraday, did he not make contact with the Royal Institution and do some serious work instead of relying on the mumbo-jumbo of improvisers who had got their mysticism hopelessly mixed up with their techniques of observation? An answer to this would associate itself with the fact that Shelley was ill-read in the literature of his own language; never seriously studied the craft of verse; seized upon the superficialities of a number of topics, and lacked the curiosity and patience to investigate any one of them thoroughly.

It may seem too much to say that ignorance was the curse of the Romantic poets. But certainly characteristics that distinguished them from major figures before their time include impatience, superficiality, a false cult of originality, a tendency to improvise rather than think. They shared the belief that a man could dissociate himself from the society of his time and still say things relevant to it. Even Keats, the least arrogant of these poets, was impeded by the fact that he hankered after classical legend yet never troubled to master Latin, Greek and the reading in mythology that should go with it. His verse, indeed, shows an interest in form and a sense of craftsmanship superior to that of his fellows. But this usually manifested itself as a sedulous imitation of those whom he took to be the best existing models. So keen was his ear and so precise his eye that in some ways he surpassed his masters. In 'The Eve of St Agnes' (1819) we have a highly particular use of the Spenserian stanza, but the particulars exist for their own sake, without the allegorical pressure we find in Spenser—at least, Spenser at his best. Similarly, the verse of *Hyperion* (1818–19) owes much to Cary's version of Dante (1812); but in Keats's poem the ordeal of the steps is a fictional event, while in the *Purgatorio* it is the contrition and the cleansing of a whole life. In grasping the actual, Keats often loses a sense of its meaning.

The hand that wrote 'Lamia' had been in close contact with Sandys's Ovid and Dryden's suave rendering of the Wife of Bath's Tale. Thus:

> Our Demi-gods, Nymphs, Sylvans, Satyrs, Fauns,
> Who haunt clear Springs, high Mountains, Woods and
>   Lawns
> (On whom since yet we please not to bestow
> Celestial dwellings) must subsist below
> (Sandys, Ovid's Metamorphoses, 1621–6)

> In Days of Old when Arthur filled the Throne,
> When Acts and Fame to Foreign Lands were blown,
> The King of Elfs and little fairy Queen
> Gambolled on Heaths, and danced on every green
> (Dryden, Wife of Bath's Tale, late 1690s)

> Upon a time, before the fairy broods
> Drove Nymph and Satyr from the prosperous woods,
> Before King Oberon's bright diadem,
> Sceptre, and mantle, clasped with dewy gem,
> Frighted away the Dryads and the Fauns
> From rushes green, and brakes, and cowslip'd lawns....
> (Keats, 'Lamia', 1819)

The youngest poet carries the palm. But, urgent though his verses are, there is something like an element of exercise here. The adaptation does not represent a decisive rehandling of the source. One might further enquire, to what end is all this technique displayed? Why do we have to be told, in 'Lamia', of a young man who marries a serpent? The whole thing seems to depend on a misreading of Philostratus by Robert Burton, Keats's immediate inspiration for the story (*The Anatomy of Melancholy*, 1621). But, for a poet so intrigued by classical legend, Keats would have done better to quarry at source. Had he troubled to read the *Life of Apollonius*, Book IV, Chapter 25, he would have found the great philosopher denouncing Lamia's palace as an illusion in the same terms as one might the Gardens of Tantalus, and condemning the nymph herself as an *empusa* or follower of Hecate. It will be seen from this that Apollonius is very much the hero of the story and that Lycius, his student, is a dupe. In his retelling, Burton invokes a good deal of sympathy for the snake-woman, and this is further stepped up by Keats. However, the moral implications of the plot—a bad one for Lamia—pull against the values expressed in the verse. And one cannot help feeling that it is for the sake of the latter that the poem exists.

Nevertheless, there is hardly anything in 'Lamia', however well done, that is not heavily derivative. And the adaptation all too often succeeds in a manner that precludes understanding. For example, Keats knew nothing of the social customs of his scene—ancient Corinth. Therefore, as Douglas Bush was the first to point out (*PMLA*, 1925), he drew for his description of Lamia's marriage feast upon John Potter's *Archaeologia Graeca* (1697–98, 1818 edition). The inquisitive will find there the curious sorts of wood Keats alludes to, the tables with their feet cast in the form of leopard's paws, and, of course, the goblets:

> The cups used by the ancient Greeks were very plain, and agreeable to the rest of their furniture being usually composed of Wood or Earth. Afterwards, when they began to imitate the Pride and Vanity of the Asiaticks, their Cups were made of Silver, Gold and other costly Materials, curiously wrought, inlaid with precious Stones, and otherways adorned.

Keats makes nothing of the point, clear in Potter, that the use of precious metals was a sign of decadence.

> Twelve sphered tables, by silk seats ensphered,
> High as the level of a man's breast reared
> On libbard's paws, upheld the heavy gold
> Of cups and goblets . . . .

An opportunity is missed because the poet failed to understand that which he imitated. The scene is rich where it could have been luxurious. 'Lamia' would have been a more interesting poem if the author had seen the *empusa* as a dangerously fallen spirit and her illusory paradise a seduction degrading to a human being.

This dichotomy is everywhere in Keats. Surface details remain sharp and clear, but we may be gravelled to understand their

significance. This is especially true of the odes. 'Ode on a Grecian
Urn' (1819) is a case in point, where elaborate imagery tends
to drown out the plot. No single urn could carry that wealth
of material. Edmund Blunden found a review of a book of
engravings in *The Examiner* whose wording, he felt, might have
given Keats the idea for the ode. But those who look at the
book of engravings itself will discover that Keats's 'Grecian Urn'
is, in fact, an ode to three Roman vases. Consider the figures
on the urn. Plate 48 of Henry Moses's *Collection of Antique
Vases* (1814) shows a very stern priest purposefully kindling a
brazier. There is in attendance a most reluctant heifer, but she
is not garlanded—those garlands may be found in Plate 7 of
the sequel, Moses's *Antiquities* (1817), where they adorn, not
the flanks of the animal, but her neck. The youth beneath the
trees is piping on a double flute in Plate 43 of Moses's *Collection*
and on the same vase is the bold lover half-turned away from
a rather disdainful maiden:

> She cannot fade, though thou hast not thy bliss,
>   For ever wilt thou love, and she be fair!

The rest of the material is more literary: a hint from *Britannia's
Pastorals* (1613–16) by William Browne:

> a lovely shepherd's boy
> Sits piping on a hill as if his joy
> Would still endure

and, from Lemprière's *Classical Dictionary* (1788, 1818 edition),
the entry for 'Hyacinthia', which ends, 'all were eager to be
present at the games, and the city was almost desolate, and
without inhabitants'.

But, as usual with Keats, the poem exists almost for its own
sake, with little meaning other than the wish to remain for
ever young and for ever living. Like the other odes, it is interesting
in its particulars rather than as a whole. To wish the poet
free of didacticism—as certainly Keats is—is not to wish him
merely a purveyor of pleasing imagery.

Strangely enough, critics have read Keats's masterpiece 'To
Autumn' (1819) in very much these terms. But a proper interpretation would work back from the last line: 'And gathering swal-

lows twitter in the skies'. This is a dying man taking his last
look at the world and grasping it with all the more intensity
because he knows it is slipping away. My interpretation is not
a biographical one, and would not be affected if I were assured
that, at the time of writing, Keats was full of the songs of
spring. The images are redolent of death: the bees are living
in a fool's paradise, autumn is personified as Time the Reaper,
the day is softly dying, the small gnats mourn, the wind now
lives and now dies, the redbreast, symbol of winter, is already
at his song—'And gathering swallows twitter in the skies'. Like
the spirit of a sick man, they are about to take their departure.
It is no coincidence that this, the finest of all Keats's poems,
is also the least derivative. Or, what comes to the same thing,
it treats its sources so creatively as to render their discussion
irrelevant. Mary Tighe—

> When from the misty east the labouring sun
> Bursts through thy fog . . .
>>   ('Written in Autumn', c. 1805)

and Thomas Chatterton—

> Oft have I seen thee at the noon-day feast
> When daised by thyself for want of peers . . .
>>   (*Aella, ante* 1770)

have been changed out of all knowledge. 'To Autumn' gave
considerable impetus to the nineteenth-century Romantics. We
find traces of it for more than half a century afterward, during
which, inexorably, the tradition thins out:

> All the west
> And even unto the middle south was ribbed
> And barred with bloom on bloom
>>   (Tennyson, 'The Lover's Tale', 1828)

> leaning backwards in a pensive dream
> And fostering in thy lap a heap of flowers
>>   (Arnold, 'The Scholar-Gipsy', 1853)

> threshold of wing-winnowed threshing-floor
>>   (Rossetti, 'Through Death to Love', *ante* 1881)

Faint and grey 'twixt the leaves of the aspens, betwixt
the cloud-bars
        (William Morris, 'Summer Dawn', *ante* 1858)

Autumn is over the long leaves that love us . . . .
        (W. B. Yeats, 'The Falling of the Leaves', 1889)

By the time Yeats was starting, the leaves had indeed fallen,
into *taedium vitae*. Nothing is more remarkable than to see this
poet, arguably the greatest of all the Romantics, pulling himself
by his boot-straps up from the rotting windfalls of the 1890s.
He had, in all conscience, little enough to learn from. But certain
areas of study had a fascination for him; for example, Eastern
mysticism. He was no more master of this body of knowledge
than Blake was of Neo-Platonism or Shelley of atmospheric
physics, but he had a surer instinct than they, and greater powers
of inference.

The story goes back to the 1850s, when a failed priest calling
himself Eliphas Levi had visited London and quickened an enthu-
siasm for the Cabala. This is a collection of esoteric commentaries,
rabbinical forgeries mostly, upon the first five books of the
Bible. One of Levi's disciples was his biographer (1896), A. E.
Waite. Another was Dr Wynn Westcott, who translated several
rabbinical texts and, in 1888, helped to found the Society of
the Golden Dawn. This was a Cabalistic off-shoot from the
Rosicrucians. Westcott's ally in this enterprise was S. L. MacGregor
Mathers, who, of all these latter-day Cabalists, influenced Yeats
the most. He, like Westcott, was something of a scholar; though
not, I think, a Hebraist. His translation of the *Clavicula Salomanis*
(1889) was made from manuscripts written in Latin, French and
Italian. Even his edition of the central Cabalistic text, the *Zohar*
(1887), was incomplete, and derived from a Latin 'original'.
But there is no doubt that this work was much frequented
by Yeats.

Perhaps we could have wished him better companions in his
youth than these associates of the Golden Dawn, though he
speaks of the Society as the chief influence upon his work until
he was forty. In *Ideas of Good and Evil* (1903) we find him
quoting from Mathers's *Zohar*, as we may call it, with reference
to the Tree of Knowledge: 'In its branches the birds lodge

and build their nests, the souls and the angels have their place'
(*Kabbala Denudata*, 1887).

This tree, in one form or another, goes through all of Yeats's
work. Its ambiguity—it is the tree of both good *and* evil—is
dramatised in the 'great-rooted blossomer' that ends the poem
'Among Schoolchildren' (*ante* 1926) 'Are you the leaf, the blossom
or the bole?' The birds that nest in the boughs represent for
Yeats, as for the Cabala, the freedom and loneliness of the released
soul. Yeats describes himself, in 'Sailing to Byzantium' (1926),
as being out of nature:

> set upon a golden bough to sing
> To lords and ladies of Byzantium
> Of what is past, or passing, or to come.

The painstaking researches of Jon Stallworthy into Yeats's drafts
(*Between the Lines*, 1963) show that his poems were revised,
and revised critically, in a manner wholly alien to the early
Romantics. But this particular image came in quite abruptly,
without reference to the protracted labours that preceded it.
Its origins are undoubtedly composite. Apart from the Cabalistic
tree of knowledge, there is a passage in Gibbon (*Decline and
Fall of the Roman Empire*, 1764–88, ch. 52) about a tree of gold
on which sat a variety of birds made of the same metal. Aeneas,
too, was guided by Venus's doves to the golden bough which
he seized as a passport to the underworld. And there is a painting,
'The Golden Bough', by Turner in the National Gallery. But
Yeats could not have organised all these disparities into a poem
without a keen sense of relevance. The golden bird exists as
an integral part of 'Sailing to Byzantium'; one cannot say the
same of the figures on the Grecian Urn.

Nevertheless, had Yeats written in the wake of a great tradition,
he need not have worked so hard, at revision as well as selection
among his sources. The dissociation of art from society that
began with the first Romantics contributed greatly to the intellectual isolation of this last of them. The pose of poet all too
often had gone along with a denial of intellect and a tendency
to take the easiest way out of a problem. Our own *reductio
ad absurdum* in the present post-Romantic age is seen in the
current proliferation of gurus. Each has his own charisma, each
is eager to teach before he has learned. It does not matter whether

these figures claim to be poets, as Allen Ginsberg does, or whether they proffer a diet of instant knowledge from the esoteric east. The *New York Review of Books* (13 December 1973) quoted a disciple of the Maharaj Ji as saying 'I used to be able to discuss Gregorian chant, and John Donne, and Cocteau, and André Breton, and Plotinus, and St Thomas, and the difference between Mahayana and Hinayana Buddhism, do you understand? But once you have received Knowledge you are incapable of having a so-called intellectual discussion.'

This is not too far-fetched a caricature of the Romantic dichotomy: the dichotomy between mind and body, education and emotion, knowledge and intuition. It usually involves an imprecise use of intellect in a frenzied hunting-up of sources to eke out a guttering imagination in the hope of bumping into what you need at the moment you need it. We do not have to wonder at the premium put by apologists for the Romantics upon 'originality', 'genius', 'inspiration' and the like. The way to Maharaj Ji was indicated long ago by the eighteenth-century melancholiacs and was taken up by the Romantic poets, greatly to the detriment of their talent. Matthew Arnold in 'The Function of Criticism' (1864) complained that the Romantics did not know enough. We can add to his diagnosis. Not only did the Romantics not know enough, but they were hardly ever in control even of that which they thought they knew.

9 The Rise of the Dramatic Monologue

The dramatic monologue has been a central form of English poetry for over 140 years. For better or worse, it is the dominant form now. Yet its antecedents are lost in conjecture.

The form is associated with the name of Robert Browning, arguably the greatest poet between Wordsworth and Eliot, and an originator so potent that his most advanced disciples are still learning from his work. Yet how did he come to make so startling a discovery as the monologue? A speech without context, a narrative implied rather than retailed, a character without the framework of plot—all this represents, at first sight, an elliptic approach strangely modern when compared with the narrative of Wordsworth or the dramatic handling of situations we find in Shakespeare.

In fact, the monologue is less startling an innovation than it appears, for it has definite antecedents in the drama. Why it looks so *dégagé* is that it flourishes where the drama, together with our understanding of that form, has decayed. Moreover, it took a considerable effort to turn monologue into literature.

But let us make some attempt to define the monologue before we go on to anatomise its history. Its best-known attribute is that it is spoken by a person other than the poet himself. But it would be possible to satisfy this condition without dramatising an aspect of a personality, and this is a crucial matter in, shall we say, the work of Browning. So we can add to our basic requirement for dramatic monologue a further one: that it should embody some revelation of character. However, there are plenty of such revelations in literature that have nothing like the feel of monologue. A recollection in tranquillity would hardly fill the bill, especially if the tranquillity was that of the poet rather than that of the speaker. What we would miss would be the presence of a dramatic situation.

Three conditions, then, should be invoked as criteria for this form, the form of the dramatic monologue. First, it should appear to be spoken by a person other than the poet. Secondly, it should reveal some aspect of character. Thirdly, it should feel like drama.

Clearly, we cannot erect an ideal to which all dramatic monologues must conform. But we can point out certain qualities inherent in the genre; that make it, in fact, possible to recognise it *as* a genre. They are the qualities that we find in outstanding monologues; in such work, for instance, as Browning's 'Fra Lippo Lippi', Tennyson's 'Ulysses', 'Philoctetes' by Lord de Tabley, 'The Mandolin' by Eugene Lee-Hamilton, Eliot's 'Gerontion' and Frost's 'A Servant to Servants'.

There are certain characteristics of these poems that can be found only in the dramatic monologue form. The fictionalising of an attitude, for example, so that it can be seen from the outside—very often the characters condemn themselves from their own mouths. This brings in a serious point: predominantly, a figure in dramatic monologue is weak, vain, brutal or all three. Characteristically—and, in this, unlike most drama—the reader is prevented from sympathising with the protagonist. This is one reason why the character portrayed has to be markedly more simple than the author who set him up. If he were not, there would be no way of seeing around him. Another point: the poem occurs at a single moment of time, a clearly defined present; it is only by recapitulation that we can take in the protagonist's past. Here is another obvious distinction between monologue and drama proper. In drama the action—even allowing for narrative inserts—is sequential. Moreover, the experience is far more complex in drama, which is why monologue form indicates a failure in the dramatic tradition.

One could say that the dramatic monologue arose out of a misunderstanding, by critics as well as playwrights, of Shakespeare's dramaturgy. There are certainly speeches in Shakespeare's plays which are revelations of character, but they are integrally

part of a context and refer too closely to other events of the
drama to be readily detachable without doing violence to the
sense. 'My Last Duchess' gives us the essential Ferrara; 'If it
were done' does not give us the essential Macbeth.

Yet one can say, in all conviction, that the drama began
a slow decline with the production of *Macbeth* in 1606. The
decline is marked, characteristically, by a progressive growth of
monologue within the play at the expense of action. In other
words, there is a correlation between defective plot and effective
monologue. The very brilliance of the individual speech distracts
attention from the play as a whole. And in that period of
decline, between 1606 and (say) 1830 or thereabouts, when the
Shakespearean theatre finally guttered out, sometimes the individual speech is so brilliant as to form a coherent monologue
on its own with little reference to a context. My contention
is that later dramatists, those of the eighteenth and early nineteenth
centuries, took this to be a virtue; and that out of this misapprehen-
sion the monologue arose.

Throughout the eighteenth century, literature and the drama
steadily diverged. Rowe, Southerne, Home, Ireland, Joanna Baillie—these make for increasingly tedious reading. When the dying
embers sputter into flame, as in various fragmentary works of
Shelley, what we have is a recollection of the speaking voice
so acute that it sounds almost independent of the narration of
which it was meant to be part:

> You will excuse me if I do not talk
> In the high style which they think fashionable;
> My pathos certainly would make You laugh too,
> Had You not long since given over laughing
> > ('Scenes from Goethe's *Faust*', 1822)

> ''Tis strange men change not. You were ever still
> Among Christ's flock a perilous infidel,
> A wolf for the meek lambs—if you can't swim
> Beware of Providence.'
> > ('Julian and Maddalo', 1818)

At this point we have to remember that Shelley was the favourite
poet of Browning. Certainly he seems to have influenced the
Browning who matters now. Browning, in fact, came out of
the wreck of the drama—all drama, including his own.

For the Romantic efforts at Shakespearean dramaturgy—I am thinking of full-scale poetic dramas by Coleridge and Byron, as well as Shelley—stand as a background to the attempt at a literary revival of tragedy which was sponsored by the nineteenth-century actor Macready. The work of many a would-be dramatist might have perished in the attic but for the energy of this honourable—and misguided—man. Bulwer Lytton, at a farewell dinner (1851), praised Macready on his retirement for having identified himself with the living drama of his time. This has an ironic quality when one considers who it was that Macready discovered. There was Bulwer himself, Sheridan Knowles, Thomas Noon Talfourd, H. S. Taylor—and Browning. Yes, for twenty nights Macready played in one of Browning's weakest efforts, *Strafford* (1837). This was the kind of play that Macready liked: static, lofty, Romantic-Shakespearean in diction, containing enormous monologues for the leading man. In the company of Bulwer and Sheridan Knowles, Browning must have seemed marginal; not one of the favourites in the stable. Their plays ran while his failed; the attempt of an impractical poet on the theatrical fringe. And yet, odd apparition though he looked, Browning belonged with the rest of Macready's forlorn hopes.

Only by being a faulty playwright could Browning become a great poet. As I have said, when the action paused, the monologue was precipitated. And there are two key situations which induced a protagonist to deliver himself of yet another soliloquy: monologue as explanation of character, and monologue as the wandering thoughts of a dying man. Characteristically, throughout the drama and its decline, the former was at the beginning of a play and the latter was generally found at the end. And it was speech such as this which eventually detached itself and turned into the dramatic monologue which could exist alone. So that dramatic monologue proper tends to be either Act i Scene i of an unwritten drama or Act v Scene iii. There is little that occurs in between.

But many different strands make up the weave of the monologue. The tendency of long speeches to detach themselves went along with the misunderstanding of Shakespeare's dramaturgy, and there were several different ways of doing this. As the drama reached a low ebb in the mid-eighteenth century, the elocutionist came into his own. As far back as 1752, Dr Dodd—better known for his forgeries—produced a popular compilation,

The Beauties of Shakespeare. He excerpted quite ruthlessly and with little regard for the surrounding drama. The great speech 'If it were done' appeared as a poem called 'Macbeth's Irresolution'. But, as I said at the beginning, this speech is not dramatic monologue. Too much of it refers to events in the play at large and so it cannot be self-supporting. When Macbeth says 'He's here in double trust', it is vital for us to know who that 'He' is. Even the name, Duncan, would not be enough. The speech, if it were monologue, would be required to establish the sanctity of Duncan, both as king and as man; as, in fact, is done in the play. Indeed, the very concept of Shakespeare as a playwright whose 'beauties' are extractable shows a critical error at the heart of Romantic tragedy—in reading as well as in writing. Another case: after her retirement in 1812, Mrs Siddons was able to make £1300 *profit* on six readings from Shakespeare. Her repertory included, among other showpieces, the Trial Scene from *The Merchant of Venice*, and this was a *pièce de resistance* also in such reader's handbooks as Bell's *Standard Elocutionist*—a compilation which went through fifty-four editions between 1850 and 1881. Bell also published a 'condensed' edition of Shakespeare especially for home recitation in 'a readable, untheatrical form'. Increasingly through the eighteenth century, a play had been considered as a succession of scenes, and increasingly speeches were heard independently of the play in which they occurred. Acting had become increasingly operatic, so that Garrick at Drury Lane had played Romeo (1750–1) and Lear (1755–6) *against* Barry playing the same parts at Covent Garden. More and more the audiences had applauded the set speech as a great aria; the actor would, as often as not, take a bow in the middle of a scene. More and more the audience thought in terms of isolated effects, so that the advocates of Edmund Kean (d. 1833) commended his performance in terms of 'points', 'shocks', 'flashes' and (that word again!) 'beauties'. The sense of dramatic continuity was sacrificed in favour of an actor's theatre which had broken up into conformable fragments the drama it was supposed to interpret as a whole; and the proliferating anthologies of Shakespearean and other 'beauties' bear this out.

The crucial anthology was Lamb's *Specimens of English Dramatic Poets* (1808), and it is hard to exaggerate its influence. The copy I used to read in the British Museum once belonged to the Victorian scholar John Addington Symonds, and his marginal notes make explicit how he saw the principle behind Lamb's compilation. 'Style was epidemic', he says, praising the Jacobeans for their 'flashes of spirit' and 'fine language'. Clearly, to see a play as a collection of flashes is to underestimate the possibilities of dramatic structure. Lamb himself claims to excerpt 'scenes of passion, sometimes of the deepest quality ... that which is more nearly allied to poetry than to wit'. But it is the more decadent Jacobean plays that allow monologue to supervene in lieu of action. The point I want to emphasise, though, is this: when such monologues are taken out of context, they startlingly resemble what Browning and his successors were to do. One of Lamb's extracts is a speech from Marston's *What You Will* (c. 1601). It is delivered by Lampatho, a kind of Jaques figure who is unimportant in a fairly chaotic plot. Yet what he speaks is, by our definition, a dramatic monologue.

Scholar and his Dog

I was a scholar: seven useful springs
Did I deflower in quotations
Of crossed opinions 'bout the soul of man;
The more I learnt, the more I learnt to doubt.
Delight my spaniel slept, whilst I baused leaves,
Tossed o'er the dunces, pored on the old print
Of titled words: and still my spaniel slept.
Whilst I wasted lamp-oil, baited my flesh,
Shrunk up my veins: and still my spaniel slept.
And still I held converse with Zabarell
Aquinas, Scotus, and the musty saw
Of antick Donate: still my spaniel slept.
Still on went I; first, *an sit anima*;
Then, an it were mortal. O hold, hold; at that
They're at brain-buffets, fell by the ears amain
Pell-mell together: still my spaniel slept.
Then, whether 'twere corporeal, local, fixed,
Ex traduce, but whether 't had free will
Or no, hot philosophers
Stood banding factions, all so strongly propped,
I staggered, knew not which was firmer part,
But thought, quoted, read, observed, and pried,

Stuffed noting-books: and still my spaniel slept.
At length he waked, and yawned; and by yon sky,
For aught I know he knew as much as I.

The same is true of other extracts: Vindice's address to his mistress's skull from *The Revenger's Tragedy* (c. 1606) by Cyril Tourneur; Luke Frugal's operatic ''Twas no fantastic object' from *The City Madam* (c. 1632) by Philip Massinger; King Henry's blessing on the young Dauphin from *The Tragedy of Byron* (c. 1608) by George Chapman—this last, looking forward, like so much else in this period, to Browning's great monologue 'The Bishop Orders His Tomb' (1845). And, like Marston's portrait of Lampatho, these are examples of prototypes that may have suggested to Browning the possibilities of the dramatic monologue as an independent form.

Lamb's *Specimens* came out in 1808, when comparatively few monologues had been written. But the next generation, that of Browning and Tennyson, was prolific in the form. Is it too much to say that, among all the elements behind this apparently original discovery, is the anthologists' way of reading drama as isolated scenes, as 'beauties'?

For the very earliest monologues to be written as independent poems came in the mid eighteenth century, when the drama was entering its last decline. Within the same ten years were published Home's *Douglas* (1756), Dodd's *Beauties of Shakespeare* (1752), Richardson's *Clarissa* (1746–8) and also the first monologues proper, Joseph Warton's 'Dying Indian' (1747) and William Whitehead's 'Fatal Constancy' (1754). This last is no more than a parody of the decadence into which heroic drama had fallen. It takes off from Rowe's *Fair Penitent* (1703), Southerne's *Oroonoko* (1695), perhaps even Whitehead's own *Creusa* (1754), in which may be seen the very faults of objurgation and inflation that he displays for our criticism in 'Fatal Constancy' itself.

But far more inherently interesting is Warton's 'The Dying Indian'. This is the first dramatic monologue to stand on its own feet within the terms that have been defined and without any supplementary context. Already the distinguishing marks are present: the dying-scene when the protagonist looks back at his past life; and—a frequent side-effect in monologue—the use of an exotic setting as a means of justifying free rein in confession.

Another side-effect is a tendency to jerkiness of utterance only just this side of melodrama:

> O my son,
> I feel the venom busy in my breast,
> Approach and bring my crown, decked with the teeth
> Of that bold Christian who first dared deflower
> The virgins of the sun; and, dire to tell!
> Robbed Pachacamac's altar of its gems. . . .

This leaning towards melodrama is a built-in propensity of dramatic monologue. It has this need to put a weight of past action upon a speech delivered in the present, and this subjects the verse to some strain, if only in handling an amount of experience disproportionate to the quantity of lines employed. Obviously the monologue as a form is incapable of dealing with the massive contexts of tragic drama. Yet, as in some sense a substitute for that form, it must seem to. Hence the need to imply a great deal more than in the time can be said. This, in its turn, requires the development of a species of shorthand—jerks, parentheses, exclamations and the like—which stand instead of the stretches of dialogue and narrative that, in other forms, would be considered structurally necessary.

So the monologue has certain qualities we would now recognise as specifically modern: ellipsis, colloquialism, and so on. Such qualities were present even in its beginning as an independent form in the mid eighteenth century, but what has become central to our tradition now we must remember would appear as marginal then. Thus it was that the hint proffered, in particular by 'The Dying Indian', was not taken up (with minor exceptions) for another forty years. Even the *Dramatic Sketches* of Francis Sayers (1790) belong really to the world of Joanna Baillie (*fl.* 1798), of plays written, but not meant to be acted. Indeed, the inert work of these closet dramatists lies between the beginnings of the monologue and the Romantics. Hence an opportunity was missed. The Romantics wasted their talents on unproducible plays; they wavered about in search of a satisfactory narrative form. Of them all, only Southey hit upon anything we would call a dramatic monologue; and, unlike his fellows, his ability was slighter than the genre demanded. Every one of his five 'monodramas' follows the line of Warton and Sayers—both of whom

Southey acknowledges as predecessors—in representing the death of the protagonist. It is only fair to add that these monodramas with their exotic heroes—Ximalpoca, La Caba—are by way of being juvenilia, dating from Southey's Oxford days of the early 1790s. Juvenilia, too, were similar efforts some twenty years later by Charles Wolfe and Thomas Lovell Beddoes, which only feebly bridged the gap between Southey's monologues and those of Browning.

It took more talent than that possessed by these early mono-loguists to bring the form from an eccentric side-issue to the centre of the stage. The elements that we have seen going into its conception—the pseudo-Shakespearean tragedy and its orators, the elocutionists with their handbooks, the anthologies, the pioneer monodramas—were so various as to demand a tremendous act of synthesis to bring about the monologue's emergence as the vehicle of great poetry.

But the fact that Browning and Tennyson were able to develop the monologue at the same time, and independently of one another, shows that it must have been immanent in the atmosphere of the 1830s. Nevertheless, the form could not be truly central until an age when the major poetic and dramatic forms had broken down.

Browning's superiority over his predecessors can be localised as a superiority of plotting. This can be seen if we compare his greatest monologues not so much with Southey or Beddoes as with his own raw material. For example, Browning shows himself in 'Fra Lippo Lippi' (c. 1853) to be a master in the art of heightening a circumstance relevant to the experiential core of his poem. In his life of the painter (2nd edition. 1568), Vasari tells the story of how Lippo was locked up by his patron, Cosimo de'Medici, as a means of getting him to finish a particular work. This anecdote—it is little more in Vasari—is given tremendous point in Browning's retelling, for he makes it the entire *raison d'être* of the monologue. Lippo explains to the guard who has stopped him in the street exactly who he is:

> Zooks, what's to blame? You think you see a monk! . . .
> Aha, you know your betters! . . . Who am I?
> Why one, sir, who is lodging with a friend
> Three streets off—he's a certain ... how d'ye call?
> Master—a ... Cosimo of the Medici,
> I' the house that caps the corner. . . .

This gets us immediately into the thick of the plot. The occasion for the monologue is the suspicion of the guard; the explanation leads us to the immediate circumstances of Lippo's breaking loose—

> And I've been three weeks shut within my mew,
> A painting for the great man, saints and saints
> And saints again. I could not paint all night—
> Ouf! I leaned out of window for fresh air.
> There came a hurry of feet and little feet ...
> And a face that looked up ... zooks, sir, flesh and blood,
> That's all I'm made of! ...

—which in its turn is a revelation of character that leads us to a narrative of his past life. But the important point to notice is that this is more than recollection: the whole is framed by the dramatic situation of the present, Lippi confronting the guards. And the 'narrative' is spoken *to* the guards—interlocutors whose reaction—'Though your eye twinkles still, you shake your head'—is implied in the text and indeed forms a counterpoint to it. These were great developments upon the preceding examples of the monologue and have not been sufficiently taken up by practitioners of the genre since.

But Browning in 'Fra Lippo Lippi' shows himself not only a master of the heightened circumstance but also a practitioner in the art of paring away. One sacrifices even striking detail in favour of preserving the experiential core. Thus Browning deliberately omits one of the most picturesque circumstances in Vasari's life of Fra Lippo: the painter's capture at sea by a Moorish galley and the eighteen months of his imprisonment in Barbary. This advanture is left out most probably because it would suggest a disruption in Lippo's life as a monk. Historians still dispute whether or not Lippo Lippi, as Vasari said he did, actually threw off his clerical habit. Certainly he was called Fra Lippo throughout his life and appears tonsured in his own self-portrait. But, in any case, for Browning's purpose, it was essential he remain a monk; for the poem is an allegory. Just as surely as the monks have doubts about this rebel troubling their ranks, so society seems to regard the value of an artist's work as not worth the nuisance of having him in its midst. This is a Romantic view, and Browning, a Romantic artist himself, represents Lippo Lippi, by reason of his art, detached from society. However, this need not make him amoral:

> For, don't you mark? we're made so that we love
> First when we see them painted, things we have passed
> Perhaps a hundred times nor cared to see;
> And so they are better, painted—better to us,
> Which is the same thing. . . .

In its turn, the art is a vision of the universe caricatured and thick with detail to make sure that we take notice: this implies that Lippo's art is beyond the confines of religion—which, if we accept the poem as an allegory, means that it is beyond the received values of society. The painter is a monk because he cannot live by painting; the monastery represents a context in which he is able to survive. In youth, Lippo tells us, with characteristic specificity, he had his share of starving:

> I was a baby when my mother died
> And father died and left me in the street.
> I starved there, God knows how, a year or two
> On fig-skins, melon-parings, rinds and shucks,
> Refuse and rubbish.

The alternative was obvious. To the monastery:

> 'So, boy, you're minded,' quoth the good fat father
> Wiping his own mouth, 'twas refection time,—
> 'To quit this very miserable world?...'

But Fra Lippo chooses to make use of the monastery rather than be absorbed by it:

> You should not take a fellow eight years old
> And make him swear never to kiss the girls. . . .

This past—Fra Lippo's poverty-stricken childhood—is beautifully evoked, but it has its place in the plot. It is the present clash with the guard that provokes the self-explanation; and the clash itself is made to seem the archetype of all manner of contretemps with society. We can recognise what is left out by having recourse to Vasari. Still, if this is not a complete life history, it is considerably more than a speech excerpted from a play.

The art of monologue, then, is at once restrictive and economical. This means that only certain kinds of character can be depicted—mostly the irresponsible, anti-social or weak—because such characters tend to get themselves into situations which require self-revelation. Another restriction tends to make for a greater degree of artistry than might have been expected: the author's judgment can only be implied, and then only in the manner of his writing; though, at his best, Browning is able to set up a creative tension between what is said and how it is being said. Most obviously of all, the action necessarily is more restricted than that of drama: the monologue we have looked at is of the explanatory Act i Scene i type.

Tennyson's earliest efforts in this line are more like Act v Scene iii. They date from the 1830s and differ significantly from the exactly contemporary monologues of Browning in being lyrical in tone and narrative rather than dramatic in technique. Rather than plunge into a dramatic situation, Tennysonian monologue tends to brood over events after they have occurred. Characteristically, Tennyson's protagonists find themselves in situations whose only logical resolution is death. This is true of 'Oenone', 'The Lotos Eaters', 'St Simeon Stylites', 'Tithonus' and 'Tiresias'; it is, perhaps, less true of his finest effort in this form, 'Ulysses' (1833). I need hardly say that the legendary figure was a hero of great cunning whose later life was a series of strange adventures encountered in his attempts to reach his homeland after the siege of Troy. Tennyson, imaginatively enough, depicts him after his adventures are done, safely ensconced on his isle, but pining for a life of action again. On closer inspection, it appears that the activity is—like the imagery of Tennyson's other monologues—something of an illusion. The static present is far more real in the poem than the adventurous past. Indeed, 'Ulysses' has this in common with 'Stylites' and 'Tithonus'; it shows a man at the term of his life. The predominant mood is one of gloom and exasperation.

> It little profits that an idle king,
> By this still hearth, among these barren crags,
> Matched with an aged wife, I mete and dole
> Unequal laws unto a savage race
> That hoard, and sleep, and feed, and know not me. . . .

—'idle', 'still', 'barren', 'aged': the verse insists upon these adjectives, and they, in their turn, show the reason for Ulysses' inactivity.

True, he has had an active past, but this also, in his recollection, is made to seem static:

> Thro' scudding drifts the rainy Hyades
> Vext the dim sea
>
> Far on the ringing plains of windy Troy.

Nor is the past particularised: what matters is not the life of heroic action but the winter of Ulysses' present discontent. A good contrast would be with the speech to Achilles spoken by Shakespeare's Ulysses in *Troilus and Cressida*, a speech to which Tennyson's poem superficially owes a certain amount. In Shakespeare the character is counselling action and all the imagery is highly dynamic. But in Tennyson the reverse is true. His Ulysses may counsel action—''Tis not too late to seek a newer world'—but the weight of imagery suggests he won't achieve it. However, the disparity between Ulysses' desires and his present weariness creates a tension which renders this monologue more interestingly complex than its fellows. It is a success, though a precarious one, to turn a heroic character into a static valetudinarian; and Tennyson has managed it.

From the 1830s and 1840s, the time of the earliest monologues of Browning as well as Tennyson, the form was established as one capable of major poetry; established, one ought to say, in terms of literature and technique rather than in critical favour, for the public mind took quite a time to catch up with this latest development in poetry. Indeed, the critics saw the Victorian age essentially as one of lyric. In a sense, it was: much of the weight of fiction was taken over by the prose novel, but this makes the verse monologue all the more important. In so far as poetry was capable of bearing serious reference to the outside world, the monologue proved to be the clue to the period. Underground as it sometimes was, submerged as critical opinion since that time has allowed it to be, the monologue nevertheless was the lifeline of English verse when poetry was in danger of losing its foothold in civilisation as a relevant art-form.

It took a little time for the example, particularly of Browning, to be grasped, rather than reached towards. Yet the period was to favour the erection of character in lieu of personal utterance, if only because it at once doubted moral issues and yet was concerned to exhibit a good front to the world. The poet might wear a stovepipe hat and go to church, but his characters lie, fornicate and murder with impunity. In Browning and his more gifted successors, a great deal of psychic energy was released, much of which had lain in abeyance since the time of Shakespeare because there was no dramatic fiction capable of giving it shape. And it is this interest in the creation of character, particularly at a psychological extreme, that typifies the school of Browning.

My mention of a 'school' of Browning may be found puzzling. It passes for fact that fifty years or more went by before monologue was resuscitated by Ezra Pound. But, as we shall see, monologue never ceased to be written. Indeed, the tradition after Browning has remarkable continuity.

Browning's most notable successors were Walter Thornbury, Augusta Webster, Aubrey De Vere Jr, Sebastian Evans, Lord de Tabley and Eugene Lee-Hamilton. The last two are fine poets unjustly neglected. De Tabley, a synthesiser rather than an innovator, learned a good deal from Tennyson as well as from Browning. His main theme is that of irrevocable loss. This is indicated by his choice of personae: Semele, Saul, Minos, Iphigeneia, Orpheus, Echo—all characters on the margin of society. Perhaps his key figure is Philoctetes—subject of both a verse drama (1866) and a monologue (1863); and the two have not a single line in common. One would infer from this that de Tabley had much to say upon the subject—the man with a wound, deserted by his friends, in exile, consumed with internal self-reproach, given to outward defiance:

> Ye have done well to leave me. 'Tis most wise,
> And friendly too, expedient, generous:
> Why this is bounty's crown; I have deserved
> No less than a sick hound . . . .

There is no doubt that the character's wound is severe enough to explain his being abandoned by his men, even though his recognition of this cannot alter the reality of his pain. This is superbly actualised in de Tabley's description of the island where Philoctetes is marooned:

Silence on silence treads at each low morn.
Pain and new pain, some glimpse of painless sleep,
And waking to old anguish and new day. . . .
I hate this island steep, this seam of beach.
This ample desolation of grey rock
Man tills not: and man reaps not, woe is me. . . .

The pain of exile and the bitterness of isolation—these are de Tabley's themes, and no wonder they have not made him popular. His greatest single gift is for the creation of atmosphere. And though this sense diminished after his early phase, after about 1870, the later poems retain a Browningesque sense of character and show considerable ingenuity in managing a plot.

Almost as neglected is Browning's other major disciple, Eugene Lee-Hamilton. He is a notable lyric poet, but shows most range and form in such dramatic monologues as 'The Mandolin' (1882) and 'Ipsissimus', 'The Wonder of the World' and 'Abraham Carew', all published in 1884. They serve to remind us how far Browning created the properties and settings used by writers of monologue. The speaker in 'The Mandolin', for instance, is a particularly venomous cardinal who tries vainly to break the affection of his ward for a low-born musician. The cardinal has the young man murdered and is haunted thereafter by his mandolin—'no sleep for eighty nights'. What compels attention is not so much the plot as its realisation: the effects of insomnia are powerfully marked—'My mind goes hazy and my temples swell'. Lee-Hamilton's catalogue of symptoms is clinically exact, even to this extent: that everything happening in the poem could have been hallucinated by a mind deranged through lack of sleep. Quite likely the sound of the mandolin was not so much the cause of insomnia as its effect. However, the cardinal cannot know that, and the whole matter is given excited realisation through his own tormented consciousness:

        Now 'tis a rapid burst
Of high and brilliant melody, which ceases
As soon as it has waked me with a leap;
        And now a sound, at first
As faint as a gnat's humming, which increases
And creeps between the folded thoughts of sleep,

Tickling the brain, and keeping in suspense,
Through night's long hours, the o'er-excited
sense. . . . .

Notice how appropriate the theme is to monologue. If anyone
other than the cardinal were telling the story, we should have
to decide whether the mandolin player were hallucination or
ghost. The best exponents of Browning's monologue were those
who did most with it. And this is true of Lee-Hamilton, whose
studies in hypochondria probe with psychological precision the
vulnerabilities of the human mind.

In the 1890s a cross-fertilisation took place between the monologue and the lyric. There flourished a whole school of poets
conventionally associated with Swinburne but who themselves
regarded Browning as their master. Ernest Dowson called the
latter poet's monologues 'masterpieces in verse' and particularly
admired—what is the key to the writing of monologues—Browning's 'tact of omission'. And Arthur Symons not only wrote
some distinguished dramatic monologues himself but produced
a whole study of Browning (1886) which was enthusiastically
appreciative. He wrote of 'Andrea del Sarto' and 'Fra Lippo
Lippi', 'to conceive a drama, to condense all its significance
and import, into some few hundred lines, this has been done
nowhere with such absolute perfection as here'. And a contemporary of Symons, John Davidson, contemplated a book of monologues called 'When Man Met God' spoken by Judas, Caesar
Borgia, Calvin, Cromwell and Cain. Of these, only 'Cain' was
written—it was published after Davidson's suicide in 1909—but
it embodies the pessimism that might have been expected from
Davidson's grim choice of subjects. However, of all these 1890s
poets, it was Lionel Johnson who threw tendrils forward into
the twentieth century and by his felicity of style decisively influenced the Imagists. His 'Julian at Eleusis' (1887) was a tightening
up and revision of a narrative that had originally appeared when
he was at school:

Caverns of haunted Ephesus! Your gloom,
Sweet with the dreamy incense, showed my youth
In earliest of mysterious ways: whenceforth,
Up mounting, brightening, labyrinths I traced
Mine homeward journey to the eternal Light. . . .

Writing such as this, together with the semi-dramatic projections of Ernest Dowson, influenced the young Ezra Pound beyond these authors' merits; and this must be their strongest claim to fame. Pound was intellectually isolated in the America of his youth and read at college T. B. Mosher's series of selections from such poets as Symons, Johnson and Dowson. These must have seemed to him England's *dernier cri*. Partly the influence was unconscious, for he insists some years later, in his Introduction to Johnson's *Poetical Works* (1915), that his effort was to improve upon the bookish dialect of these poets of the 1890s and to write 'the language as spoken'. Yet, if we look at Pound's early work, we can see how these poets helped to bridge the gap between himself and Browning by giving him access to a lyrical–descriptive form of monologue in which, characteristically, the speaker harks back to a happier past:

> I am homesick after mine own kind,
> Oh I know that there are folk about me, friendly faces,
> But I am homesick after mine own kind....
>
>   ('In Durance', 1907)

This, unrealised though it may seem, was the plasm from which Pound fashioned his later poems and from which, in his turn, Eliot learned as well. It must rank as one of the creative endeavours of the twentieth century, Pound's adaptation of the dramatic monologue. Critics do not seem to realise how many times in his early years Pound essayed this form. There are thirteen examples in his first four slim volumes, all written before 1912. Some, indeed, are excessively Browningesque ('Scriptor Ignotus', 'Fifine Answers') and the only one that keeps its place in the anthologies is the robust 'Altaforte' of 1909:

> Damn it all! all this our South stinks peace.
> You whoreson dog, Papiols, come! let's to music!
> I have no life save when the swords clash....

But a richer quarry than Provence proved to be China, as was shown by the 'Exile's Letter' of 1915, and even more rewarding than that was Ancient Rome. The remarkable series of monologues known as *Homage to Sextus Propertius* (1917) feels like memoir or epistle more than dramatic speech; yet there is no lack of drama in the various situations:

> But in one bed, in one bed alone, my dear Lynceus
> I deprecate your attendance;
> I would ask a like boon of Jove. . . .

The creation of character lies in that wry, uneasy tone. What may be failure of technique in the original Latin of Propertius, Pound turns to self-critical irony in his English transcription. But, even so, just as the 1890s are important for their influence on Pound, Pound himself, it is increasingly certain, will continue to be read for his influence on Eliot.

Eliot was experimenting with monologue very early on. 'The Death of St Narcissus', written in 1912, looks like monologue, and might have been, too, but for the need to kill the protagonist off in the last stanza. 'Prufrock' (1910–11) was written before 'Propertius' and, like that poem, it turns hesitancy into a dramatic device. After meeting Pound, Eliot developed rapidly. 'Gerontion' (1920) uses the monologue form with a freedom previously equalled only by Browning himself. Yet it is a poem written against Browning's technique. Browning accumulates effects: Eliot disperses them. The facts of Gerontion's life refuse to cohere. We never know who he is or what his connections are. In fact, at the end of the poem we know less about him than at the beginning. The whole framework flies apart. Any attempt to follow up this particular technique would make for incoherence. Eliot wrote other and more traditional monologues, such as 'Journey of the Magi' (1927), but equally, though in a different direction, these represent, for all their qualities, a dead end.

In spite of that, the monologue continued to run its course, though after 1920 this lay mostly in America. Robert Frost ignored Eliot and filtered the tradition through the subtle example of Edward Thomas. The latter poet wrote what look like dialogue poems, but it is noticeable that 'Wind and Mist' (1915), for example, is dominated by a central personality as surely as the monologues of Browning and the dialogue poems of Hardy, Thomas's most immediate master. From such examples Frost took the form to a point that has hardly been equalled. I am thinking, among other works, of 'The Pauper Witch of Grafton', 'The Census-Taker', 'Wild Grapes' and 'A Servant to Servants'

(1914). The speaker in the last-named poem is a woman trapped in a travesty of home-making—cooking and cleaning for a bunch of men hired by her unfeeling husband. She is painfully conscious that her strength will not last as long as her succession of tasks. The climax of the poem is a story she tells of her father's brother who was insane and confined in a wooden cage in the attic:

> He'd shout and shout
> Until the strength was shouted out of him,
> And his voice died down slowly from exhaustion.
> He'd pull his bars apart like bow and bowstring,
> And let them go and make them twang until
> His hands had worn them smooth as any oxbow.
> And then he'd crow as if he thought that child's play
> The only fun he had. I've heard them say, though,
> They found a way to put a stop to it.

The situation of the speaker is similar to that of the madman. Love has turned to derangement, life to confinement, strength is on the wane. The poem is couched in verse so nervous and live as to indicate a direct continuity from Browning. That image of the bow and bowstring with its suggestion of lethal intent baulked by imbecile impotence should not be wasted upon us. The poem is a study in weakness, but couched in a verse idiom that matches the best of the English and American traditions of living speech.

In this inheres Frost's superiority to his successors. Randall Jarrell was his most persuasive advocate (*Poetry and the Age*, 1955), but he could not translate his critical insights into verse. And Robert Lowell suffers from an over-restrictive approach. One could say that it is not the persona in Lowell that interests the author of *Life Studies* but the Lowell in his various personae. Nevertheless, he had a galvanic influence on the younger British poets. His crudities and jerks meant more in the late 1950s than the academic suavities of many respected seniors.

> It's the injustice ... he is so unjust—
> whiskey-blind, swaggering home at five.
> My only thought is how to keep alive.
> What makes him tick? Each night now I tie

> ten collars and his car key to my thigh ...
> Gored by the climacteric of his want
> he stalls above me like an elephant.
>   ('"To Speak of the Woe that is in Marriage"', 1959)

And it cannot be coincidence that, in the ten years after *Life Studies* reached Britain in 1959, more than 400 monologues were published by poets such as George MacBeth, Peter Redgrove, Edward Lucie-Smith and Peter Porter; to name only the leading exponents of the form.

At first sight, these British poets of the 1960s seem to be more objectively dramatic in their form than the Americans. I suspect this to be a sign of the effort needed to break down and reconstruct the unsatisfactory verse techniques prevalent in their formative years. Direct resort to Eliot and Pound had not done much for their elders. The initial problem was to match the fictional properties of the monologue with the urgency to be found in poets like Owen and Rosenberg, whose premature deaths had truncated British poetry. George MacBeth has a poem, 'Report to the Director' (c. 1960), which shows the efficiency of a mass-extermination, expressed in the crisp tones of a visiting inspector:

> I doubt if anyone smelled
> A rat in the whole building, or heard as much
> As a squeak from a plimsoll. They moved like professionals
> From start to finish. I'd say it was all good work.
> They certainly do things with the minimum fuss.
> I'd recommend we exonerate the whole depot.

But once such a synthesis was accomplished—most notably by MacBeth himself and by Peter Redgrove—the monologue form seemed too restrictive to embody contemporary experience. So the next problem is how to escape from the cruder exigencies of the monologue without losing the correlative necessary for dramatic speech. Perhaps a resolution to this difficulty is indicated by a glance back at Browning, some of whose technical resources, even now, remain to be exploited. It is clear that much of his power lies in his sense of audience, and, to create such a sense, he developed a vocabulary of nods, becks and gestures, indicating a reaction to the words of his speaker:

Nay, we'll go
Together down, sir
('My Last Duchess', *ante* 1842)

Then, you'll take
Your hand away that's fiddling on my throat
('Fra Lippo Lippi', c. 1853)

You turn your face, but does it bring your heart?
('Andrea de Sarto', c. 1853)

Draw round my bed: is Anselm hanging back?
('The Bishop Orders His Tomb', 1845)

This vocabulary seems to me developed from the stage directions
embodied in the verse of Shakespeare—'What, man! Ne'er pull
your hat upon your brows'. It will be interesting to see whether
the range of such stage directions will stretch much further.
Of course, various extensions are still possible. The American
poet Anne Stevenson has a book called *Correspondences* (1974)
which is an epistolary novel in verse and includes speeches or
monologues in the form of letters written by seven generations
of a mid-Western family. The basic form is varied in a number
of directions: a religious fanatic addresses God, a bride before
her wedding writes a memorandum to her married self, a dying
woman's imaginary journal recalls her thwarted life, her husband
after her death confides to her memory the letter he dared
not write her when she was living:

Ruth, in our thirty-six years lost to eye-strain and
    bad temper
you never spoke to me once of what I know.
I neither dared nor dared not to speak to you, though
sometimes your inattentions drew black words like
    swarming insects
swimming in held-back tears through my desperate
    paragraphs. . . .

The whole is contained within a framework of the present composed of letters and responses flying back and forth across the
Atlantic. This is one of the more decisive attempts in our own

time to bring the sense of a reacting audience into the form of the monologue.

Throughout the twentieth century there has been this quest for a new personalisation; an adaptation of the monologue that would contain some of the attributes, not only of epic and tragedy, but, currently, of prose fiction as well. A good deal of the most distinguished writing of our time has been successfully transplanted to radio and it may be that this prefigures a kind of radiophonic poetry which could continue to exist independently of the medium. The present interest in the speaking voice, both in recital work and in broadcasts, may very well be a genuine recrudescence. In any case, the monologue, or some version of it, is likely to be with us for a considerable time to come. We had better welcome it, since the more traditional forms which it has supplanted seem unlikely to reassert themselves for our approval.

10 Eliot, Whitman and American Tradition

Few critics have attempted to answer the question most often asked by those who grew up to find the revolutionary young poets of the 1920s embalmed as elder statesmen of the 1950s. Is Eliot really a great poet? What are the indisputably major poems and how do we read them? Why—a question so far ignored by all Eliot commentators—why has Eliot had so little influence on the younger English poets?

This last question is even more relevant now we can see that the period 1918–1955 produced in England little more than a few good but essentially minor poets. And the fact that the emphasis must now be placed on (for example) Empson, Graves and Betjeman, rather than the fashionables with whom we were plagued in our youth, does not render the question any the less relevant.

There are certainly points of difficulty in Eliot's technique that make it possible to understand at least some of the resistance to his poetry when it first started to come out. J. C. Squire's review of *The Waste Land* is well-enough known: 'a grunt would serve equally well' (*London Mercury*, 1923). And, as Mrs Leavis has pointed out (*Scrutiny*, 1943), George Gordon's inaugural lecture as Professor of Poetry at Oxford (1934) was little more than a series of gibes at Eliot as representative of the 'moderns'. Still, these men were not fools. Granted that their reaction was a mistaken one, ought we not to enquire how exactly the mistake came about?

One could say that there are points of difference between Eliot's poetry and that of his English predecessors. If we suggest Langland, Chaucer, Shakespeare, Wordsworth and Eliot are among our greatest poets, it is the last-named that appears to be the wild card in the pack. All the others had a high regard for plot and a logic that carries them through the aesthetic variability of their poetry. Eliot, on the other hand, seems to work rather by suggestion, qualitative progression, evocative catalogue.

This is best illustrated from 'Gerontion' (1919). Ostensibly the poem appears to be a monologue spoken by an old man deploring his futile life. But the more we look at this poem, the odder it all gets. Nobody requires a detailed biography of the protagonist, but it is quite in order to enquire who exactly he is. The references to his past are singularly inconclusive:

> I was neither at the hot gates
> Nor fought in the warm rain
> Nor knee deep in the salt marsh, heaving a cutlass,
> Bitten by flies, fought.

So now we know what he didn't do. But nothing in the poem gives us very much evidence of what it was that he did.

The impatient reader may rejoin that this is precisely the point of the poem: it is about an old man who has accomplished nothing. And I am far from suggesting that this takes away from the credit of 'Gerontion' as a literary work. But it is necessary to concede that it is a literary work operating in terms very different from those of Chaucer, Shakespeare, Wordsworth: different from, in fact, English dramatic narrative.

What is so extraordinary about the poem is the way in which it actively evades telling a story:

> In depraved May, dogwood and chestnut, flowering
>   judas,
> To be eaten, to be divided, to be drunk
> Among whispers; by Mr. Silvero
> With caressing hands, at Limoges
> Who walked all night in the next room;
> By Hakagawa, bowing among the Titians;
> By Madam de Tornquist, in the dark room
> Shifting the candles; Fräulein von Kulp
> Who turned in the hall, one hand on the door . . .

Who are all these people? No further mention is made of them. Yvor Winters calls this mode of fictionalising pseudo-reference: naming characters and alluding to events which are not specified in detail within the poem and have no existence outside it (*In Defense of Reason*, 1947, pp. 48 ff., 87 ff.). This is very distinct from the clearcut narrative of (say) *Othello* or 'Michael'.

Obviously, then, the effect of 'Gerontion' is going to be different from that of previous English poems. Instead of history we are given hints; instead of characters, implication. Using Winters's terminology once again (*ibid.*, pp. 57 ff.) we proceed not by chronological nor even dramatic narrative but by qualitative progression.

This means that the poem moves, if it moves at all, not through logical connections but through images associated emotionally and suggestively. Often this works in terms of catalogue:

> De Bailhache, Fresca, Mrs. Cammel, whirled
> Beyond the circuit of the shuddering Bear
> In fractured atoms. . . .

These names are all foreign and suggest, in some obscure way, decadence: the author assumes we know whom he is talking about, and certainly names such as 'de Bailhache' have some kind of aristocratic significance, but apparently they have all come to an explosive end, 'in fractured atoms'. A similar effect is gained by Scott Fitzgerald in his list of those who came regularly to the Great Gatsby's parties (1926, ch. 4). It is all rather like reading a faded yellow newspaper account of Edwardian junketing or debauches during the Prohibition period. Except that here what might have been an accidental Happening is given an artistic force and direction.

So the point of 'Gerontion' is that it has no point; the character of the speaker is to be devoid of character. He cannot be defined by his past history since he appears to have none. He cannot be characterised by his present circumstances: they do not exist. F. R. Leavis has remarked (*New Bearings in English Poetry*, 1932) that the few details we are given about Gerontion's environment— the decayed house, the goat coughing, the woman keeping the kitchen—co-exist rather than coalesce into an achieved situation. Nor can Gerontion be defined by his associates: they have no relationship to each other in his wandering mind and he does not remember enough about them to make them actual. It is a nice example of a definite evocation of indefiniteness.

This is by no means an isolated example in Eliot of an apparently idiosyncratic approach to poetic form. Indeed, as an early poem, it is rather more traditional in its performance than later, and greater, works.

Ash Wednesday (1927–30), for example, defies any sort of description in conventionally literary terminology. Plot and character have no place here as categorising terms. Indeed, it has often seemed to me that the method of modern literary criticism, with its emphasis on linguistic analysis rather than structural survey, was developed to explain and justify poems such as this.

It would be an escape on the part of a critic to define *Ash Wednesday* simply as a collection of religious lyrics. Yet what else is it? Some progression there seems to be, certainly. The unnamed protagonist begins in weariness of spirit, has a vision of a garden that proves to be dangerously seductive, struggles away from it in a series of crises typified by mounting a twisted flight of stairs, surveys the vision once more from the vantage point of an achieved equipoise, questions it in terms of increasing bewilderment, finishes in resignation tinctured with hope. Or at least that is how I should characterise Sections I–VI of *Ash Wednesday*.

But it cannot be said that anything is decisively *told* to us. On the contrary, all is indecisiveness and suggestion:

> Because I do not hope to turn again
>
> Who walked between the violet and the violet
>
> This is the time of tension between dying and birth . . . .

If, even, we take the most dramatically fictional section of the poem, no. II, we will find any plot suppressed in favour of a vibrant atmosphere, a series of evocative images:

> Lady, three white leopards sat under a juniper-tree
> In the cool of the day, having fed to satiety
> On my legs my heart my liver and that which had been
>   contained
> In the hollow round of my skull. . . .

Clearly it would make no sense to ask, as we might of Chaucer or Wordsworth, what those leopards are, what they represent. But equally I think Leavis is abdicating responsibility when he declares they have only a heraldic function (*New Bearings*). Rather I see them as suggesting an impulse of destruction; which renders the Lady's association with them highly equivocal.

What then of the Lady? The scattered bones of the protagonist say

> Because of the goodness of this Lady
> And because of her loveliness, and because
> She honours the Virgin in meditation,
> We shine with brightness.

Any attempt to tie her down to a fixed quantity disperses before this haze of evocation, this built-in paradox—the bones scattered *because* of her goodness and beauty. But this, again, is the point of the poem. We do not know, and cannot know, who the Lady is. Like the Romantic poets—Blake, Keats and Shelley—Eliot is asking questions rather than proffering answers.

But his manner of doing so is greatly different from that of his predecessors. Whereas Blake dramatises a tiger, Keats a dying man listening to the nightingale, Shelley a wind as both creative and destructive impulse, Eliot shows us a priestess-like figure in a decidedly contradictory context. And, if we turn to enquire:

> The Lady is withdrawn
> In a white gown, to contemplation, in a white gown.

Just how subtle this refusal to define a situation is can be seen if we relate the passage to the source from which it was almost certainly drawn. Everyone recognises the relationship with Canto xxx of the *Purgatorio*, but there is another factor involved. Eliot, it is well known, was in his earlier years a virtually tireless reviewer of middlebrow books—novels, detective fiction, and the like. Since he did many of these for his own magazine, *The Criterion*, it is reasonable to conclude that he wrote them from personal preference and that such matters would form part of his habitual reading. Certainly echoes from such sources persist in poems which at first sight seem to be very distinct from them in technique and approach. Little, it would seem, would connect *Ash Wednesday* with the plodding realism of H. G. Wells. Yet consider this passage, from 'The Door in the Wall' (1906):

> It was very difficult for Wallace to give me his full sense of that garden into which he came.
>
> There was something in the very air of it that exhilarated, that gave one a sense of lightness and good happening and well-being.... And everything was beautiful there.
>
> Wallace mused before he went on telling me. 'You see,' he said, with the doubtful inflection of a man who pauses at incredible things, 'there were two great panthers there. ... And I was not afraid. There was a long wide path with marble-edged flower borders on either side, and these two huge velvety beasts were playing there with a ball....
>
> 'Then presently there came a sombre dark woman, with a grave, pale face and dreamy eyes, a sombre woman, wearing a long soft robe of pale purple, who carried a book, and beckoned and took me aside with her to a gallery above a hall. ... She took me to a seat in the gallery, and I stood beside her, ready to look at her book as she opened it upon her knee. The pages fell open. She pointed, and I looked, marvelling, for in the living pages of the book I saw myself; it was a story about myself, and in it were all the things that had happened to me since ever I was born'. ...

Here we have the main properties of this section and some of the one that follows. I have deliberately omitted the connecting links of realistic narrative, and so the story seems much better than in fact it is. It is surprising how many evocative details in modern middlebrow fiction add up to a fragmentated poetry: one could almost construct the townscape of 'The Love Song of J. Alfred Prufrock' (1910–11) and 'Portrait of a Lady' (1909–10) from the fog swirling over the roofs of Conan Doyle's Sherlock Holmes stories (1887 *et seq.*). And here, too, we have a vibration beyond the immediate prose narrative: it is this vibration that gives the story what life it has, and Eliot has abstracted the vibration from 'The Door in the Wall' while suppressing the actual plot.

This vibration, however, evokes a feeling beyond its immediate particulars. What is this garden, this mysterious garden where the beasts lie down and are calm, where everything is peaceful and holy? One thinks, inevitably, of the Garden of Eden; itself a foreshadowing of what many people still conceive to be Heaven: a place where no work is done, where all is given over to meditation. And it is clear enough where *that* notion comes from: the archetypal image of the womb, in which the embryo floats, calm and protected, safe from all responsibility and the incessant attrition of life.

It is this, turning back to the text, that gives the second section of *Ash Wednesday* such power. And it is a power which can be felt without knowledge or acknowledgement of its sources, though these may have to be adduced if we are to make exegesis intelligible.

But why, the reader may ask, has Eliot not spelt out his situation in detail—why, in particular, has he not told us that the garden is viewed with the eye of childhood? I would suggest that this is because he has not the certainty that faith in a biblical myth would give him, or the lack of self-criticism everywhere exhibited in the prose of an H. G. Wells. He is not certain, at the point reached by Section II, that the garden is an escape from adult responsibility and is therefore to be grown out of and thenceforward avoided. Moreover, he has not the certainty of the English narrative tradition.

But the poem does progress, albeit (as Winters would say) qualitatively, and by Section III we have a struggle away from the garden and all it represents and by Section IV an equipoise that enables him from a great height—from the gallery, as it were—to look back at it. Again, a highly idiosyncratic view is put forward, made available by a method which has no parallel in earlier English narrative poets.

The method is taken to its extreme in the *Four Quartets*. This is Eliot's attempt at a *Prelude*: a spiritual diary 1934–42; an exploration of the dark night of the soul. Unlike Wordsworth, Eliot dissolves his narrative into a play of images and phrases with an emotive rather than a logical connection.

It is true, of course, that there is a surface formality of organisation, and writers such as Hugh Kenner (*The Invisible Poet*, 1959) have gone on to no small extent about this. But they should also have admitted the obvious corollary: that the poem was given such external shape because it is almost devoid of narrative progression.

Few readers will admit to being unable to specify what each of the Quartets is about or to explain how each differs from the others. The work, if indeed it is one, is the result of a process of accretion. According to Hugh Kenner, Eliot's revision of *Murder in the Cathedral* (1935) left him with a quantity of fragments excised from the play because they were unsuited to the theatre. From internal evidence they would seem to have been concerned with the problem of choice and the nature of reality. A visit to a deserted mansion in Gloucestershire precipitated these fragments into a sustained meditation upon the past which became 'Burnt Norton' (1935). A further meditation was conceived concurrently with another play; but, along with the conception of 'East Coker' (1940), came the idea that this and the poem already written could be extended into the series that eventually was called the *Four Quartets*.

In spite of the title, the Quartets are best thought of separately. One imitates another, but with increasing artificiality; and the proportion of waste matter to poetry increases, too, as the reader proceeds. 'East Coker' is a sensitive elegy over the middle years of life and is therefore flawed by its incongruously violent fourth section. 'The Dry Salvages' (1941) is spoiled by functionless lapses into High Table conversation and so may be considered in terms of its better individual parts, especially the fine sestina on the fishermen. While 'Little Gidding' (1942), apart from its terza rima on *il miglior fabbro*, is the failure of the four. A willed assertiveness of metaphor gives rise to a considerable amount of local confusion. The sense of exaltation that appears intermittently is not associated with anything that can be seen to occur in the text. Nothing is given to us concretely enough to justify the final proclamation, 'All manner of thing shall be well ...'. One can infer what has happened. Quartet has imitated Quartet, and 'Little Gidding' is an attempt to rescue the *Four Quartets* from the sense of defeat that, if they were taken as a whole, would mark them out as a failure.

That is why one would choose rather to look at the unequivocally great poem among them, 'Burnt Norton', on its own. It is difficult, but its difficulty is not, like that of 'Little Gidding', a result of technical failure. Rather it arises because 'Burnt Norton' is a poem of a peculiar kind, embodying attitudes so paradoxical as to resist direct expression. Therefore the language is deployed in a pattern of contrasts that have great local vitality but which, since the process has little to do with traditional verse narrative, exact considerable toll of the critic's power of rationalisation.

The poet begins by explaining in a register derivative from the F. H. Bradley of *Appearance and Reality* (1893) that an experience which has not happened is undiscussable:

> What might have been is an abstraction
> Remaining a perpetual possibility
> Only in a world of speculation.

The tone is ironic; the proposition is there to be rejected. For he then evokes just such an experience which, he assures us, has no basis in his past. However, the vivacity of the register he uses to evoke this—a mode very different from the imitation of Bradley—is such as to put the experience concretely before us:

> Footfalls echo in the memory
> Down the passage which we did not take
> Towards the door we never opened
> Into the rose-garden. . . .

It is a use of poetry to create what, Bradley claims, could not possibly be there. Through this paradox, the poet is able to admit us to a mystical illumination after he has said that it never happened to him. In this way he turns his back on an apparently arid past in favour of one rich with a meaning denied to his arid present.

It is as though an experience is assumed never to have taken place, and, at the same time, is set before us, an actual moment. And this 'moment' manifests itself as an association of images which look as though they might progress into narrative, but, in practice, never do. As in *Ash Wednesday*, a plot is suppressed in favour of evocative vibration. Here again we may have passing reference to a probable source, first pointed out by John Heath-Stubbs in a symposium on Eliot edited by Tambimuttu and March (1948). Eliot's 'Burnt Norton' has properties in common with Kipling's 'They' (1904): a secret garden with a lily-pond and children hiding in shrubs and trees. The datum of Kipling's story is that the children are hallucinated or invoked by a grave and courteous lady who, because she is blind, will never marry

and will never have children of her own. Eliot's analogy seems
to be that in spiritual blindness one does not possess such history
as one had, while with spiritual insight one possesses even that
which never occurred. The world of speculation, denied by Bradley, is acted out in this urgent verse with its restless play upon
words:

> Go, said the bird, for the leaves were full of
>   children,
> Hidden excitedly, containing laughter.
> Go, go, go, said the bird: human kind
> Cannot bear very much reality.
> Time past and time future
> What might have been and what has been
> Point to one end, which is always present.

Once more, it is not necessary to acknowledge the source of
the poem, if indeed it really is one, but acknowledgement is
a way of defining the singular blend of resignation and hope
one finds in the verse here.

This singularity of subject-matter rendered it impossible for
the poet to state his paradox directly. And it was more than
personal idiosyncrasy that stopped him from making the attempt.
It is true that Eliot was never much of a hand at telling a
story. The earlier poems hint at plots, perhaps imply them,
but never spell them out. And when we come to the late plays,
where a story really is to be told, the inadequacies in plotting
are so crude as to cause embarrassment. It is not for me to
belabour a great writer with his worst work: to point out the
way in which the narrative proceeds in *The Cocktail Party* (1949)
in convulsive jerks; or to detail the concatenation of coincidence
that brings the characters in *The Confidential Clerk* (1954) together—if 'together' is the word. In even a passing consideration
of these plays we see at once why in the earlier poems Eliot
chose to keep his characters—Mr Silvero, Hakagawa, Madame
de Tornquist et al.—apart.

But I am inclined to think this is not merely a matter of
idiosyncrasy. Or, if it were, it meshed in extraordinarily well
with the tradition in which Eliot wrote.

For I am far from believing Eliot to be the new departure
he is commonly considered. Granted that his *procédé* is markedly

unlike that of the great English narrative poets, this does not necessarily make him the quintessence of modernism: turning all established practice on its head and producing an entirely new form of verse.

Those who think that this is what Eliot did can usually be found considering—and over-valuing—Eliot at his most eccentric: the Eliot, that is to say, of *The Waste Land* (1922); that jumble of wild and sometimes misleading allusions, leaps from rhetoric to realism, lapses—for me, welcome ones—into that grave slow music which is curiously Eliot's own:

> A woman drew her long black hair out tight
> And fiddled whisper music on those strings . . . .

But even in *The Waste Land* there are to be found points of method similar to the approach of the great poems; of, that is to say, 'Gerontion', *Ash Wednesday* and 'Burnt Norton'. Most notably, these are the suppression of plot in favour of evocative vibration; phanopoeia—that is to say, the emotive play of images; qualitative progression, whereby properties link up without following a narrative line; a tendency towards implication by means of catalogue or montage; free verse.

None of these is new to the English language, though they had not previously been used successfully by English poets. This is not a conundrum: the inference is clear. What English critics of the 1920s resisted in Eliot's verse, and in some cases denounced, was not its quality of modernism. There is no world in which Eliot co-exists with Tzara, Dada and the Sitwells. It was not a young English poet the Georgians were fighting against, but a young American poet.

Once this is taken into account, all becomes clear. *The Waste Land* and *Ash Wednesday* cannot be related with any persuasiveness to English narrative precursors because there is no sense in which they can be termed English narrative poems.

How the United States came to develop its native speech is a matter for the sociologist and has no place in my argument here. One could suggest that differences of climate and landscape were bound to make for the development of a nucleus originally English away from its roots; which, in the case of the United States, appear to be (via the Pilgrim Fathers) the Bible, Shakespeare, possibly *Pilgrim's Progress*. One could also say that pressure of immigration, even when it did not centrally affect that nucleus—for Eliot was a Boston Brahmin—played a crucial part in altering the complexion of the nation as a whole. Certainly, throughout the American nineteenth century, England drifted progressively further away.

But for my purpose it would be sufficient to show that Eliot had predecessors, and at least one of them very distinguished indeed; so that what has been termed 'modernity' in his work should rather be regarded as the development of a decisively American tradition.

Who, long before Eliot, worked through evocative vibration, phanopoeia, montage, free verse and the rest? The answer is obvious: Whitman. And if we further enquire why this palpable fact was not noted by critics and editors as intelligent as Leavis, Roberts and Empson, we can only point to one of the salient characteristics of Eliot's work: that he, more than any other poet, has succeeded in constructing his own literary history. Unfortunately, it is largely fictional.

'The most individual parts of a poet's work may be those in which the dead poets, his ancestors, assert their immortality most vigorously' wrote Eliot in 'Tradition and the Individual Talent' (1919). We may agree. But in Eliot's case the ancestors we would wish to acknowledge are not those which he claims for himself; not, that is to say, Baudelaire, Laforgue, Corbière, nor even Tourneur, Middleton and Webster. The characteristic form and approach of his own verse has little in common with either French symbolism or Jacobean drama.

Baudelaire, for example, has a very strong narrative line. Consider 'La Charogne' (1843), where the young couple stumble across a decaying corpse and a moral point is made from the confrontation: nothing ambiguous or equivocal there. Or the famous 'Spleen' (1857), where the poet projects a sustained simile as a means of defining his mood. Nothing Eliotesque about that: the simile describes a country in clear detail. The young prince of the poem is not the Fisher King, nor Tiresias, either: in Baudelaire the particulars of the country are described efficiently, one arising out of another; while in The Waste Land the wildly contrasting images are juxtaposed to effect a deliberate jarring of the sense.

Nor do I find a much closer relationship between Eliot, on the one hand, and Corbière and Laforgue on the other—even though he praised them highly. 'Cantique du pardon de Sainte-Anne' (1873) is spoken very much in the character of a ballad-singer present at a festival. Here again, the situation is defined, the particulars cohere. Where Corbière departs from the immediate particulars of the festival, he moves into a kind of jovial prayer— once more, far removed from the rhetoric of *The Rock* and *Murder in the Cathedral*, and equally foreign to the inturning agonies of self-examination in *Ash Wednesday*.

Of the three French poets I have named, Laforgue seems to have meant most to Eliot. But the protagonist in 'L'Hiver qui vient' (1886) is defined not just as the poet himself but as a quirky and personalised individual. So the catalogues which certainly occur in the poems are linked not just by atmosphere but also by the personality of the central character—almost the reverse procedure to that undertaken by Eliot with his shadowy Tiresias in *The Waste Land*. In general one would say that Corbière and Laforgue, like Baudelaire, plot more clearly, write more lucidly, give more idea of who's doing what to whom, than Eliot does.

It is true that Eliot wrote some straight imitations of French poets such as Gautier. But 'The Hippopotamus', 'A Cooking Egg', even the Sweeney poems, are hardly central to Eliot's slender output. And no one at this stage is likely to take seriously 'Conversation Galante', still less the poems actually written in French.

Possibly the debt to the Jacobeans is slightly more difficult to fend off. But I doubt it. Tourneur and Middleton are both remarkable for plot-construction: the speed and certainty of *The Revenger's Tragedy* (c.1606) has little parallel with the introspective verse of Eliot. It is true that 'Gerontion' falls into direct imitation of *The Changeling* (c.1622). But a great deal has happened before that speech of Beatrice–Joanna confessing to her father. It does not have to take upon itself the responsibility of implying the plot of a whole tragedy. And in any case I cannot see much formal relation between the speech of a young girl at the close of an event-packed drama and the monologue of an old man, separate from any drama at all and wandering disconsolately about the ruins of a wasted life.

One might be on firmer ground with Webster (*fl.* 1613). Here indeed the drama is broken-backed and the poetry intermittent. But, whereas Eliot uses this as a literary device, with Webster it is rather a matter of bad craftsmanship, of patchy sensibility. One should admit without too much shame to not knowing exactly what Webster's plays are about. But there is a difference between the darkness of obfuscation and that of suggestive ambivalence. Gerontion's motives may be mixed; they are not, like those of Bosola, muddled.

So we can dispose of Eliot's account of his literary history as being one of his own less elusive fictions. It is difficult to see why he had to be so circumspect about all this. Possibly it had to do with his leaving America, giving up American nationality, even disguising a naturally strong and vigorous speaking voice with a curious intonation approximating to that sometimes deemed to be used by senior clergy of the Anglican denomination. Certainly Eliot managed, in reading aloud, to ruin with it some of his best poems.

In brief, seen as an English poet Eliot makes no sort of historical sense at all: springing fully armed from nowhere, writing a verse at odds with all that we hold best in the English tradition, influencing younger poets, if at all, measurably for the worse.

But Eliot taken as an American poet is something different again. Seen in that context his stature, great in any circumstances, seems actually to increase. What I propose to stress mainly is the Americanness of American poetry: an area, in other words, shared by all the major American poets. But even if, for the moment, we keep to a direct relationship between Eliot and Whitman, the verbal parallels are numerous and striking.

We must take Eliot at his most individual if we are to make much of a case. The sort of thing—it can almost be an irritating quirk of style—which M. C. Bradbrook called haughty humility (in *T. S. Eliot*, ed. B. Rajan, 1947) is seen, for instance, in 'East Coker':

> You say I am repeating
> Something I have said before. I shall say it again.
> Shall I say it again?

But Whitman, in 'Song of Myself' (1855), has

> If you do not say anything how can I say anything?
>
> Do I contradict myself?
> Very well then I contradict myself....

This is, equally, characteristic of Whitman: its confidence, its ease. Yet there is more than a passing resemblance here, of one poet to the other. Both, for example, admit—and use—what in English poets might be a fault.

Again, in 'Burnt Norton', we find Eliot enjoying what we have come to think of as a curiously Eliotesque form of paradox:

> Neither movement from nor towards,
> Neither ascent nor decline

But in Whitman we find just such a collapsing of geography to cast a doubt on the validity of time and distance in favour of the reacting self—'If they are not just as close as they are distant they are nothing' ('Song of Myself')—which in its turn recalls Eliot's 'End of the endless / Journey to no end' in *Ash Wednesday*, and so back to Whitman:

> Not I, not anyone else can travel that road for you. . . .
> Perhaps you have been on it since you were born and
>   did not know.   ('Song of Myself')

Such plasticity of locale, often taken to be a modern trait, is thus seen to be a Whitmanesque—more properly, an American—one.

Equally striking is the likeness of the images the two poets use. We have already glanced, in passing, at Section III of *Ash Wednesday*. Let us now quote from it:

> At the first turning of the second stair
> I turned and saw below
> The same shape twisted on the banister
> Under the vapour in the fetid air . . . . ('Song of Myself')

But Whitman also mounts a stair:

> My feet strike an apex of the apices of the stairs.
>   . . . still I mount and mount.
> Rise after rise bow the phantoms behind me,
> Afar down I see the huge first Nothing, I know I was
>   even there,

I waited unseen and always, and slept through the lethargic
   mist,
And took my time, and took no hurt from the fetid
   carbon. . . .

The stairs, the mounting, the phantom below, the fetor—all
are common to both passages. It is hardly coincidental.

Resemblances in imagery are coupled with similar syntactical
patternings in both poets. Examples are numerous. *The Waste
Land* has

After the torchlight red on sweaty faces
After the frosty silence in the gardens
After the agony in stony places . . .

which not only compares with Whitman's 'silent sea of faces'
in the Lincoln elegy but also with his

After the sea-ship, after the whistling winds,
After the white-gray sails taut to their spars and
   ropes . . . .   ('After the Sea Ship', 1874)

which in its turn recalls, in its patterning, not only the end
of *Ash Wednesday*—'the white sails still fly seaward'—but also
'Marina' (1930), with its ship imagery—

What seas what shores what grey rocks and what islands
What water lapping the bow . . .

from which we can go back to Whitman's 'Salut au Monde'
(1856)—

What waves and soils exuding?
What climes? what persons and cities are here? . . .

For all Whitman's confidence of tone, there is the same questioning
of experience: America, land of sudden contrasts and unexplored
frontiers, is not so easily set down as the damp and foggy
island we call Britain.

Perhaps it is this variousness of landscape that has produced
the most characteristic American tendency of all, towards what

I have termed montage. The disparity of landscape, of fauna, brings out an urge to assemble properties, to count them, to heap images one on top of another. Eliot, in *Murder in the Cathedral*, has 'The horn of the beetle, the scale of the viper, the mobile hard insensitive skin of the elephant, the evasive flank of the fish . . .'; or again, in 'Burnt Norton':

> The crying shadow in the funeral dance,
> The loud lament of the disconsolate chimera.

Truly, this is a country where anything can happen—where sounds are full of significance, often potentially hostile. Whitman, too, has this, in 'O Magnet-South' (1860)—'the bellow of the alligator, the sad noises of the night-owl and the wild-cat, and the whirr of the rattlesnake . . .'—and, in 'Our Old Feuillage' (1860): 'the howl of the wolf, the scream of the panther, and the hoarse bellow of the elk'. And notice, too, here as elsewhere, the tell-tale article: taken by Rostrevor Hamilton in his book on the subject (1949) to be a characteristic thumb-print of modern poets, but in fact a concomitant of this cataloguing trait in the American language.

The poem of Whitman's that most decisively influenced Eliot is without doubt the elegy on the death of President Lincoln (1865-6). To anatomise this would be to go into all of Eliot's poems in needless detail. But it is legitimate to point out two or three of the more striking parallels between the poets. And in doing this we may show something of Whitman's great distinction—a distinction even now all too grudgingly admitted on this side of the Atlantic.

The poem collapses intimations of the American landscape and memories of the Civil War into a montage mourning the death of a great and wise man. As we would expect, in absence of narrative logic, the landscape images are given to us with great and evocative intensity. Indeed, the whole poem is built around three symbols. And these recur, as subdued vibrations, throughout the corpus of more recent American poets; and Eliot is no exception.

Even thé first line, 'When lilacs last in the dooryard bloomed', is echoed by Eliot: 'In the rank ailanthus of the April dooryard . . .' ('The Dry Salvages'). And the lilac is perhaps the flower most mentioned in Eliot:

> Now that lilacs are in bloom
> She has a bowl of lilacs in her room

says Eliot, in 'Portrait of a Lady'. One need hardly mention

> April is the cruellest month, breeding
> Lilacs out of the dead land . . . .   (*The Waste Land*)

Sydney Musgrove in his penetrating study of Eliot and Whitman (1952)—to which, I must acknowledge, I owe some of my examples—says that Lincoln died in April and so may have served Eliot as a modern and familiar instance of the annual cycle of birth and death. However that may be, certainly lilacs are a mourning flower, an elegiac flower; and the lilac is one of the major symbols in Whitman's poem:

> In the dooryard fronting an old farm-house near the
>   white-washed palings,
> Stands the lilac-bush tall-growing with heart-shaped leaves
>   of rich green

> But mostly and now the lilac that blooms the first,
> Copious I break, I break the sprigs from the bushes

> Yet the lilac with mastering odor holds me

> Passing, I leave thee lilac with heart-shaped leaves,
> I leave thee there in the door-yard, blooming,
>   returning with spring

—an intimation that the symbol of Lincoln's death is also a symbol of resurrection: what he stood for has not died.

All this derives from the very first line of Whitman's poem. Let us look at the second: 'And the great star early drooped in the western sky in the night'. Here we have the second of Whitman's great central images, symbol of hope ebbing away, of the night coming in. This re-echoes all over Eliot's 'Hollow Men' (1924–5); is used, indeed, as a kind of refrain:

> the wind's singing
> More distant and more solemn
> Than a fading star

Under the twinkle of a fading star

   this valley of dying stars

   the perpetual star

—always, notice, in close association with the idea of a man dying. In Whitman, too, the image recurs over and over, as an intimation of sorrow yet to come:

O western orb sailing the heaven
Now I know what you must have meant as a month since
   I walked . . . .
As you drooped from the sky low down as if to my
   side . . . .

I cease from my song for thee,
From any gaze on thee in the west, fronting the west,
   communing with thee,
O comrade lustrous with silver face in the night.

And the third great image of the poem is that of the bird, the solitary singer, hidden from sight, who in this poem represents the hope of acceptance:

In the swamp, in the secluded recesses,
A shy and hidden bird is warbling a song.

Solitary the thrush,
The hermit withdrawn to himself, avoiding the settlements,
Sings by himself a song.

Song of the bleeding throat,
Death's outlet song of life, (for well dear brother I know,
If thou wast not granted to sing thou would'st surely
   die.)

This, too, occurs all over Eliot—always as a symbol of hope: most memorably, perhaps, in 'Marina'—'the woodthrush singing through the fog', but also as an insistent bird-call in 'Burnt Norton':

Quick, said the bird, find them, find them

Into our first world, shall we follow

The deception of the thrush?

Go, said the bird, for the leaves were full of children,
Hidden excitedly, containing laughter.

In Eliot the bird acts as either an incitement or a warning—that
'go' could mean 'follow' or it could mean 'be off'; and neither
we nor the poet can tell which. In Whitman the bird is related
to the poet: singing out of pain—'song of the bleeding throat'—
and who, if he could not sing, would die. And the song is
definitely a call:

Sing on there in the swamp,
O singer bashful and tender, I hear your notes, I hear
    your call,
I hear, I come presently, I understand you.

Even though the song may at first seem a song of woe, it
compels identification with its utterance:

Sing on, sing on you gray-brown bird,
Sing from the swamps, the recesses, pour your chant
    from the bushes,
Limitless out of the dusk, out of the cedars and pines.
Sing on, dearest brother, warble your reedy song....

The song compels him away from the star, image of sinking
despair and night, and eventually gives voice to one of the
loveliest lyrics in the whole of Whitman: an acceptance of death,
as of life, as part of the natural order of things. 'The voice
of my spirit tallied the song of the bird', he says, and the
bird sings,

Come lovely and soothing death
Undulate round the world, serenely arriving, arriving,
In the day, in the night, to all, to each,
Sooner or later delicate death....
Over the treetops I float thee a song,
Over the rising and sinking waves, over the myriad
    fields and the prairies wide,
Over the dense-packed cities all and the teeming

wharves and ways,
I float this carol with joy, with joy to thee O death.

The American Civil War is remembered, with all its 'battle-corpses, myriads of them' to the accompaniment of this 'victorious song, death's outlet song'—'That powerful psalm in the night I heard from recesses', uniting the memories of the past, the landscape of the present, the hopes of the future in associating to itself the other symbols, which tell the poet that all the suffering and death has not been in vain:

Comrades mine and I in the midst, and their memory
    ever to keep, for the dead I loved so well,
For the sweetest, wisest soul of all my days and
    lands—and this for his dear sake,
Lilac and star and bird twined with the chant of my
    soul,
There in the fragrant pines and the cedars dusk and dim.

With a poem like this before us, why is not Whitman generally regarded in Britain, as in America, as a great poet? All the critic need do, one would think, is read it. But it operates in a manner very distinct from Whitman's British contemporaries, Tennyson, Arnold and Swinburne; to say nothing of the great masters of their craft, the English narrative poets. This poem cannot be read as a simple sequence, the one event succeeding another to form a chronological whole. Rather it should be said that it coheres around its central symbols—the lilac, the star, the thrush—to evoke, rather than narrate, the Civil War and its hero—Whitman's hero, and the hero of a democracy.

But such a procedure would not puzzle our critics if they found it in a modern poet; it does not seem to puzzle them in Eliot. Merely it is that such a use of symbolism has been taken to be an essential characteristic of twentieth-century art, and therefore they were not looking for, and did not expect to find it in, the work of a nineteenth-century poet.

This problem cannot be shelved by saying that Whitman was seventy years or so ahead of his time. Such symbolism, such breaking down of narrative logic, can be found in the work of the great novelists who were his American contemporaries.

What, for example, are we to make of Captain Ahab in *Moby-Dick* (1851); what of the whale? Ahab taken out of context is a monomaniac, as most contemporary reviewers remarked; what happens when we put him into context? Taken as a simple story of the sea the novel—I nearly said dramatic poem—makes no manner of sense. But Lawrence interpreted it as the civilised will hunting down the animal blood-consciousness (*Studies in Classic American Literature*, 1924). And Winters termed it a perversion by man of the vengeance which is, properly, a Divine Right (*In Defense of Reason*, 1947). Even incidentals provoke such modes of interpretation: the squid, with its arbitrarily intertwining tentacles, symbol of flux and uncertainty; the mother-whales suckling their young, representative of the natural flow of life disturbed by Ahab's incursion into their untroubled seas.

Much the same interconnection of images—call it catalogue, montage, phanopoeia, what you will—can be found, too, in Hawthorne's *Scarlet Letter* (1850), 'Major Molyneux' (*ante* 1851), 'Young Goodman Brown' (1835); in the work, too, of lesser artists such as Thoreau and Emily Dickinson. This is a literature emerging from the sway of Scott and Wordsworth, just as America itself emerged from British colonialism. It is insular indeed to treat such a literature as ancillary to that of the English tradition.

But there are other, more tangible, reasons for our reluctance to accept Whitman as sign and prototype of an American literature and our consequent failure to put Eliot himself into perspective. Some of this is Whitman's own fault; most is that of the critics of his time.

Not that twentieth-century critics have shown much more discernment. Leavis dismisses Whitman along with Dreiser as being alienated from the European tradition (*'Anna Karenina' and Other Essays*, 1967). More damagingly still, Marius Bewley says that his 'exalted and stultifying afflatus' exerted a damaging influence on American letters (*The Complex Fate*, 1952). Still, Dr. Leavis has never committed himself to a wholesale appraisal of American literature—his remarks on Melville and Hawthorne, for instance, are only in the nature of pointers. And Mr Bewley has the remarkable gift of being interestingly wrong about almost every writer on whom he touches: Wallace Stevens, Robert Lowell and Scott Fitzgerald are only three that spring to mind.

But what of Lawrence? He, more than any other Englishman, seems to have understood Whitman. He says 'Whitman is a

very great poet, of the end of life. . . . The poet of the soul's
last shout and shriek, on the confines of death' (*Studies in Classic
American Literature*). But he also attacks 'I am he that aches
with amorous love', saying, 'Walter, leave off. You are not
HE. You are just a limited Walter. . . . Chu–chu–chu–chu–chuff!
Reminds one of a steam-engine.'

However, what Lawrence was talking about here is an exceed-
ingly bad poem, three lines long, that Whitman perpetrated
in the 1860s. By that time some, at least, of the rot had set
in; to be halted, momentarily, by the Civil War: because, with
the exception of a few of the *Drum-Taps*, the Lincoln poems
and the superlatively fine Civil War prose, the essential Whitman
is to be found in *Leaves of Grass*; especially that section now
called 'Song of Myself'.

It is one of the mysteries of literature that this is hardly
ever read in its original form. Critics as learned as Allan Rodway
and poets as Whitman-oriented as Bill Butler have expressed
surprise to me that there was more than one edition; and, granted
there was, that the one differed so much from the others.

Let us consider what critics have disliked in Whitman—the
quality that Marius Bewley, among others, calls afflatus. Do
we not find it here?:

> Here or henceforward it is all the same to me, I
>   accept Time absolutely.
> It alone is without flaw, it alone rounds and completes
>   all,
> That mystic baffling wonder alone completes all.
> I accept Reality. . . .

He had better, replied one stern American critic. But we can
see the faults in this passage without such prompting. Abstract,
quasi-philosophic, rhetoric unbacked by the pressure of implication—this is the sort of poetry that is felt to be typical of
Whitman. However, the point to remember is that it does not
appear in the first edition of the poem. There the equivalent
is one single line—and that, a good deal more tentative: 'One
time as good as another time ... here or henceforward it is
all the same to me.' And that is all. No absurdity about 'accepting
reality' whatsoever.

Or, to take a passage supposedly redolent of another of Whitman's vices—relentless egoism:

> My tongue, every atom of my blood, formed from this
>   soil, this air,
> Born here of parents born here from parents the same,
>   and their parents the same,
> I now thirty-seven years old in perfect health begin,
> Hoping to cease not until death.
>
> Creeds and schools in abeyance,
> Retiring back a while sufficed at what they are, but
>   never forgotten,
> I harbor for good or bad, I permit to speak at every
>   hazard,
> Nature without check with original energy.   (1881)

In fact Whitman was not thirty-seven when he wrote this; it, too, is a later addendum—a preliminary statement of intention before embarking upon his great poem.

Even the familiar beginning is an accretion upon the original. The first edition reads, simply, 'I celebrate myself', without the repetitive 'and sing myself'. The changes are symptomatic: they, like the additions, indicate a desire to explain, to force home—possibly, as unsympathetic readers might say, to bully or assert.

Every now and again, for instance, Whitman has added statements of intention with no equivalent in the original and little organic connection with the body of the text. Thus, at different points, we find lines such as the following:

> Absorbing all to myself and for this song
>
> And of these one and all I weave the song of myself
>
> Now I tell what I knew in Texas in my early youth . . . .

It could be argued that most of the changes are not additions such as these but changes in verbal emphasis. Thus, 'As the hugging and loving bedfellow sleeps at my side through the night, and withdraws at the peep of the day with stealthy tread' is the revised version of 'As God comes a loving bedfellow and sleeps at my side all night and close on the peep of the day'. It is obvious that 'hugging' unnecessarily stamps home 'loving' and that 'peep of day' implies withdrawal and that therefore the theatrical 'stealthy tread' is not needed. Changes such as these are in the direction of inflation and melodrama, and they are typical of Whitman's attempts at verbal revision. Over a long poem the effect of the changes is to blur and muffle.

Almost invariably the direct and concrete phrase is replaced by one abstract and rationalising. So the cumbrous 'And more the reminders they of life untold, and of freedom and extrication' has, as its original, the colloquial 'And go on the square for my own sake and for other's sake'. And for 'I hear all sounds running together, combined, fused or following' read 'I hear all sounds as they are tuned to their uses'.

Even when the revised version compresses or omits, it usually does so in the interests of abstraction:

> Eleves, I salute you! come forward!
> Continue your annotations, continue your questionings

is two lines, indeed, but the second is a kind of hold-all for the following in the original:

> I see the approach of your numberless gangs ... I
>   see you understand yourselves and me
> And know that they who have eyes are divine, and the
>   blind and lame are equally divine,
> And that my steps drag behind yours yet go before them,
> And are aware how I am with you no more than I
>   am with everybody.

'Continue your annotations', in retrospect, seems a poor equivalent for 'I see the approach of your numberless gangs'.

The reason for Whitman's lack of confidence in his own original is not far to seek. He was sophisticated enough to realise that his work represented a considerable development on the existing tradition: though, as Winters has pointed out, many of his ideas are to be found in Emerson, Whitman wrote in a far less conventional and British-oriented language. Moreover the publication of *Leaves of Grass* was a curiously individual venture: sponsored by Whitman himself, indeed partly printed by him, it received, when it came out in 1855, only three favourable reviews. All three were written by Whitman.

The rest of the critics joined in a chorus of shocked disfavour. 'We, who are not prudish, declare that the man who wrote p. 79 of the *Leaves of Grass* deserves nothing so richly as the executioner's whip' (*Critic*, 1856); 'a mass of sentimental filth' (*Criterion*, 1855); 'he must be some escaped lunatic raving in pitiable delirium' (*Boston Intelligencer*, 1856)—these are not extreme but characteristic instances of Whitman's critical reception.

The critics' understanding failed in two distinct areas. One is the question of the verse—the ear attuned to Longfellow, Holmes and J. R. Lowell simply could not hear the pattern of Whitman's metric: more than one critic—including Henry James some years later (1865)—compared it with the 'excited prose' of Martin Tupper. It is, in fact, based on an analgam of the Authorised Version, the testimonies of his mother's Quaker friends, and the writings of such freethinking rationalists as Frances Wright (*fl.* 1822; see F. O. Matthiessen, *The American Renaissance* (1941), pp. 536 ff). But more important still is the fact that critics failed to recognise the dramatic nature of the poem with which they were dealing. The 'I' of *Leaves of Grass* is as much a persona as Shakespeare's Hamlet.

There is a distinction, of course: the distinction to be observed throughout major American literature. Shakespeare's persona is defined by a more or less concrete plot, whereas Whitman's is dispersed throughout the poem. Instead of plot or chronology we get a phanopoeia of emotionally related images.

Central to these is the symbol of the grass. This represents life: common, growing where it can, spreading everywhere—and yet various and extraordinary even in its ubiquity:

> A child said, What is the grass? fetching it to me
>   with full hands;
> How could I answer the child? ... I do not know what
>   it is any more than he.

> I guess it must be the flag of my disposition, out of
>   hopeful green stuff woven.

> Or I guess it is the handkerchief of the Lord,

> A scented gift and remembrancer designedly dropped,
> Bearing the owner's name someway in the corners, that
>   we may see and remark, and say Whose?...

Here Whitman achieves a remarkable identification of disparate
qualities: the common grass is seen to be rarely scented and
to be a complex creation in its own right. At the same time
it is identified with the persona himself and with the Creator
who made them both. Significantly, the question which sparks
off this recognition of relationship comes from the fresh sensibility
of a child.

The speaker in the poem is, then, only in a sense Whitman
himself; more relevantly, he is a working-class American and
representative therefore of all Americans; and, through America,
of life itself.

The poem is not simply one about nature. A good deal of
it is given to a passionate exploration of America; once more,
a relating together of disparities. Whitman moves, by qualitative
progression, from a recognition of the grass, through scenes wild
and less wild—the trapper's wedding, the runaway slave, the
country town—to the remarkable celebration of the People, beginning

> The pure contralto sings in the organloft,
> The carpenter dresses his plank ... the tongue of his
>   foreplane whistles its wild ascending lisp ....

At first sight, these two images appear to have nothing to do
with each other. But, apart from the alliterative links that seem
to be inseparable from great poetry in the English language,
both the contralto and the carpenter are fulfilling themselves,
and, odd though it may seem, through song, by giving tongue.

In much the same way a concept of dance or organised movement unites these particular instances of Whitman's American
montage:

> The groups of newly-come immigrants cover the wharf
>   or levee,
> The woollypates hoe in the sugarfield, the overseer views
>   them from his saddle;
> The bugle calls in the ballroom, the gentlemen run for

> their partners, the dancers bow to each other;
> The youth lies awake in the cedar-roofed garret and harks
> to the musical rain . . . .

Ostensibly this is all catalogue: the tell-tale naming 'The . . . ,
the . . . , the . . . .' In fact, however, there is a pattern through
all these contrasts: the pattern of qualitative progression. Thus
the immigrants serve as a momentary focal point for the images
that follow: what they see is America. The slaves at their drudgery
are given an almost balletic quality by the context in which
they appear; followed closely by the energy and purpose of
the ballroom, as though the dance were itself work; and the
music of the dance flows on into the next line to influence
the quality of the rain. Work, dance and music become an
entity without our losing our sense of the disparities involved
in such resolution.

From the lowest to the highest, all are involved in this dance
of life:

> The prostitute draggles her shawl, her bonnet bobs on
> her tipsy pimpled neck,
> The crowd laugh at her blackguard oaths, the men jeer
> and wink to each other,
> (Miserable! I do not laugh at your oaths, nor jeer you,)
> The President holds a cabinet council, he is surrounded
> by the great Secretaries . . . .

The last line restates the basic pattern of the first two in grave
and respectable terms: just as the prostitute is surrounded by
a jeering crowd so the President is surrounded by his officers.
The shock of the contrast is heightened by this implied relationship
of circumstances; and, beyond them, the fact that they all make
up America.

Immediately following upon this taste of the sublime we are
brought down to conformability:

> On the piazza walk five friendly matrons with twined
> arms;
> The crew of the fish-smack pack repeated layers of
> halibut in the hold,
> The Missourian crosses the plains toting his wares and his
> cattle,

> The fare-collector goes through the train—he
>   gives notice by the jingling of loose change,
> The floormen are laying the floor—the tinners are
>   tinning the roof—the masons are calling for mortar,
> In single file each shouldering his hod pass onward
>   the laborers;
> Seasons pursuing each other . . . .

Qualitative progression: just as the matrons are interlinked one with another, so are the repeated layers of halibut—acted out by the echo in the line itself. The concept of the fishing-smack leads us on to the idea of travel, and so we see first the cattle-drover, then the fare-collector. The idea of motion is contrasted with an idea of stasis—a house built. But motion is not quite lost: it is time to pack up, and, in a line whose inversion gives it a Miltonic dignity, the labourers leave for home. Indeed, one connecting factor throughout the entire section is that it all appears to take place between evening and nightfall, so that it ends in a gathering night beautifully symbolised in the Indian names with their association of desert and loneliness—'The torches shine in the dark that hangs on the Chattahoochee or the Altama-haw'—which itself makes more welcome the bright oases of light where patriarchs sit at dinner with sons and grandsons, and where, finally, both city and country sleep.

But further even than this is the sense of identity Whitman projects: the identity of these people with each other, despite social and regional disparities, and with himself, the observer seeing everything and subsuming it—'Walt Whitman, an American, one of the roughs, a kosmos'. So this section, like the entire poem, is a montage: contrasting disparities and yet showing their interconnections.

The poem turns on this central section relating the people and regions of America. It is held together throughout by the symbol of grass as life. And not by this only, but also by the way in which the poet uses his persona in the poem: in worshipping his own body he is worshipping America. Moreover, the poem is linked by the persona's seeing eye. What Eliot, on his own testimony, attempted with Tiresias in *The Waste Land*, Whitman, far more successfully, brings off here. The substance of the poem is what the persona sees—'I am the man . . . I suffered . . . I was there.'

Much of the technique and language used was immanent in the America of Whitman's time, though he was certainly the first to bring it into full life in verse. However, he was among a most remarkable group of near-contemporaries, including Melville, Hawthorne and Thoreau. And if his work received short shrift from the critics, as indeed that of Melville did, this is only a sign that America had not awakened to a full consciousness of its cultural identity: critics tend always to see things through the eyes of the generation previous to them.

But Whitman certainly defined the literary possibilities of that culture, as the successful montages of Hemingway and Fitzgerald and the unsuccessful ones of Dreiser and Wolfe only go to show. However, he lacked a decisive interpreter: the position pre-empted by George Santayana as intermediary between the nineteenth century and the twentieth should have been occupied by someone who understood American literature and who did not attempt to emasculate its barbaric yawp into some Italianate ideal.

The early twentieth-century has many writers in America evading their literary heritage: Robinson, Ransom, Santayana are only three examples that come to mind; notice that they are all minor poets. But there was a group of writers stemming from Harvard which did take some account of the American tradition, even though their work is to some extent flawed by an education oriented too far in the direction of Europe.

Conrad Aiken, for example, seems to have understood what Whitman was after. Certainly as a critic he retrospectively took issue with James on the subject (*A Reviewer's ABC*, 1958). And as a poet he is at his best in frankly Whitmanesque poems such as 'Mayflower' and 'Hallowe'en' (c. 1955)—both, notice, American themes. He also exerted a strong influence on Eliot, as the most glancing comparison between his *Senlin* (1918) and Eliot's work (including 'Prufrock', *The Waste Land*, and 'Burnt Norton') will show.

But, attractive as he often is, nobody is going to take Aiken today as much more than historical portent. Perhaps Ezra Pound is more to the point. His best work comes early, when he was working on a relatively small scale and with a definitely characterised point of view, as in *Mauberley* (1920) and *Propertius* (1917). In these, and even earlier efforts in a similar vein, he, too, influenced Eliot. Perhaps his most important way of doing

this was by making Whitman more dramatic and providing
an American equivalent of Browning. Pound is a writer of dramatic monologues, one might say, but he works through un-
Browningesque and very rapid contrasts:

> When, when, and whenever death closes our eyelids,
> Moving naked over Acheron
> Upon the one raft, victor and conquered together,
> Marius and Jugurtha together,
>   one tangle of shadows.
> Caesar plots against India,
> Tigris and Euphrates shall, from now on, flow at his
>   bidding,
> Tibet shall be full of Roman policemen,
> The Parthians shall get used to our statuary
>   and acquire a Roman religion . . . .

The effect of contrast is obtained, in this instance, by the impres-
sionistic juxtaposition of fragments from various Propertian elegies—II xii a, III v, III iv are drawn upon for this passage alone.
Elsewhere, Pound stage-manages register and rhythm to provide
an iridescent poetry of evanescence and mutability. Much of
this is found in his Cantos—a sequence which ostensibly seeks
to compare various past civilisations with that of the present,
much to the latter's disadvantage. However, the Cantos are best
read as an anthology of lyrics and fragmentary speeches, most
of the best of which occur in I–xxx:

> And you, Pentheus,
> Had as well listen to Tiresias, and to Cadmus,
>   or your luck will go out of you.
> Fish-scales over groin muscles,
>   lynx-purr amid sea   (II, 1917)

> For the husks, before me, move,
>   The words rattle: shells given out by shells
>   (VII, *ante* 1925)

> In the gloom, the gold gathers the light against it.
>   (XI, *ante* 1925)

Thirty and forty years later, Pound was still recurring to these early themes:

> O Lynx, guard this orchard,
> Keep from Demeter's furrow   (LXXIX, *ante* 1948)

> A blown husk that is finished
> but the light sings eternal.   (CXV, *ante* 1962)

In Eliot, in Whitman, in Pound we have this tendency to collect images, to try and create a unity out of disparity. And this I have called a characteristically American approach. If this point is accepted, it will make nonsense of many of the accepted groupings and categories of writers; especially Rahv's time-honoured Paleface–Redskin syndrome (*Image and Idea,* 1957). Gone is the concept of the white-collared Eliot as contrast with the rough-necked Whitman; and it can be seen that, for all their uneasy genuflections towards Europe, the major American writers of the twentieth-century inhabit the same ambience. Perhaps, if they did not, they would not be major.

One can define this characteristically American quality in Wallace Stevens. The sophistication is there, without doubt, but if we look at his best work we shall see the familiar Whitman–Pound–Eliot phanopoeia at play. In 'Sunday Morning' (1915) we have a progression which works against the customarily-recognised laws of fiction. The poem follows no logic more certain than that of a woman's dream. That is to say, it works by the juxtaposition of contrasted images and seeks to show some kind of relationship among them:

> Complacencies of the peignoir, and late
> Coffee and oranges in a sunny chair,
> And the green freedom of a cockatoo
> Upon a rug mingle to dissipate
> The holy hush of ancient sacrifice.
> She dreams a little, and she feels the dark
> Encroachment of that old catastrophe,
> As a calm darkens among water-lights.
> The pungent oranges and bright, green wings
> Seem things in some procession of the dead,
> Winding across wide water without sound.
> The day is like wide water without sound,

> Stilled for the passing of her dreaming feet,
> Over the seas, to silent Palestine,
> Dominion of the blood and sepulchre. . . .

Wherever one breaks off the quotation it seems an indignity, so suavely does the verse flow. Yet it is built of disparities: two quite different sequences of imagery are involved here. One— the oranges, cockatoo, rug—represents sensual ease, and the other— calm, water-lights, wide water, blood, sepulchre—represents the spiritual insight which sensuality engrosses and denies. The two sequences are held in equipoise by the persona through whose mind they pass. It is not being intentionalistic to remind ourselves that this poet, so often thought of as looking away from America, never in fact set foot in Europe in his life.

Whitman, Eliot, Pound, Stevens—our great 'modernists', so wrongly called; in fact a fine flowering of a great culture—is there no other name to be added? Crane, we may feel, died too young: as Winters had occasion to remark, even 'The River' (late 1920s), his masterpiece, portraying the folk of America in terms of the Mississippi, tends to disperse into its component images. And *Paterson* (1946–60), William Carlos Williams's attempt at an American epic, similarly seems to me to break down to unrelated lyrics: 'Jostled as are the waters . . .', 'Patch leaped . . .', 'The province of the poem . . .'. But there is one name, I am certain, that should be put forward at this point; and that is Robert Lowell.

Here the distance from Whitman will seem great indeed: much happened in the century which separated their births; the creation of the United States as an independent culture, no less. And it is interesting to see how this poet struggles to escape from his imprisoning—Europeanised—culture into a more characteristic American speech. The earlier work, on which Lowell's reputation was built, is rhetoric of a high order, and does, indeed, exhibit the American montage which we have already seen operating in Whitman, Eliot and Pound. But the metric even of 'The Quaker Graveyard at Nantucket' (1945) is circumscribing, and sometimes even inexpressively ugly. Distinguished poem though it is, one must view it, in the light of Lowell's later work, as very much a 'literary' production. *Life Studies*, by contrast, works through an intuitive collocation of sights, sounds and feelings.

Life Studies (1959) was received with blank incomprehension in the British press. Critics such as Frank Kermode, Charles Tomlinson and Donald Davie must look back at their reviews of the book with something like remorse. If the American tradition never went any further—though it has—it would have reached an impressive climax here. One recalls the brilliant vignettes of 'Czar' Lepke—'flabby, bald, lobotomized'; of Uncle Devereux Winslow—'his trousers were solid cream from the top of the bottle'; and the portrait in depth, tragi-comic, of Commander Lowell, the poet's father:

> whenever he left a job
> he bought a smarter car.
> Father's last employer
> was Scudder, Stevens and Clark, Investment Advisors,
> himself his only client. . . .

Most evocative of all, 'Skunk Hour' is a montage of images designed to reflect a mood of self-disgust and, behind it, a decadent society—the hermit heiress, the fairy decorator, the love-cars, all destined to be replaced by more vigorous organisms:

> skunks, that search
> in the moonlight for a bite to eat.
> They march on their soles up Main Street:
> white stripes, moonstruck eyes' red fire. . . .

These co-exist in the poem in much the same way as do Eliot's pseudo-references in 'Gerontion'. Once more we have in montage the uniting of apparent disparities into a single entity.

Eliot, Pound, Stevens and Lowell, then, stand clear as the American poets who most deserve attention in the twentieth-century. And the similarities in their approach to literature and technique are not mere accident. This amounts to what, in fact, I would call a definable American tradition in poetry. To define it, as I have tried to do here, will not necessarily make the individual poets seem any better, though it may. But we shall never understand why they are as they are unless we see them in some kind of tradition. Most frequently the qualities that critics find in their work are described as modernism. If this chapter has done its work, henceforward we shall recognise that quality as Americanness.

11 The Growth of English Modernism

A conventional account of the rise of modern poetry would, I suppose, run something like this. The Georgians of Sir Edward Marsh's anthologies represented the last lap of Victorianism; sheltered subjects and literary diction. English poetry was shocked out of such torpor by the Imagists; insistence on experiment, free verse. The resistance to 'modernism', so called, was overcome by the mature work of T. S. Eliot in *The Waste Land* and of Ezra Pound in *Hugh Selwyn Mauberley*. But their work has never been satisfactorily implemented in English poetry. Hence the thin poetic haul of the last thirty years.

There is a lot in this that one can agree with. Yet it seems to me far from the whole truth. And, indeed, a certain amount of dissatisfaction with this account has been shown already. In a broadcast of 1961, George MacBeth clearly showed that the Georgians were not so whimsy-whamsy as popular accounts, and popular anthologies, have suggested. He maintained that the links between the Georgians, such as Lascelles Abercrombie, and the modernists, such as Eliot, were closer than had been suspected. In Mr MacBeth's opinion, the true division was in terms of subject matter—whether, for example, the poet was committed to violence as a mode of purgation or whether he was himself half in love with it.

But this, again, may be only part of the truth. It is one thing to show that both Eliot and Rupert Brooke were influenced by the Metaphysicals. It is quite another to demonstrate that they made comparable use of that influence. One may suggest, too, that Pound's attitude towards the First World War was a very different matter from that of his fellow non-combatant Lascelles Abercrombie.

There is a third account of the rise of modernism which has become rather fashionable. It can be located in the critical work of academics who are also practising poets. Examples that come to mind are John Holloway (*The Colours of Clarity*, 1964) and Graham Hough (*Image and Experience*, 1960). Their account of modernism would suggest that it was interesting while it lasted, and even salutary, but that its impetus is now spent. For them, this is an age of consolidation rather than experiment. From this view, it is only a step to regarding Eliot and Pound as eccentric side issues. Yet, in a sense, they are—at least, as far as English poetry is concerned.

It is not often enough remembered that Eliot was an American by birth and upbringing. Of course, he lived in England for many years, was a naturalised citizen and had associated himself with a number of characteristically English institutions. Even his intonation was impeccably English—and, in its way, this was a disadvantage. One could say, for example, that Eliot's urbane reading of his own verse rather muffled its colloquial, experimental and, I would add, very much American qualities.

For one thing, Eliot characteristically wrote in free verse. This form has never sat very happily on the English language, as the nineteenth-century attempts of Southey, Arnold and Henley show. Yet Eliot brings it off. How?

Again, Eliot's work exhibits the characteristic American qualities of free association or phanopoeia and autobiographical content. English verse, however, has been at its best as fiction: an arrangement of what is external to the poet to convey the tension or release within. Yet Eliot's work succeeds. Why?

Associated with the problem of Eliot is that of Ezra Pound. This poet has a name for being erudite, cosmopolitan. Yet even in his most polyglot cantos he is most himself in colloquial American speech. For instance, in Canto xcvi (*ante* 1959) Pound describes Justinian's law reforms in the tones of the Idaho of his boyhood.

It may well be that both Eliot and Pound have been read with too English an accent. To my ear, the rhythms of 'Sweeney Agonistes' (1924–7) are akin not only to those of demotic American speech but also to the attempt of the Beat poets to write a genuinely popular poetry. And doesn't such a lyric as 'My little island girl' very much anticipate the innovations of 'Poetry and Jazz'?

To go further than this: one could say that the experiments of Eliot and Pound have not fallen on stony ground in the United States. R. P. Blackmur (*Language as Gesture*, 1952) has demonstrated the influence of the *Four Quartets* (1936–42) on Wallace Stevens's 'Notes toward a Supreme Fiction' (1941–2). The grinding personal verse of Pound, in *Mauberley* (1920) as in the Pisan Cantos (1948), seems to me, raised to the nth power of concentration, to be right behind Lowell's *Life Studies* (1959). But, of course, American poets have always excelled in the public presentation of the minutely personal. One thinks of Whitman, who wrote in what has always been agreed to be a distinctively American language. I would never deny that Eliot and Pound, who derive so much from Whitman, are fine poets. But is it not time to insist that they are fine *American* poets? And that therefore the influence they may be expected to have on English poets is limited?

Certainly it is true to say that the influence of Eliot and Pound on English poetry has, so far, been damaging. The American language lends itself peculiarly to the assemblage of images in an emotional rather than a logical connection. Whitman's catalogues (and, indeed, those of F. Scott Fitzgerald) would convey next to nothing if compiled by an Englishman—or even an Irishman, as so many dead pages in Joyce's *Ulysses* only go to show. Yet free association in free verse was what was recommended to a rising generation of poets in the 1930s by that most astringent critic of modern poetry, F. R. Leavis.

New Bearings in English Poetry (1932) is a model of approach to the modern poets with which it deals—in many respects. But it was written at a chaotic period in English literature. That we are now able to challenge some of Leavis's formulations is, in no small part, due to the efficacy of his work as a critic. He must, however, be held responsible for the view that English poets could do nothing better than to learn from the experimentalism of the modernists; by which he particularly meant Eliot and Pound. And, although he has deprecated the talent and influence of W. H. Auden, Leavis must be seen as part of the same movement—a movement which sought to graft Eliot's essentially American experimentalism on to English poetry.

And so we have Auden writing long poems such as 'Easter, 1929' with a distinctively *Waste Land* mood and landscape; Louis MacNeice, closest of all the 1930s poets to Eliot technically, trying to produce a spiritual diary (1938) in the mode of *Four Quartets*; and the weakest of them, Day Lewis and Spender, sticking odd Eliot properties on to a characteristically Georgian nostalgia, traditionalism—even patriotism. The 1930s poets adapted Eliot's vatic utterance to their own leftish brand of doom; but they all grew out of it.

Stephen Spender and Cecil Day Lewis—how did their reputations come about? More important, how did they, along with Louis MacNeice, come to be joined with W. H. Auden, a poet of really considerable talent? Most important of all, how did the work of these four come to be acclaimed as a renaissance in English poetry?

The renaissance, it is now plain, was stillborn. A revaluation of the 1930s would establish William Empson, Robert Graves, Norman Cameron and perhaps John Betjeman as the most interesting new poets then writing; that is, apart from Auden himself. And the whole does not amount to more than an orbit of rather minor satellites. What is most immediately noticeable is that they lack any sort of a sun.

Auden himself was incapable of supplying the necessary energy. For one thing, he himself was poorly chanced for survival. Some of his early poems are at once synthetic and impenetrable:

> Between attention and attention
> The first and last decision
> Is mortal distraction
> Of earth and air,
> Further and nearer,
> The vague wants
> Of days and nights,
> And personal error. . . .   ('Easy Knowledge', 1930)

The tone is, in cant phrase, 'significant'—but significant of what? Do all these abstractions really refer to anything beyond themselves? And this riddling nicety—'Between attention and attention'—is it really making any sort of valid distinction? It is easy enough to see where it all derives from:

Between the idea
And the reality
Between the motion
And the act
Falls the Shadow   *For Thine is the Kingdom* . . . .

Eliot's 'Hollow Men' (1924–5), no less. And Eliot's hollow men
were what the poets of the renaissance were to become.

For, if we look at the periodicals of the time, we shall find
singularly few of the rave notices that literary historians have
led us to expect. On the contrary, it seems as though the editor
of *The Criterion* had a busy private line to Oxford and Cambridge
—spying the coming man before he had come, as A. S. J.
Tessimond, a neglected poet of the time, was to write.

Auden's play *Paid on Both Sides*, dedicated to Cecil Day Lewis,
appeared in *The Criterion* in January, 1930; 'Four Poems' by
Stephen Spender, dedicated to W. H. Auden, appeared in October,
and were followed by three more a year later. Meanwhile reviews
by the coming men began to appear: Auden on psychology,
Spender on belles lettres. It was not a revolution in the palace
so much as a tacit capitulation. The Editor of *The Criterion*,
of course, was T. S. Eliot.

Not all the new young men were untalented. The reviews
by Empson and James Smith are still worth looking up, and
Paid on Both Sides has a sustained brilliance that Auden never
was to achieve again. What one objects to is the way these
reputations were made: there is about it all a distinct air of
fait accompli. Whatever F. S. Flint or Peter Quennell said in
The Criterion's poetry chronicles, Auden had come to stay. And
with him came a good deal else.

Because, it's no good pretending, a great deal of bad verse
was published, and not so much held up to acclamation as
passed by default. There it was, the new writing, and that was
all there was to say about it. Even the more traditionalist *London
Mercury* had an article solemnly discussing the young poets in
terms of a new range of emotion: 'the reader's receptive faculties,
then, have to be sharpened'. But what one may question is
the whole mode of reading involved.

There is no doubt that Eliot did a great deal to disrupt English
poetry, as distinct from that of the Americans. He claims descent
from the Jacobean playwrights and Laforgue, but the most evident

ancestor is Walt Whitman. Whitman's abstractions and random collocations have a raw life of their own, a form even through their formlessness; and this has remained highly characteristic of American poetry ever since. *The Waste Land* (1922) is, indeed, a heap of broken images: this is its meaning, and, to some extent, its distinction. But that kind of writing has never worked well in England. And so Eliot's revolution seems nowadays not so much modernistic as alien.

This is borne out by a look at English poetry written before his influence became a *sine qua non* for young poets. Who wrote this, for example?:

> Sixty odd years of poaching and drink
> And rain-sodden waggons with scarcely a friend,
> Chained to this life; rust fractures a link,
>   So the end. . . .   (c. 1923)

Hardy? Edward Thomas? In fact, it is the earliest Auden—Auden before the influence of Eliot. And I do not think that it is accidental that this gifted poet showed himself at the very first in the direct line of Hardy and the war poets; that is to say, in the mainstream of English poetry. But in the absence of any strong direction—Hardy was very old and the war poets had not survived—English poetry became Americanised, and the result was the brilliant obscurity of Auden's first (1930) volume.

Auden himself came out of it all rather well, which only goes to show how difficult it is to extinguish an original talent. Many of his 1930s poems have a warmth of moral indignation that irradiates the distorted language in which he felt constrained to write. There are moving passages in 'Easter, 1929', in *The Orators* (1932), even in *The Dog Beneath the Skin* (1935). He is seen at his best in an interim selection, *Some Poems* (1940). And it seems to me that Auden's reputation will have to rest mainly upon the poems which exist as finished wholes. Many of these are to be found in his sequences, 'In Time of War' (1938) and 'The Quest' (1940). Not surprisingly, they are couched in the unEliotesque—and very unAmerican—form of the sonnet.

Other poets were not so lucky: at least in their achievement—for their success, of course, was assured. The earliest Spender reads like Eliot's 'Preludes' sucked in and spat out again:

Moving through the silent crowd
Who stand behind dull cigarettes . . .
The promise hangs, this swarm of stars and flowers,
And then there comes the shutting of a door . . . .

(1933)

But Auden soon replaced Eliot in his work, and it gained a
new—but suspiciously general—exaltation:

oh young men oh young comrades
it is too late now to stay in those houses
your fathers built where they built you to build to
   breed
money on money   it is too late . . . .   (1933)

This is shrill, and the sense is governed by the sound, as witness
the functionless outbreak of alliteration in the third line quoted.
Compare it with the Auden poem from which it obviously
derives:

Seekers after happiness, all who follow
The convolutions of your simple wish,
It is later than you think. . . .   ('Consider', 1930)

One would have thought that such a comparison would have
stamped Spender as a second-rate derivative, but nothing of the
sort. The resemblance assured him of a currency among those
who wanted to know what, in poetry, was the latest thing.
Even his anthology pieces do not very much transcend the sort
of verse I have quoted. Image after image defies visualisation,
and offers little to any other kind of reading. The end of 'I
think continually' is characteristic in its evasive rhetoric:

Born of the sun they travelled a short while
   towards the sun,
And left the vivid air signed with their honour.   (1933)

The reputation of Cecil Day Lewis seems to have grown
less rapidly, though it is interesting to see that the *London Mercury*
backed him most heavily of all the new young poets. Perhaps
this was an involuntary tribute to his Georgian temperament:

the modernism of his work never seems more than a superficial overlay. *Transitional Poem* (1929) came out with the usual *Waste Land* sort of notes, but, in spite of its pretensions, was quite evidently a collection of harmless lyrics:

> It is becoming now to declare my allegiance,
> To dig some reservoir for my springtime's pain,
> Bewilderment and pride, before their insurgence
> Is all sopped up in this dry regimen. . . .

The allegiance is most immediately, of course, to Auden; but the quatrains and rhymes take us back to a world before Eliot. Day Lewis mentions charabancs as well as hedgerows, but then so did Sir John Squire, and it is open to doubt whether either of them realised that there were more subtle ways of being modern. Later on, Day Lewis was to coarsen the fabric of his verse and produce this sort of claptrap:

> Look west, Wystan, lone flyer, birdman, my bully
>   boy!
> Plague of locusts, creeping barrage, has left earth
>   bare:
> Suckling and centenarian are up in air,
> No wing-room for Wystan, no joke for kestrel
>   joy. . . .
>
> (*The Magnetic Mountain*, 1933)

But, towards the end, Day Lewis gave up what must always have been an unequal battle. Those who thought him one of the new modernists lived to see him read and remembered for poems such as his later 'Sheep Dog Trials in Hyde Park' and 'View from a Window' (1961): gentle, discursive, countrified in that urban way beloved of Squire and the *London Mercury*.

Louis MacNeice is something of a different proposition. Unlike his two contemporaries, he seems to have been able to go direct to Eliot. Just as early Auden sometimes reads like Edgell Rickword's parodies of Eliot, so early MacNeice often looks like those of Henry Reed:

> But I, Banquo, had looked into the mirror,
> Had seen my Karma, my existences

Been and to be, a phoenix diorama,
Fountain agape to drink itself for ever
Till the sun dries it. . . .   (*Blind Fireworks*, 1929)

However, to do MacNeice justice, he seldom in his later work
takes himself as solemnly as this. His last volume, *The Burning
Perch* (1963), is a craftsmanlike collection. One reason why even
his work of the 1930s has worn better than that of his contemporaries is because he is, on the whole, unsentimental and often
genuinely witty:

> The country gentry cannot change, they will die in
>   their shoes
> From angry circumstances and moral self-abuse,
> Dying with a paltry fizzle they will prove their
>   lives to be
> An ever-diluted drug, a spiritual tautology. . . .
>   ('An Eclogue for Christmas', 1933)

But, one's tempted to remark, Auden did this sort of thing
much better; and this brings us to the crux of the whole problem.
   The renaissance of the 1930s rested largely on the shoulders
of one man: W. H. Auden. And, as we have seen, he himself
had ignored his earliest influences and embarked upon a misdirected
course. His consequent idiosyncrasies were therefore erected into
a style for modern poetry, and one has only to look at the
Preface to Michael Roberts's *Faber Book of Modern Verse* (1936)
to see how rooted the misconception became. Modern poetry
was to be obscure, condensed, fantastic in diction, freed from
logic. The result was that a lot of minor talents, such as Kenneth
Allott and Charles Madge, wrote themselves out for want, among
other things, of a viable tradition; and the revolution ended
in Dylan Thomas and the New Apocalypse, when poetry in
England ceased to mean anything even to an educated reader.
   The conventional account of the last fifty years would suggest
that the social realism of the 1930s was succeeded by the romanticism of Dylan Thomas, George Barker and the New Apocalypse.
In fact, of course, the resemblance between these two 'schools'
is obvious. Both indulged in longish autobiographical poems full
of private allusion, usually in free verse, often of considerable
obscurity, indulging in a scolding rhetoric unparalleled since

the best days of Shelley. Pound could get away with this; in
the Usura Canto (*ante* 1937), for example, or in 'Pull down
thy vanity' (Canto LXXXI, *ante* 1948). And Eliot could admit
his reader to his inner vision in 'Burnt Norton' (1935) and
not for a moment seem posturing or rhetorical. But then Eliot
and Pound are Americans; and their 'modernism' is only suited
to an American language. In English poetry of the 1940s, obscurity
grew so fast and rhythms broke down to such an extent that
the whole attempt at modernism collapsed in the nerveless verse
and chaotic imagery of the New Apocalypse. Hence, of course,
what came to be known as the Movement.

This was largely academic in origin—an attempt by several
poets who were also critics to consolidate English verse. In comparison with Dylan Thomas, or even with early Auden and
Spender, the poems of the Movement were self-contained, formal,
and sought to be unrhetorical. Like most schools of poetry,
the Movement proved too constricting for its more talented
members. Philip Larkin, Kingsley Amis, Donald Davie and Thom
Gunn wrote in the 1960s better than they ever did before, but
not in a Movement style. That style, abstract and gnomic, produced
little of real value. But the Movement was a necessary spring-clean-
ing whose real achievement may have been to arouse interest
in a number of poets of the 1930s who had been unjustly neglected.
The most impressive of these is probably William Empson. His
verse represents a concern for form, and this is an integral quality
in the best English poetry. Without it, it turns into something
very like prose.

This concern for form is a characteristic of a development
in our poetry which has not, I think, been separately recognised.
Perhaps it is best called English modernism—as opposed to the
American brand of Eliot, Pound, Stevens and Lowell.

The chief heroes of English modernism died sixty years ago,
in the First World War. I am thinking particularly of Edward
Thomas, Wilfred Owen and Isaac Rosenberg. They seem to
me quite distinct from the Georgians, on the one hand, and
the modernists, on the other. Their deaths were probably as
great a set-back as those of the young Romantics, Shelley, Keats
and Byron, even though, it is true, their achievement is less.
And their deaths were a set-back for much the same reason.
Their uncompleted work was not sufficient to prevent the tradition
of which they were the latest development from falling into

misunderstanding and neglect.

Only a superficial classification would relate Edward Thomas to the Georgians. His poems certainly belong to an English tradition. But it was one that had been much misunderstood, as was shown by the cool reception of Hardy's *Wessex Poems* in 1898. This tradition was as much one of prose as of verse: the tradition of Cobbett and Jefferies—on whom, as a critic, Thomas had written most eloquently. Indeed, it was Thomas's own prose that led his friend, Robert Frost, to suggest that he should try his hand at poetry. Thomas never actually followed Frost's advice to write up his nature studies into free verse. But there is no doubt that much of Thomas's strength is that he has no time for the merely 'poetic'. His poetry really is 'a valley of this restless mind'. He objectifies his inner emotions in terms of landscape, or even fiction. That is to say, Thomas will often act out his feelings in terms of story, scene and character, rather than state it in his own person. And this brings him close to the writings of the finest poetic realists—Wordsworth, for example, whose best work is in narrative form, and is akin to the great nineteenth-century novelists, themselves the heirs of Shakespeare. This inclination towards fiction rather than auto-biography or lyric is characteristic of much good English poetry.

Palgrave's attempt to exclude all but lyric from the canon of English verse gave us a singularly denuded *Golden Treasury* (1861). Hardy, who had grown up in the age of Palgrave, was concerned to point out rather deprecatingly—in his introduction to *Wessex Poems*—the fictional element in his own verse. And perhaps it was this element of fiction in Thomas's work, as well, that disturbed the Georgians. It is notable that the lyric 'Adlestrop', rather a conventional production, was for years Thomas's prime anthology piece, as 'The Darkling Thrush' was Hardy's. There is nothing so decisively great in Thomas's output as Hardy's cycle 'Veteris vestigia flammae' (1912–13). But no more than for Hardy does the countryside represent for Thomas an escape. Thomas has been much admired for his powers of observation and presentation of particulars. And they are remark-able. But more remarkable still is Thomas's placing of war as a senseless evil against the life-giving rhythms of the countryside. This can be seen in his poem entitled 'As the Team's Head-brass' (1916). Here, the certainty of the ploughman's coming and going is contrasted with the delays and uncertainties of the war. The lovers going into the wood, the ploughman harrowing the clods, are an assertion of life against maiming and death. And the war's encroachment on these rhythms is symbolised by the fallen tree that, if the ploughman's mate had returned from France, would have been moved long ago. The relationship with Hardy's war poems is clear enough. One thinks most immediately of 'In Time of "The Breaking of Nations"' (1915)—where there is also a pair of lovers and a ploughman.

The difference between Thomas and even the better Georgians is that his work is an advance on that of the poetry of a previous generation. His is a genuinely modern sensibility. His view of life has none of the heroics easily assumed by those who never saw action, or who joined the army in a spirit of public-school patriotism. But Thomas had little chance to produce trench poetry. His best work was written before leaving for France, while training as an officer. He had time to contrast the English countryside he was forsaking with the Front—known only by hearsay and implication—to which he was going. And he was killed soon after reaching it.

There were Georgians who saw more action than Thomas; most notably Siegfried Sassoon. And Sassoon's poems certainly include much first-hand reaction to experience. But I am not so sure that his technique is equal to his sensibility. In 'Break of Day' (1918) he presents an escape from battle into the memory of a happy day's hunting. Here we have the detailed realism for which Sassoon was to become famous. No doubt this is a strong poem if compared with the early, and now suppressed, war poems of Graves. Graves is prone to smother his action in whimsy and allusion. But, if we think of Edward Thomas, Sassoon's tone seems over-insistent; and perhaps the most telling comparison is with Wilfred Owen.

It cannot be too often stressed that Owen's technique is not just a matter of half-rhyme. Half-rhyme had been used before in English; though not, it is true, so systematically. Owen's genius can be localised in the actual function of the play of the vowels. They mute those over-confident metres which Owen, in common with other war poets, inherited from the previous, more peaceful, generation. He makes them as exploratory and tentative as his feelings about war. In comparison, Sassoon's verse seems too assured for its content. It is impossible to feel that 'Strange Meeting', for example, will ever date.

Owen's verse, like Thomas's, is akin to fiction rather than lyric. He will adopt a persona, as in 'Strange Meeting' (1918), where he acts as interlocutor; or he will don the mask of narration or of dramatic monologue. Even when he seems to be speaking more directly, as in his poem 'Exposure' (1917), he will use the first person plural rather than singular. So that he seems to be speaking for all the soldiers of the war, not just himself. His details are never merely descriptive. In 'Exposure', they are selected to create an atmosphere and a human attitude—the cold, and the soldiers waiting. It is rather too simple to regard Owen as the poet who hated war. His verse has a distinctively modern ambivalence. In 'Exposure', as well as a grim endurance on the part of the troops, there is a desire for action—a desire which is mocked by the way in which the weather is presented in this poem through a metaphor of war: dawn massing in the east her melancholy army.

Owen recognises with startling modernity that death can be as certain out of battle as in it, and dispiritingly inglorious. His poems are the defeat of lyric; anything but a subjective cry of pain. We are not asked to take an interest in something just because it was happening to Wilfred Owen. A point is made, through the evocation of a war, about war itself. Owen's landscape has all the conviction of Sassoon's with a dramatic quality which Sassoon never achieved. Not one death is expressed in Owen's work, but many:

> Tonight, His frost will fasten on this mud and us,
> Shrivelling many hands, puckering foreheads crisp.
> The burying-party, picks and shovels in their shaking
>   grasp,
> Pause over half-known faces. All their eyes are ice,
>   But nothing happens. ('Exposure')

Like Owen, Isaac Rosenberg characteristically uses the plural first person. But he appears to use words, as D. W. Harding remarked (*Scrutiny*, 1935), without any of the usual couplings—as though the poetry were formed at a subconscious pre-verbal level. Although as authentic as Owen's stretcher-party, that of Rosenberg is alarmingly unexpected:

> A man's brains splattered on
> A stretcher-bearer's face;

> His shook shoulders slipped their load,
> But when they bent to look again
> The drowning soul was sunk too deep
> For human tenderness. . . .   ('Dead Man's Dump', 1918)

One can see why Gordon Bottomley, Rosenberg's first editor, was so hesitant about publishing this poetry. And why, even when it was published, it took so long to make its way. Even the iambic metres have been abandoned in this plasm of verse.

Rosenberg's technical innovations cannot be so readily discussed in terms of a past norm as those of his fellows. One can hear in the lines of Owen's 'Strange Meeting' the rhythms of the Induction to 'The Fall of Hyperion' (1819); but muted down, made tentative by the half-rhyme. The poem gains much of its strength through adapting familiar material to an utterly new situation. Keats's goddesses occur, too, in Rosenberg's 'Daughters of War'. But that is as far as resemblance goes. The myth is created in strikingly individual terms—a kind of sprung verse, for example, developed quite independently of Hopkins. To find Rosenberg's antecedents, one has to look at the juvenilia, as one does with Hopkins's surprisingly Keats-like fragments (c. 1866). The mature poems resemble nothing but themselves—though there are signs that gifted poets of our own time, such as Ted Hughes and Peter Redgrove, have learned from them. It would be absurd, then, to call Rosenberg a traditionalist, except in the sense that he is in the tradition of Keats and Shakespeare. His sprung verse, use of myth, are wholly unlike anything produced by the 'traditional' Georgians. It is as though an overmastering experience had blasted out a new form:

> The old bark burnt with iron wars
> They blow to a live flame
> To char the young green days
> And reach the occult soul; they have no softer lure—
> No softer lure than the savage ways of death. . . .
>   ('Daughters of War', 1918)

Nobody could call this traditional in manner or content. Yet it is certainly not modernist, if by modernist one thinks of a play of images, a montage in free verse. If Rosenberg's verse has affinities, it is not with Eliot or Pound but with the apocalyptic prose of Lawrence. Not, indeed, with Lawrence's verse, which seems to go more diffuse as it gets further from Hardy and nearer to Whitman. Rosenberg, unlike the modernists, does not go in for phanopoeia or free association. His poems exist through images, but never for them. And the poems are not autobiographical, though they may be a projection of his inner feelings, in terms of myth. Rosenberg projects outwards. As in 'Daughters of War', he creates a fiction in which feelings are acted out. Like Thomas and Owen, he conveys his emotion through poems about something other than himself.

These poets used forms and, at the same time, changed them. Thomas used Wordsworthian blank verse that had also learned from nineteenth-century novelists, and so could absorb further narrative and symbolic properties. Owen muted the rhythms of the Romantics by the use of pararhyme, and applied the Romantic sensuousness to a new and grimmer end. Rosenberg manipulated events even more resourcefully than the others, and revitalised dramatic blank verse into a sprung rhythm that has not been fully exploited even now. They all marked an advance not only in technique but in sensibility. The world of 1911 must have seemed very remote in 1915. A glance at the newspapers of the time would establish the difference in terms of an increased sense of strain, a wedge driven between the generations, criticism of hitherto accepted values by the young. But it was only the exceptional writers who could get much of this into their verse. In the last analysis, the success of Thomas, Owen and Rosenberg as poets could be attributed to their recognition of the need to adapt the old forms to express new experience.

This should differentiate them on the one hand from the American modernists, who broke forms down, and, on the other, from the Georgians, who relied on them even when they proved inapplicable to modern experience. But Thomas, Owen and Rosenberg died young, and, after the war in which they died, a debate broke out about which was the right path for poetry. The alternatives offered were American modernism, as represented by Eliot, Pound and the Imagists, and traditionalism, as represented by Abercrombie and Squire. As Mr MacBeth has reminded us, this debate was quite irrelevant to the facts. This, indeed, was seen at the time by that most penetrating reviewer, John Middleton Murry. In reviewing two volumes, one from each of the opposed schools (*Athenaeum*, 1919), Murry said that there was no distinction

between them, and the only distinction he himself would be
prepared to recognise was one of quality. Such quality was found
in the only good poem in either of the volumes: it was Owen's
'Strange Meeting'.

But this distinction was not made by Leavis in *New Bearings*
or Michael Roberts in the influential anthology *The Faber Book
of Modern Verse*. Leavis and Roberts got rather taken in, it
seems to me, not by Eliot's poetry, but by his position *vis
à vis* tradition. They thought that Eliot would be more of a
healthy influence than he could possibly be, at least on Englishmen.
Leavis and Roberts were examples of progressive opinion at
the time. Other *loci classici* are the contemporary undergraduate
magazines, such as Cambridge's *Experiment* (c. 1929), edited by
Empson and Bronowski. And this, in its turn, led to the misapplica-
tion of the talent of many young poets, notably the so-called
Auden group. Out of this came the misunderstanding of the
stream of consciousness which eventually led to the confused
writings of the 1940s; when it became the fashion for writers,
even some of undeniable talent, to switch off their intellect before
they started composing.

Poets of Auden's generation could have saved themselves by
learning less from Eliot and Pound and more from Thomas,
Owen and, perhaps especially, Rosenberg. But history was against
them. My main thesis, I suppose, is that English poetry in the
twentieth century has had four atrocious strokes of luck. They
are worth enumerating. First of all, that the wrong emphasis
should have been placed on the work of one great Victorian
who could have had a useful influence—I mean Hardy. Secondly,
that the Georgians, for the most part, should have chosen to
regard tradition as a resting-place rather than a launching-pad.
Thirdly, that three of the poets who *were* developing an essentially
English modernity should have been killed in the war—their
publication, too, was delayed and incomplete. And, lastly, that
Eliot and Pound should have chosen to start an essentially American
revolution in verse technique over here rather than in the United
States, and so filled the gap which the death of the war poets
left with an alien product whose influence has been a bad one.

But, over the period since the First World War, some talented
poets stuck out against this. John Betjeman ignored Eliot and
did what no Georgian ever really managed: married a modern
sensibility to a Victorian verse technique. Andrew Young carried

on the Georgian mood, but with a first-hand reaction to experience and a metaphysical wit most of the Georgians lacked. Of these poets, Norman Cameron now seems to be one of the most valuable. But his hard economical verse excludes so much of life that he hardly seems to be a man of our own time. And what I have said of Cameron would do very well for Robert Graves too. There has been a tendency to erect Graves into a great modern poet. But he does not seem to me to have done much more than refine the Georgian techniques. Much of what Mr MacBeth finds to admire in the Georgians at their best will be found in the work of Graves. His place is with Sassoon and Blunden rather than with Owen and Rosenberg. What one misses in Graves is a real sense of the world we live in. His keen eye is directed inwards. His verse represents, for all its formal toughness, a retreat from a concern with man as a social animal into a species of pastoralism. Though more skilled than Cameron, he seems to me inferior in sensibility.

Auden could have saved himself by learning more from Owen and less from Eliot. But William Empson is a different case entirely. His imitators in the Movement laid stress on all the wrong aspects of his verse—the tedious refrains, the occasional stiffness of form. Empson's better poems are probably his early ones: for example, 'To an Old Lady', and 'Part of Mandevil's Travels' (c. 1928). His best later poems are those like 'Let it Go' and 'Success' (c. 1935) which were not imitable by the technical means at the disposal of most of the Movement writers. Empson is not a straightforward traditionalist. As Owen did, he uses forms in such a way as to make them new. With all this, his subject matter is restricted and his *oeuvre*, though intense, is narrow.

Neither those who passively imitated Eliot nor those who explicitly reacted against him have produced a very rich crop of poetry. But Empson, who did neither, is an example for the poet of today in more ways than the obvious one. The work of a gifted poet who owes little directly to him, Philip Larkin, shows many of the qualities one finds in Empson's work and in the sonnet sequences of Auden. Larkin is a formalist in so far as he uses rhymes and writes in regular metres. But his rhyme is not the clanging full rhyme which suited the self-confidence of a Swinburne rather more than the self-doubt of a Francis Thompson, let alone of an Elroy Flecker. Larkin uses mainly pararhyme in his poem 'Church Going' (c. 1951), creating, in the varying degrees of rhyme he utilises, the unease in church, not of a worshipper, but of an agnostic.

This is done even more subtly by a rather younger poet, Peter Porter. He uses degrees of pararhyme to secure different degrees of emphasis. Here is an example, from his poem 'Metamorphosis' (1959):

> This new Daks suit, greeny-brown,
> Oyster-coloured buttons, single vent, tapered
> Trousers, no waistcoat, hairy tweed—my own:
> A suit to show responsibility, to show
> Return to life—easily got for ten pounds down
> Paid off in six months—the first stage in the
>   change.
> I am only the image I can force upon the town.
>
> The town will have me: I stalk in glass,
> A thin reflection in the windows, best
> In jewellers' velvet backgrounds—I don't pass,
> I stop . . . .

Notice the pattern of pararhyme here. In the remainder of the stanza, 'glass' rhymes with 'mask' and 'last'—mocking the assurance of his attitude, 'I am myself at last'. In the same way, the vowel of the 'town' echoes throughout the first stanza before it comes clanging in on the keyline, 'I am only the image I can force upon the town'. The rhyme here is made all the more blatant by alternating with unrhymed lines. The rhythms, too, are flexible. The basic unit is a five-stress line, but there is no syllable count. The first line of the first stanza, 'This new Daks suit, greeny-brown', has only seven syllables for its five stresses, while the last line, 'I am only the image I can force upon the town', has fourteen—from diffidence to brash self-confidence, one might say.

There is a poem by another contemporary, Peter Redgrove, called 'Bedtime Story for my Son' (1955), which chases a rhyme through many kinds of assonance and half-rhyme, just as the couple in the poem chase the ghost of a child, and catches up with it only in the last two lines, as the couple do:

Love pines loudly to go out to where
It need not spend itself on fancy, and the empty air.

Of course, it is cruel to isolate metre and rhyme in this way, particularly when one is sure the poet himself did not. But it is a way of bringing home a point: that what is best in English poetry generally and in the present generation of English poets is this vigour within the discipline of shape—freedom through reshaping a form rather than breaking it down. Inevitably, there are poets such as Charles Tomlinson who are trying to carry on the technique of the American modernists, just as there are poets, like David Holbrook, who have pushed traditionalism further than ever the Georgians did. But they seem to me to be fighting against the genius of the time and the language. D. J. Enright, Philip Larkin, Ted Hughes, Peter Porter and Peter Redgrove—to name only five of our best contemporary poets—did not get together in a huddle to find out which form they ought to write in. Their feeling and experience come out in the way I have described, a way that is neither modernism nor traditionalism—perhaps because it is the only way it can come out in English poetry at present. It is a way that relates back to Owen, master of the half-rhyme, and through him back to the Keats of the 'Fall of Hyperion' and back to Shakespeare. Another line could be traced through Redgrove and Hughes through Thomas and Rosenberg to the blank-verse fictions of the Romantics, Shakespeare and even back to the medieval poets. Either way, it is the central line of English poetry. And I cannot see much good work being done far away from it. Like any tradition, however, it is alive only as long as it can be re-created. But I am not being optimistic when I say that it seems to be in process of re-creation, after a long quiescence, at the present time.

12 The Poetry of Barbarism

There are certain qualities, inherent in the English language, that are brought out strongly in the work of its greatest poets. Such qualities, indeed, define the nature of the work such poets can do. The resources at a writer's disposal will be seriously warped if he attempts to make English sound like Italian; if he seeks to avoid the letter 's'; if he concentrates upon the image at the expense of the total structure. All this may seem obvious, yet ambitions such as these have been explicitly voiced by poets in the past; and other examples of self-limitation could be cited. More positively, one can say that the character of English is to be tactile, even kinaesthetic. Its poetry is full of muscular movement and packed with interacting consonants. This last is a very remarkable characteristic. It means that climaxes of intensity tend towards distinct alliterative patterns. This is a norm in medieval verse, of course, but even there it can be shown to act out the sense, and this demonstrative capacity is the basis of the essentially expressive nature of English verse:

> Hunger in haste thoo hent Waster by the maw
> And wrung him so by the womb that all watered his
>   eyen.
> He buffeted the Bretoner about the cheeks,
> That he looked like a lantern all his life after
>
> *(Piers Plowman*, c. 1377)

Thay bowen bi bonkkes   ther boghes are bare,
Thay clomben bi cliffes   ther clenges the colde.
The heven was uphalt,   but ugly ther-under;
Mist muged on the mor,   malt on the mountes
　　　　　(*Gawain and the Green Knight*, late 14th century)

All the stored vengeances of Heaven fall
On her ingrateful top! Strike her young bones,
You taking airs, with lameness　　　　(*King Lear*, 1605)

Heart, I will drag thee hence, home, by the hair;
Cry thee a strumpet through the streets; rip up
Thy mouth unto thine ears; and slit thy nose,
Like a raw rochet!　　　　　　　　(*Volpone*, 1605)

O'er many a frozen, many a fiery Alp,
Rocks, caves, lakes, fens, bogs, dens and shades of death
　　　　　　　　　　　(*Paradise Lost*, 1667)

Obscure they went through dreary shades, that led
Along the waste dominions of the dead:
Thus wander travellers in woods by night,
By the moon's doubtful and malignant light
　　　　　　　　　　(Dryden's *Aeneid*, 1697)

Meanwhile the precipices rang aloud;
The leafless trees and every icy crag
Tinkled like iron　　　　　　　(*The Prelude*, 1805)

I starved there, God knows how, a year or two
On fig-skins, melon-parings, rinds and shucks,
Refuse and rubbish.　　　　　('Fra Lippo Lippi', 1853)

But examples are legion. This is an English packed with sharp
particulars that are thrust close upon each other, again to interact
and so form an entity. Words are deployed vigorously enough
to bring their areas of connotation into creative relationship.
Such an English each great poet quarries for himself from the
triumphs and the débris of the past. That is why there is a
family resemblance between poets as temperamentally different
as Shakespeare, Jonson, Milton, Dryden, Wordsworth and Brown-

ing. They have, fully or in part, rediscovered the mimesis and expressiveness which was the achievement of the great medieval poets. In doing this, they have repudiated rootless experiment, alien linguistic patterns and passive convention.

The tradition is alive in so far as it is being re-created today. It is all too easy to accept the current evaluations and to decide from them that ours is a barren period. Scenes, trends and fashions mean nothing: at any given time, most of what is written will be rootless and lifeless. What is said to be happening is not necessarily the same as what is happening: rumour need not be consonant with the event. We must look for the best work, remembering that, at any time, it need not be that which is most applauded. By the same token, the twenty or so decent minor poets working in any period require no especial emphasis, other than a concession that their work provides a welcome and necessary background.

The major work, what there is of it, will be of a different kind altogether. It seems to me, as a deliberated judgement, that Peter Redgrove is the most imaginative and vital poet of the last thirty years. His first book, *The Collector* (1960), puts the work of his immediate predecessors into perspective. In this light, we see the bachelor limitations of Philip Larkin's poetry of regret; the decent journalism proffered in lieu of poetic satire by D. J. Enright; the early lyricism of Ted Hughes, whose romantic engagement with the deaths of small animals led, inevitably, to the melodramatic inflation of *Crow*.

The distinction of Peter Redgrove does not lie solely in his superior deployment of language, but some such consideration would be a convenient point from which to start an appreciation of his work. His verbal efficacy can be pointed out in his descriptive writing, though there is nothing merely descriptive about such metaphor as this:

> the sightless worm
> Like soft successive links of a spring
> Wants to pile out and slubber for hours
> In the moist slow shade among the twigs. . . .
>
> ('A Leaf from my Bestiary')

The fusion of perceptions—the 'successive links' which want to 'pile out'—show us at once the worm-like qualities of a

spring and the spring-like qualities of the worm. Description
is not quite the word for this: it is a recreation of nature
where man-made object and natural object interfuse and comment
upon each other:

> A jagged curling bedstead, like a nest of snakes
> ('A Search')

> A shiny beetle like a boot
> Its laces waving in the air ('Aid')

> Somebody is throttling that tree
> By the way it's threshing about ('A Storm')

> Small elephant on wings with dabbing trunk,
> Almost a circus animal . . . . ('Flies')

Such verse, composed of disparities, has the quality of fusion;
it admits no easy distinction between artefact and nature.

This is worked out in greater depth in Peter Redgrove's second
book, *The Nature of Cold Weather* (1961). Here, man is shown
in relation to the winter and the wilderness. The title poem
is a dialogue between two voices. The first treats of a concept
of home:

> Now the air is stuffed with feathers and we walk
>   on wool,
> The barking radios tethered to their territories . . . .

The indication is that such cosiness forms a barrier against the
full range of vital experience. The tame man, decoyed out for
one last walk before winter sets in, is reassumed into the frozen
countryside. The second voice, the voice of winter, gains in
strength as the poem progresses, and speaks for the cold weather
in a dramatic verse seldom equalled since Wordsworth—the
Wordsworth of the Ice Skater and the Ascent of Snowdon:

> the flesh
> Squeezes pain downwards, bleaching skin into my heart,
> My innermost things, underground.
> Two ponds of blank grey ice with grizzled reeds,

> A heaped-up chine with two dark rabbit holes,
> A slash of almost-frozen stream with meeting teeth,
> Clashing and tinkling, with brisk beard tugging at
>   its banks . . . .

The anthropomorphism sees man as metaphor of nature and, inevitably, nature in metaphor of man—'Sight is beneath the ice like fish or stones . . .'. This has a decisive function. The ice giant eventually breaks up and becomes physically part of the soil—'His withered limbs lie as short-ice in the grass . . .'. Peter Redgrove sees this as part of a natural cycle—the sun shines on the green meadows and 'the playing children come'. The poem ends with an acknowledgement of defeat which is, in fact, a recognition of our 'losing war' with nature. Over and over again, Redgrove's work shows that we have become abstracted from life and so have lost nature—*our* nature, as sentient and responsive creatures.

This I take to be the meaning of the prose-poem with which this second volume ends: 'Mr Waterman'. Here, water itself becomes, in all its flexuous versatility, the rival of a middleclass suburbanite for the favours of his wife. The qualities of water in its various shapes are rendered tellingly—it changes to

> a charming dolls'-house of glass, with doors and windows opening and shutting; a tree that thrusts up and fills the room; a terrifying shark-shape that darts about between the legs of the furniture, or lurks in the shadows of the room, gleaming in the light of the television tube . . . .

The virtuosity of the narration is all the more remarkable when one reflects that the story is told by the troubled householder—placed by his conventionality ('I don't know what rent to charge him'). This character is evidently a man of fact, and that he retails such extraordinary facts as these gives the fantasy an unexpected plausibility. But the contrast goes deeper than that. For how can mortals compete with a creature as fascinating as this Mr Waterman, who 'can be as stubborn as winter and as gentle as the warm rains of spring'?

The poem is a dramatic monologue, basically, interrupted by the deflating comments of an uncomprehending listener—significantly, a psychiatrist. And Redgrove's work has consistently tended towards the larger forms. A great deal is included in this poetry which used to be the province of fiction or drama. This, I think, is a sign of its peculiar strength. Before ever fiction or drama were serious forms in English, poetry accommodated the whole range of human experience, not just the lyrical marginalia. After the Romantics, indeed, the only poetry that mattered in critical consideration was lyrical; hence the cramping limitations of Palgrave's *Golden Treasury*. However, we live at a time when drama seldom rises to the level of articulacy and when fiction is a commercialised industry, largely ancillary to the cinema and television. Therefore there are signs that poetry has begun to come once more into its own. If it does so, it will probably be more a dramatic and fictionalising poetry than one of 'pure' lyricism.

Peter Redgrove has shown himself adept at the smaller forms. Strangers to his work could do worse than begin with his best short poems, such as 'Bedtime Story for my Son', 'Foundation', 'For No Good Reason', 'Ghosts', 'The House in the Acorn', 'Only Resting', 'The Curiosity Shop', 'The House of Taps'. These are so beautifully articulated that they do much to subsume the frequently obsessive nature of Redgrove's vision. But the narrative and dramatic forms give him greater scope, and his ultimate poetic ancestors are the great medieval allegorists. The title poem of his book *At the White Monument* (1963) shows this. Like 'Mr Waterman', it is essentially an interrupted monologue—the poet himself calls it an interview. An official is sent by the town council to investigate a local park in which stands a white monument. Apparently the place is infested by a strange figure who claims that he has a job to do there. The dialogue takes place, in so far as it is a dialogue, between the official and the stranger; and the latter is very strange indeed, with his unwinking lashless eyes and smoking nostrils set in a copper-coloured bladder of a head.

This confrontation gives the guardian of the monument a chance to tell his story. The park, he insists, is *his* park; and the monument, *his* monument. Originally, the site held a manor house that sheltered many families. But the wind constantly boomed and battered through the chimneys, and this drove everyone away except his beloved wife and himself. He was forced to think of a way to stop the noise. He decided to block the great central shaft, and got up on to the roof and poured down load after load of concrete until the sound of the wind ceased. This seemed to work, and he descended to ground level and re-entered the house to tell his wife the good news. But her parlour was sealed off behind its stone wall, and she herself entombed at the base of a tall shaft that spitted the house—the filled-in central chimney.

The account given by the stranger to the council official is accompanied by many grimaces and gestures that act out his theme, and these in their turn are mimed by the inventive and graphic language:

> He shuffled and skipped as the beam of heat hit his
> back,
> And skipped out of the way of the puff and crackle
> underfoot,
> As he told how wet slag sparked the power, and his
> hair puffed out in a flash,
> Past a coxcomb of flames from the old kitchen range
> Weltering and glittering in its lead, and since
> He has never lost the smoke in his nostrils.

He goes on to say that he got himself clear just as the house exploded and fell. It left him burnt and hairless, as now we see him. All that remained finally, rising up from his wife's tomb, was the shaft of the great chimney. Rain and weather annealed and glazed it over the years, while he created the park that surrounded the monument to his monstrous folly—the white monument. The poem offers two alternative solutions. The guardian refuses to be moved on and says he will kill to keep the job. But he also says that, before long, all the louts of the town will pull down his elaborate screening and set fire to the monument:

> And the gas will flame again the heart of her sun
> And he run through the flames to her and pass
> Into the wall with a puff like thick powder
> Only the shadow left, running, with arms outstretched.

The poem is alight with an exuberance kept under control by close verbal cohesion. Here, for example, we have an imagining—a man running through a wall—which is brought off by the power of phrase. The operative phrase in especial is 'a puff like thick powder'. This describes not, as most poets would have done, the wall, but the disintegration of a body in rapid motion. It is a remarkable example of poetic tact. Moreover, we have the way in which the body passing into the stone is brought in relation to normality: the implied metaphor is that of the image left upon the retina after a sudden flash of light. Further, the idea is prepared for by the previous encounter with fire, when the house first catches alight. Some of the key words of the finale are anticipated there, in several of the same relationships:

> his hair puffed out in a flash
> Past a coxcomb of flames . . . .

This therefore acts as prolepsis and gives the happening at the end, the man passing through the wall, an effect of narrative progression.

I take the poem to be an allegory of the way in which the artist's life is subsumed into his art, which thereby becomes a monument formed from the ruin it has caused. But powerful though the allegory is, the signs of the grotesquerie that distorts a good deal of Redgrove's later work are already here. They are even more present in an unpublished prose version broadcast in 1963. And, consequent upon this production, more and more of Redgrove's poetry approximated to the prose poem.

A remarkable instance is 'The Sermon', which occurs in '*The Force*', *and Other Poems* (1966). Here, again, we have the interrupted monologue which has proved to be so fertile a poetic form. In this case, a parson stands for the poet or seer of our time, and puts forward an extreme form of pantheism while being heckled by an increasingly horrified congregation:

But God cannot die, and by the same token no more can we! Remember that whatever happens cannot hurt us, because we *are* God—not hurt us permanently anyway. Brothers—and I am speaking to God—do not sit about wailing here for God's second-coming-before-it-is-too-late—he is already here, and We will be There, each of us a shard of him, a ward of him, a bright, piercing, secure, razor-sharp splinter of him,

and heaven ... where no moth nor rust ... Matthew 6 ...
We are already Here ... and More of Me arrives every day! ...

Much of this inclusive power lies in Redgrove's ability to confound fruitfully the notions of God in the first and second persons singular *and* plural with the characters of the congregation and the minister. But he is precariously near loss of control. If the poem succeeds, it succeeds as a pantheist's nightmare, with such possibilities as it evinces taken to extremes.

And nightmare is certainly a presence in Redgrove's latest work; held in check in smaller forms, like 'The House of Taps', but unleashing itself in some of the larger works, such as the title-poem of *Dr Faust's Sea-Spiral Spirit* (1972), which remains obscure, even to the *aficionado*. This is true also of the large-scale prose fantasies, by the press erroneously termed novels, but actually a rehearsal of obsessive visions in the manner of a dream. Almost every page bears witness to having been written by a man of genius. But the fact that I invoke this Romantic concept rather than offer a wholesale interpretation may suggest that Redgrove's obsessions have at last got the better of him:

> The pond came like a glass udder walking on its teats down to the sea's edge for its blessing.
> The faithful chaplain bit off a finger and ran with it carried in his mouth. To bless the people. She suckled the child through her warty witchnipple. To bless the people. The king's wizards lost their heads, pumping into the skyhead from seven faithful channels. To bless the people. ...
>
> (*In the Country of the Skin*, 1973)

> If they did indeed one day lie at the bottom of the sea's branches, bedded in sea-flesh of ooze, skeletons full of windows through which the sea-life swum, the moist-air currents fashioning the great stem from which the white clouds budded and the clear rain fruited, all the water of the world would flow past the bones of the lovers, and this water-shrine of pleasure was good practice for that state of being. 'One thousand black-coated clergymen are at this moment raising me to their lips and gargling with me in preparation for their Sunday sermon,' she said. ...   (*The Glass Cottage*, 1976)

One wonders whether more can be expected from Peter Redgrove than a luxuriant wilderness of such fantasies. The *oeuvre* is already there, of course, in his first six books of poems, but the proportion of poetry to obsession has been worsening through the years. His is, irrespective of his age at the time of writing, a young man's work. One phenomenon of post-Romanticism is that a poet begins to die in his early thirties. Redgrove has done better than his contemporaries and near-contemporaries, most of whom expressed all they had to say in a single book—usually, their first. This is typical of a deficiency: they had no conceptual framework for their imaginings. No body of thought was re-created in their work in the sense that Chaucer re-created Boethius or Langland William of Ockham. The poet who relies on indivi-dual fantasy may well find himself outgrowing it or will be constricted by its failure to grasp the continuing flow of events around him. Yet there is little excuse for such a reliance: the obvious intellectual framework in our time is the sense of history. Here we are indeed fortunate: we know more than our prede-cessors, not only in the sense that they are what we know, but also in that research has opened up channels to the past hitherto thought inaccessible. The wealth of information ready to our hand is greatly superior to that which Shakespeare had, even though his reading included Plutarch, Geoffrey, Holinshed and Buchanan.

One poet who is aware of this is Francis Berry. His first book dates from a year after Redgrove's birth—from 1933—but he has a surprising amount linguistically in common with the younger writer. Mr Berry is a master of the long poem, and his best writing has been done in that genre. Because of this, he has been under-represented in magazines and anthologies, and his reputation has yet to match the high opinion which so great a critic as G. Wilson Knight (*Neglected Powers*, 1971) has formed of his work.

Francis Berry does not always choose to write about an obviously crucial event. He seeks a legend with which he can empathise, and this, in its turn, depends upon his own area of preparedness. Such a legend is utilised in his first really important poem, *The Iron Christ* (1938). It celebrates the averting of war between Chile and Argentina in 1902. Instead of fighting, the two countries melted down the cannon that guarded their respective fortresses at the frontier. With this metal, they cast a statue of Christ which was erected on the highest point of the Andes, between the two countries, as a symbol of peace.

The incident is a curious and moving one, but it would not work as a poem unless the author had rendered his narrative graphically. However, like his younger contemporary, Mr Berry has access to a mimetic language whose very rhythm struggles to get the statue up the mountainside:

> The driver turns his face, his arm to throttle
> Levering steam, but, with a cursing, spin
> The driving-wheels, skidding upon raw rails,
> Circuiting vainly, then grab, heel over rods,
> Pistons pant, valves hiss, wheels grip, groan, grab . . . .

The title poem of *Fall of a Tower* (1943) is less obviously based on history. It suggests the black night that is liable to overtake an emergent Christian on the brink of conversion. The poem describes a town dominated and overshadowed by a church; we may take this to be *the* Church. This gives the narrative of the attempt by a man called Edmund to blow up the building a mythopoeic quality. Once more we have the deploying of highly mimetic language in order to render a story in graphic terms:

> Struts straddle; West Front
> Walks apart, begins ungainly waddle,
> Collapses on its face; brick and mortar
> Flee yelling from their stocks . . . .

Murdock (1947) approaches its subject more elliptically. The poem looks like the chronicle of the unending affray between two brothers. But the tone of the verse very much invokes Wilfred Owen, and the peculiar legend implies material related to the First World War. We are shown the effect of fraternal conflict upon a world depicted in terms of a village. It is an extended 'Strange Meeting'; and, as such, it is a poem suffused with memories of the archetypal struggle of Cain and Abel:

> We of this Village know our heavy Wood
> Haunted by Brothers in their furious Mood.
> Two Brothers, locked and pledged to nightly Duel,

THE POETRY OF BARBARISM

Fight under Trees, hidden at fullest Moon.
Though dumb, their Blows do toss upon the Gale;
Their Groans disturb us at our Murdock Fires;
Their sobs are heard through Falls of Autumn Rain. ...

The title poem of Francis Berry's 1961 collection, *Morant Bay*, deals with a negro uprising in Jamaica which was put down ruthlessly by Governor Eyre in 1865. Unlike many commentators on such outbreaks, Mr Berry does not jump to conclusions, even though his source is Lord Olivier's *Myth of Governor Eyre* (1933) which is highly critical of the governor. On the contrary, Mr Berry is concerned to see the affair in perspective. The motive behind the outbreak was racial friction, but Mr Berry reminds us that this is no abstraction but a conflict between specific people. He concentrates on the three principal figures: Governor Eyre, whom he sees as a courageous white man incapacitated by his distaste for the Blacks; G. W. Gordon, a Coloured rentier seen as embittered by ill-treatment from the Governor; and Paul Bogle, deacon of the native Baptist church, seen as driven into rebellion by superstitious rage.

The rebellion started over a triviality—the non-payment of a fine. But, by the time the Governor got round to looking into it, as Mr Berry tells us, 'it was too late to do anything but be stupid and brutal'. A number of white volunteers were killed, and so was the Chief Justice. In retaliation, 537 black men were hanged in batches of nineteen each evening—except, Mr Berry points out with grim irony, Sunday.

What is so impressive about this poem is that, despite the prejudiced account on which he drew, Mr Berry does not take violent sides. To condemn, he says, is to become a member of those we condemn. Instead, he seeks to understand the situation. And he does so in terms of his own keen sense of original sin, to which we are all subject, an *obeah* 'whose magic undergoes all manner of transfer, / But cannot be cast out'.

As in Mr Berry's other major poems, the history is set before us in such colourful detail that we have to accept it as a whole. The exotic coloration is instantly compelling:

On the other side of the ravine
Rises the opposing flank of another spur,

Its sandstone swooned from the blurs of that sun,
Dotted with thorned scrub, roots bedded in stone,
On which the red spider darts or the lizard waits
Before his next scurry with a sobbing throat. . . .

The voices, too, sound across the years. One thinks of the impassioned prayer of the black Deacon Bogle and the equally
impassioned response of his congregation:

'Der he be
In dat King's House, an' he eat—'
In dat King's House, an' he eat.
'He eat fishes an' he eat meat,'
He eat fishes an' he eat meat,
War-o, heavy war-o. . . .

Francis Berry has shown remarkable powers of self-renewal
over the forty-five years since his first book. With *Illnesses and
Ghosts at the West Settlement* (1966), his recreation of voices entered
a new terrain. This is the Greenland colonised at the end of
the first millenium AD by Eirik the Red. But Greenland itself
is a precipitating factor in the poem. The basic theme is woman's
helplessness in the face of intransigent men and events. The
central character is Eirik's daughter-in-law, Gudrid—the young
wife taken out to Greenland. Her voice comes across the centuries
in characteristically tentative cadences:

'. . . Illnesses and Ghosts.
You founded Greenland. I've seen enough of your
    Greenland
And I want the sun for a while, husband or no husband.
I want the sun because I am so cold, you know I am
    so cold
That I could hear that particular sound again.
        Oh I am so old
Before I am hardly girl. Dear Father, Father-in-law,
    help me. . . .'

The Greenland of this poem is not only cold; it is disease-ridden.
Plague strikes down the little settlement and smashes the sanctions
that govern even a primitive society. The hapless remnant that

stay there are confused and demoralised. The fevered Grimhild drags herself from the coffin where she has been put as dead to creep under the blankets where the delirious Thorstein, Gudrid's husband, lies. Gudrid goes over, in spite of herself, to her husband's namesake, Black Thorstein. Dying, her husband cries out,

> '. . . look here, Gudrid, Gudrid darling,
> Beware that man with his arm towards your waist.
>   Marry again,
> But don't marry a Greenlander—for that man
> Sitting beside you on this bed
> Is black, vile, low,
> Whatever his name. . . .'

Gudrid, almost the sole survivor of the settlement, returns, widowed, with a shipload of black coffins, to her father-in-law. The whole poem is couched in terms of a recollection by the dead Gudrid hovering as a ghost above the settlement where she suffered so dreadfully a thousand years ago—interrupted, from time to time, by gruff interpolations from the long dead

> 'Eirik the Red, *the* Eirik
> Who made this land, who found this land, who named this land
> Greenland. . . .'

It is questionable whether any contemporary poet can offer so great a range of technique and subject-matter. But these characteristically exotic settings are, it must be remembered, a means of staging a penetration into the motives behind human actions. The story does not, however, end with Greenland. Francis Berry's most recent major work, not published at my time of writing, was broadcast in 1971. It concerns Shah Jehan, who built the Taj Mahal in memory of his wife. Here is the voice of another woman, the dead Mumtaz, interrupting her husband's thoughts, accusing him of wishing her dead in order to create his immemorial dome:

> 'I died because you wanted me to die.
> Or thought you did ... sometimes. For I could read
> That silent thought in the way you looked

At me ... sometimes. It made me sad—for you,
Because I surmised you would be desolate
And helpless ... I gone. And that you would regret
That thought you had allowed me to discern ...
Sometimes ... though you should have not. . . .'

Note the pondering metre, the quiet dwelling upon the word 'sometimes'. This is a verse sparser than that we are used to from Mr Berry. And, indeed, 'The Near Singing Dome', as the poem is called, may be part of a still larger work-in-progress. The reputation of Francis Berry, who wrote this and *Illnesses and Ghosts*, *Morant Bay* and *The Iron Christ*, may continue to grow slowly; it is certain, in any event, to endure.

It is a remarkable fact that Francis Berry and Peter Redgrove pursued their poetic concerns separately. Neither had cognisance of each other's work during the period when their respective styles were being formed. It is in a deeper sense than that of mutual imitation that they can be said to belong to the same tradition. Redgrove had studied Isaac Rosenberg and Edward Thomas with great care, and they, in common with other war poets, lead back to the blank-verse fictions of those Romantics who ultimately stem from Shakespeare. And Redgrove had his own, intense, first-hand reading of Shakespeare. He had also been deeply influenced by the medieval volume of the *Penguin Guide to Literature*, which included Berry's edition of *Gawain and the Green Knight* together with a telling essay on the subject. Francis Berry himself is a medievalist, a Shakespeare scholar, and a student of Wilfred Owen, whose work he put to such effective use in, for example, his poem 'Murdock'. For the rest, it is reasonable to assume that a sensitised talent will take from the possibilities of language in his time such elements as are necessary to his vision; and that the vision of one such talent, individual though it will necessarily be, may in certain particulars resemble that of another. Such a context provides an explanation for the community between these two poets. This can be located in the characteristically graphic imagery that each of them manifests and in their mimetic rhythms. It is also a matter of using, as a basic form, the interrupted monologue—present in framework, past in narrative; dominated by one characteristic voice, but involving others in argument, in agreement, in mock or in wrangle. In each of these poets one has the sense, not only of individually fine poems, but of an *oeuvre*.

How different from this is the minor poet, whose isolated vignettes, well shaped in themselves, tend to have the air of items detached from a context. The reader, in assenting to their qualities, wonders why they were brought to his attention. This is true of a number of American poets of the post-Lowell generation: Richard Wilbur, Howard Nemerov, Anthony Hecht, Frederick Seidel. But there is an instance—a poet whom otherwise one would associate with these—when the ideas have coalesced, if only once; and the result is a major poem.

Galway Kinnell began as an accomplished poet in the wake of Robert Frost and John Crowe Ransom. His later work leans heavily on a Whitmanesque mysticism shot through with reminiscences of François Villon, whom he has translated brilliantly (1965). However, Whitman is used to far more concrete purpose in Kinnell's masterpiece, 'The Avenue Bearing the Initial of Christ into the New World' (1960).

This apparently cumbrous title gives us a useful approach to the poem. The initial of Christ—as though the avenue were lettered rather than numbered—is the mark of Cain the scapegoat, set on all Jews wandering over the earth ahead of the pogrom and débouching *en masse* into the East Side of New York; *their* kingdom. In Whitman there is a sense of liberation, of far horizons; but Galway Kinnell uses the older poet's violent disruption of logic as a means of creating a sense of confinement. On the literal level, his poem describes a community—a ghetto, if you like—where the preponderance of Jewish elements subjugates the customs of other immigrants into their adopted country:

> Even the Puerto Ricans are Jews
> And the Chinese Laundry closes on Saturday . . . .

Here we have the heaving, sweating life of an enclosed community—enclosed by the pressure from all sides surrounding it. This is a place where no one would choose to live unless they were denied the choice of living anywhere else. The refuse from outside has streamed here, causing this little world to consolidate. The richness of its débris, its accumulation of properties, informs the poem. In the pushcart market, on Sunday,

> The sun beats
> On beets dirty as boulders in cowfields,

> On turnips pinched and gibbous
> From budging rocks, on embery sweets,
> Peanut-shaped Idahos, shore-pebble Long Islands and
>   Maines,
> On horseradishes still growing weeds on the flat ends,
> Cabbage lying about like sea-green brains
> The skulls have been shucked from . . . .

The Jewish shopkeeper nails fish on to the wood in order to gut them:

> He scrapes the knife up the grain, the scales fly,
> He unnails them, reverses them, nails them again,
> Scrapes and the scales fly. He lops off the heads,
> Shakes out the guts as if they did not belong in
>   the first place,
> And they are flesh for the first time in their
>   lives. . . .

Through such images of torment, Kinnell shows how people prey upon their fellow-creatures. This passage about the fish is juxtaposed with what looks like a form letter sent out to relatives of victims who died in the prison camps:

> Dear Frau _____
>   Your husband, _____, died in the Camp Hospital on _____. May I express my sincere sympathy on your bereavement. _____ was admitted to the Hospital on _____ with severe symptoms of exhaustion, complaining of difficulties in breathing and pains in the chest. Despite competent medication and devoted medical attention, it proved impossible, unfortunately, to keep the patient alive. The deceased voiced no final requests.
>
>   Camp Commandant, _____.

The dry prose contrasts violently with the heightened imagery of the fishmonger and the market. By such means the ghetto of the East Side is made to seem a simulacrum of all ghettos, pales, prison camps, even those of the Holocaust itself.

Level after level of paradox peels off in this poem. The Jew, alleged crucifier of Christ, himself a Jew, proscribed for that persecution, harried through the world, finds only a temporary

peace in a ghetto which is also a prison camp, before he is
harried on again. The dying cadences of the finale evoke a
sense of retrospect. Here we have art of the highest order:

> Since Providence, for the realization of some unknown purpose,
> has seen fit to leave this dangerous people on the face of
> the earth, and did not destroy it . . . .

> Listen! the swish of the blood,
> The sirens down the bloodpaths of the night,
> Bone tapping on the bone, nerve-nets
> Singing under the breath of sleep—

> We scattered over the lonely seaways,
> Over the lonely deserts did we run,
> In dark lanes and alleys we did hide ourselves . . . .

> The heart beats without windows in its night,
> The lungs put out the light of the world as they
> Heave and collapse, the brain turns and rattles
> In its own black axlegrease—
>   In the nighttime
> Of the blood they are laughing and saying,
> Our little lane, what a kingdom it was!
>   Oi weih, oi weih.

Whitman, it can be seen, made the decisive intervention in a
tradition that, however, ultimately stems from those most potent
progenitors of American literature, the Authorised Version of
the Bible, and Shakespeare.

But there are other ways of travelling to that rare but distinctive
modern achievement, the poem of some length. This eye for
detail matched with a sense of form may be seen in the poetry
of Patrick Kavanagh. Irish by birth and upbringing, he came
out of a line of descriptive writing which traces some of its
origins to the translations of Dryden, earthier than his original
work; the poetic realism intermittently found in Pope; the struggle
for exactitude that went on in the work of the poetic realists
proper—Langhorne, Goldsmith, Cowper—which was transformed
into Wordsworth's distinctive vision and which otherwise found
its highest reach in the work of Crabbe and Clare. Although

through most of the nineteenth century this was a prose tradition—
one thinks of Cobbett, Jefferies and Hardy—the decisive intermediary work of Edward Thomas and one or two intelligent war
poets brought the rhymed couplet into the twentieth century.
Patrick Kavanagh, however, probably went direct to Pope (his
favourite poet) and Clare: his equivalent for the couplet was
a kind of loose quatrain. In this metre, frequently diversified,
he obtained effects similar to those of the English poetic realists,
together with a sharpness of wit very much his own:

> May came, and every shabby phoenix flapped
> A coloured rag in lieu of shining wings;
> In school bad manners spat and went unslapped—
> Schoolmistress Fancy dreamt of other things. . . .
>
>   ('After May', 1936)

> A poplar leaf was spiked upon a thorn
> Above the hedge like a flag of surrender
> That the year hung out. I was afraid to wonder
> At capitulation in a field of corn. . . .
>
>   ('Temptation in Harvest', 1947)

Patrick Kavanagh's first book, *Ploughman* (1936) was an impressive
performance, and alone would have served to put him securely
in a line of nature poets. But 'The Great Hunger' (1942) is
something else again. It is a long poem about frustration and
deprivation in a starkly rural setting:

> Come with me, Imagination, into this iron house
> And we will watch from the doorway the years run
>   back,
> And we will know what a peasant's left hand wrote on
>   the page.
> Be easy, October. No cackle hen, horse neigh, tree
>   sough, duck quack. . . .

Patrick Kavanagh left a poor hill farm in County Monaghan
to become a freelance writer in Dublin and London. 'The Great
Hunger' is a kind of apologia to the people he left behind.
It gives a hypothetical portrait of himself as he might have
been had he stayed—a sixty-five year old bachelor, ridden with

ignorance and prejudice, bent to the labours of his barren hills. He begins with a deliberate building up of place and atmosphere:

> Clay is the word and clay is the flesh
> Where the potato-gatherers like mechanised scarecrows
>   move
> Along the side-fall of the hill—Maguire and his men.
> If we watched them an hour is there anything we
>   can prove
> Of life as it is broken-backed over the Book
> Of Death? Here crows gabble over worms and frogs
> And the gulls like old newspapers are blown clear
>   of the hedges, luckily.
> Is there some light of imagination in these wet clods?
> Or why do we stand here shivering? . . .

Place and atmosphere build up at the expense of the men at work in these fields. The Great Hunger of the poem is the Irish Famine in a figurative, but deadly serious, sense. This is the deprivation of love, intellect, imagination most of all. These men are prey to a sterile religion, bound to a meaningless routine of labour:

> Watch him, watch him, that man on a hill whose spirit
> Is a wet sack flapping about the knees of time.
> He lives that his little fields may stay fertile when
>   his own body
> Is spread in the bottom of a ditch under two coulters
>   crossed in Christ's Name. . . .

Outwardly, the central figure is dehumanised into clay, a wet sack. But his inward agony is dramatised, largely in retrospect, in a manner that renders it highly specific. All this is done in terms of time and place; the poem is a masterpiece of structure. Section I is set in the present—significantly, the season is October. Sections II and III are transition passages, a commentary on the whole life of the poet's *alter ego*, Maguire. Section IV finds him near the present, in a cold April; but halfway through this section the poem goes into a prolonged retrospect which carries its central figure from his youth onward, through memories of happier times, set in various remembered springs and summers, seen, however, through the medium of disillusioned age:

Once one day in June when he was walking
Among his cattle in the Yellow Meadow
He met a girl carrying a basket—
And he was then a young and heated fellow.
Too earnest, too earnest!   (IV)

      One summer morning
Again through a hay-field on her way to the shop—
The grass was wet and over-leaned the path—
And Agnes held her skirts sensationally up,
And not because the grass was wet either   (VII)

Nobody will ever know how much tortured poetry the
      pulled weeds on the ridge wrote
Before they withered in the July sun   (IX)

I remember a night we walked
Through the moon of Donaghmoyne,
Four of us seeking adventure,
It was midsummer forty years ago.
Now I know
The moment that gave a turn to my life.
O Christ! I am locked in a stable with pigs and
      cows for ever.   (XII)

A cry in an agonised first person—this is the last of the personalised
retrospects of summer and it is the climax of the poem. It
is embedded in a grim February that is almost at the unhappy
present: Maguire's old mother has died, and he is his own man,
too late, at last. Section XIII is a transition passage, a further
generalised comment on the peasant's life. And in the final section,
XIV, we complete the cycle by reaching the autumn where the
poem began. Here we take leave of the peasant, dehumanised,
subjugated by his bleak landscape:

He stands in the doorway of his house
A ragged sculpture of the wind.
October creaks the rotted mattress,
The bedposts fall. No hope. No lust.
The hungry fiend
Screams the apocalypse of clay
In every corner of this land.

The cumulative effect is one of threnody over a life wasted by forces greater than itself, and this gives the poem, so packed with descriptive detail, its poignancy. The poignancy is held in check, however: only at climactic points is the peasant heard in his own person, and then usually in indirect speech. The form of the poem, both in its loose stanza pattern and in its structure based upon the seasons, keeps the underlying passions under restraint. An essential pattern, therefore, is never lost. The tradition in which Kavanagh writes requires of him, as it did of Crabbe and Clare, an extraordinary blend of talents and opportunities. There has to be knowledge and observation of the countryside; a sophisticated ear for rhythm; access to a fount of vital language.

It is unlikely that the achievement of 'The Great Hunger' will be repeated. There are a number of poets who have managed something of this poise; most of them from the environs of these islands, some with origins that are Celtic. But even the best of these—Seamus Heaney, say, or George Mackay Brown— tend to simplify, and in this way they define the limitations of a genre which Patrick Kavanagh transcends. They observe man without the complications of metropolitan life; what they produce is a kind of pastoral. This, in its turn, links up with the simple bestiary which is the attractive but limited stock in trade of such poets as Ted Hughes. The escapist tendency is obvious.

The advantage retained by Patrick Kavanagh, on the other hand—and by Redgrove, and Berry—is that they draw upon resources of natural description without sacrificing their awareness of modern complexities. There is nothing backward-looking in the themes of these poets, though their language can be related to medieval sources. This language, like that of most good poetry in English, is onomatopoeic. It recreates in sound sensations of pain or labour; it mimes violent or difficult body-movement and action; it actualises experience in muscular rhythms; it grasps firm particulars in concrete and realised imagery. There is an effect as of separate entities—images, properties—so closely packed as to bring about a fusion. My words are adapted from Francis Berry's characterisation of the language of *Sir Gawain*, but it would do equally well to describe an English tradition that goes back well before Langland, though the *Visio* is one decisive realisation and *Sir Gawain* another. And it relates to Berry's own work and that of his greater contemporaries and predecessors. What we have in such work is the alliterative mode rehandling the facts of contemporary life. This poetry depicts the war between man and nature—neither simply defined as mutually exclusive; or it narrates the incessant attrition of violence between man and man. Of course there are scores of reliable versepeople who produce collections acceptable to the sensibilities of the usual reviewers; and one would not be without them. But the work crucial to our tradition is the poetry I have sought to define in this chapter: the poetry of barbarism. The work of those others, for all their virtues of decency and good sense, is the poetry of decay.

Index

(The names of English and American poets are printed in bold type, as are the more important entries after their names)